Prejudice in the Modern World

Almanac VOLUME 2

Prejudice in the Modern World

Almanac VOLUME 2

Richard C. Hanes, Sharon M. Hanes, Kelly Rudd
Sarah Hermsen, Project Editor

U·X·L
*An imprint of Thomson Gale,
a part of The Thomson Corporation*

Detroit • New York • San Francisco • New Haven, Conn. • Waterville, Maine • London

Prejudice in the Modern World: Almanac

Richard C. Hanes, Sharon M. Hanes, Kelly Rudd

Project Editor
Sarah Hermsen

Rights and Acquisitions
Margaret Abendroth, Tim Sisler

Imaging and Multimedia
Dean Dauphinais, Lezlie Light, Mike Logusz

Product Design
Jennifer Wahi

Composition
Evi Seoud

Manufacturing
Rita Wimberley

LIBRARY OF CONGRESS CATALOGING-IN-PUBLICATION DATA

Hanes, Richard Clay, 1946–
   Prejudice in the modern world. Almanac / Richard C. Hanes, Sharon M. Hanes, and Kelly Rudd; Sarah Hermsen, project editor.
      p. cm. — (Prejudice in the modern world reference library)
   Includes bibliographical references and index.
   ISBN-13: 978-1-4144-0204-8 (set hardcover: alk. paper)—
   ISBN-10: 1-4144-0204-X (set hardcover: alk. paper)—
   ISBN-13: 978-1-4144-0205-5 (v. 1 hardcover: alk. paper)—
   ISBN-10: 1-4144-0205-8 (v. 1 hardcover: alk. paper)—[etc.]
   1. Toleration—Juvenile literature. 2. Prejudices—Juvenile literature. 3. Intergroup relations—Juvenile literature. 4. Ethnic relations—Juvenile literature. 5. Race relations—Juvenile literature.
I. Hanes, Sharon M.   II. Rudd, Kelly, 1954–   III. Hermsen, Sarah.   IV. Title.
   HM1271.H36 2007
   303.3'85—dc22   2006036955

ISBN-13:

978-1-4144-0203-1 (set)
978-1-4144-0204-8 (Almanac set)
978-1-4144-0205-5 (Almanac vol.1)
978-1-4144-0206-2 (Almanac vol.2)
978-1-4144-0207-9 (Biographies)
978-1-4144-0208-6 (Primary Sources)
978-1-4144-0209-3 (Cumulative Index)

ISBN-10:

1-4144-0203-1 (set)
1-4144-0204-X (Almanac set)
1-4144-0205-8 (Almanac vol.1)
1-4144-0206-6 (Almanac vol.2)
1-4144-0207-4 (Biographies)
1-4144-0208-2 (Primary Sources)
1-4144-0209-0 (Cumulative Index)

This title is also available as an e-book.
ISBN-13: 978-1-4144-1057-9; ISBN-10: 1-4144-1057-3
Contact your Thomson Gale sales representative for ordering information.
Printed in the United States of America

10 9 8 7 6 5 4 3 2 1

Table of Contents

Of the many kinds of emotions and feelings a person may hold, prejudice is perhaps one of the most common yet complex. Prejudice is a negative attitude, emotion, or behavior towards others based on a prejudgment about those individuals with no prior knowledge or experience. Prejudice can be extremely harmful, oversimplifying diverse aspects of human nature and making broad generalizations about entire races and cultures. These generalizations are frequently based on stereotypes. The use of stereotypes employs negative images of others. Such negative stereotypes may lead to certain forms of behavior including discrimination or even hostile violent acts. This kind of use of generalizations and stereotypes becomes especially critical when people in power, or seeking political power, manipulate through the media the stereotypes of social groups they wish to dominate, or perhaps eliminate. People in these stereotyped groups often become less valued socially. They are frequently made scapegoats, blamed for the problems affecting society in general, even if they have nothing to do with it.

Prejudices usually form very early in life; they are shaped by family, schools, and society in general. Prejudice can assume many forms based on the kinds of traits that others are being prejudged by. Racial prejudice focuses on physical biological traits, such as skin color. Religious prejudice considers the beliefs held by others or what religious denomination they are associated with. Ethnic prejudice identifies people who share common backgrounds or social customs. Nationalism is a form of prejudice that focuses on the political systems others live under. Sexism is a gender prejudice against men or women. Sexual orientation prejudices are usually against people who are homosexuals or transgendered.

Some prejudices focus on disabilities of others, ranging from physical handicaps to mental disabilities to mental illnesses.

Normally, people—both as a group and individually—are acting out multiple forms of prejudice at any one time. One group of people may hold prejudices and discriminate against another group because of combined religious and ethnic prejudices, racial and social class prejudices, or gender and disability prejudices. Similarly, any multiple combinations of prejudices are possible and may even occur in different combinations in the same individual over time. No matter the complexity of prejudice, one simple fact exists—prejudice has long been one of the greatest barriers and most destructive forces in human history.

Prejudice has been a major influence on human relationships throughout the history of humankind. Not only has prejudice existed throughout the history of civilization, it has dominated certain historic periods and historical events, such as the invasion of Christian armies into the Muslim-held Holy Lands beginning at the end of the eleventh century, the sixteenth century religious upheaval of the Reformation in Europe, and the Holocaust in World War II (1939–45) in the mid-twentieth century. Despite this influence of prejudice throughout history, the actual concept of what prejudice is did not develop until the twentieth century, when the study of prejudices gained recognition.

Slavery, colonialism, and world empires had largely ended by the early twentieth century. However, racial discrimination, particularly against those groups previously enslaved, ethnic conflicts, and international conflict driven by nationalism remained major influences on the course of modern history. Instances where the consequences of prejudice were most apparent included the racially discriminatory Jim Crow laws of the American South, the extermination of European Jews by Nazi Germany in the Holocaust, ethnic conflicts in former Yugoslavia in Eastern Europe, genocides in the African states of Rwanda and Somalia, and religious conflicts in Northern Ireland and the Middle East.

The nature of prejudice-driven discrimination and violence has changed over time. Efforts by national governments, human rights watch groups, and international organizations, such as the United Nations, have made strides in combating prejudice through various educational and humanitarian programs. However, it appeared that prejudice would continue as a major influence and source of conflict in the world into the twenty-first century.

Features

Prejudice in the Modern World: Almanac offers twenty-two chapters in two volumes. The first eleven chapters explore the many different types of prejudice, their history, what causes these prejudices in people and societies, and their consequences. The types of prejudice described in detail include ethnic, racial, religious, class, gender, sexual orientation, nationalism, and disabilities. Each chapter contains a list of additional sources students can go to for more information; sidebar boxes highlighting people and events of special interest; and a Words to Know section that introduces students to difficult or unfamiliar terms (terms are also defined within the text). Over 120 black-and-white photographs help illustrate the material. Both volumes begin with a timeline of important events in the history of prejudice and a Research and Activity Ideas section. The volumes conclude with a general bibliography and a subject index so students can easily find the people, places, and events discussed throughout *Prejudice in the Modern World: Almanac.*

Prejudice in the Modern World Reference Library

Prejudice in the Modern World: Almanac is only one component of the three-part Prejudice in the Modern World Reference Library. The other two titles in this set are:

Prejudice in the Modern World: Biographies presents the life stories of twenty-five diverse and unique individuals who played key roles in the history of prejudice. Some were prominent national leaders in fighting well-established prejudices while some promoted prejudices in order to pursue their own political and economic gain. Other figures were activists combating the various types of prejudice. Profiles include Paul Kagame, president of Rwanda; Saddam Hussein, president of Iraq; Golda Meir, prime minister of Israel; Wilma Mankiller, chairperson of the Cherokee Nation; social activists Gloria Steinem, Cesar Chavez, Mine Obuko, and Mahatma Gandhi. Other biography subjects range from Nazi German military leader Heinrich Himmler, the primary instigator of the Holocaust, to the Dalai Lama, the Tibetan spiritual leader who promoted religious tolerance.

Prejudice in the Modern World: Primary Sources tells various stories in the words of the people who fought prejudice, acted out prejudices, and those who were the victims of prejudice. Sixteen excerpted documents touch on a wide range of topics on prejudice.

Included are excerpts from published diaries, national magazine and news articles, reports produced by the United Nations and human rights watch groups, published interviews, and Web sites dedicated to the elimination of prejudice in everyday life.

A cumulative index of all three titles in the Prejudice in the Modern World Reference Library is also available.

Acknowledgements

These volumes are dedicated to our new granddaughter Jenna Grace Hanes. May she grow up to enjoy a world far less shaped by the destructive consequences of prejudice.

Special thanks are due to Dr. Mick Bollenbaugh and Matt May for their contributions to the *Almanac* volume.

Comments and Suggestions

We welcome your comments on *Prejudice in the Modern World: Almanac* and suggestions for other topics to consider. Please write: Editors, *Prejudice in the Modern World: Almanac,* U·X·L, 27500 Drake Rd. Farmington Hills, Michigan 48331-3535; call toll free: 1-800-877-4253; fax to (248) 699-8097; or send e-mail via http://www.gale.com.

Timeline of Events

632 Conflict erupts among Muslims after the death of Islamic Prophet Muhammad leading to a major split between Sunni and Shiíte Muslims over who should rightfully succeed Muhammad.

1095 The first of a series of Crusades is launched into the Middle East by an alliance of Christian armies from Europe determined to recapture lands lost to Muslim populations.

1200s Genghis Khan and his sons carry out possible genocides throughout much of Europe and Asia systematically killing millions of civilians.

1492 European explorer Christopher Columbus arrives in San Salvador leading to a mass killing of native peoples throughout the Western Hemisphere over the next several centuries through military conquest, introduction of foreign diseases, and general hardships caused by the loss of traditional homelands and resources.

1534 King Henry VIII of England breaks ties with the Roman Catholic Church, whose seat of power is in Rome, and establishes a new church, the Church of England also known as the Anglican Church; this revolt against Catholicism results in the birth of Protestantism and future religious conflict.

1624 British colonists arrive in India and gain control over much of India by 1858.

1648 The Treaty of Westphalia marks the initial rise of nation-states in Europe, replacing religion as a main organizing force of populations and leading to the growth of nationalistic prejudices.

1770s The ideas of social class and wage labor emerge as industrialization begins in British textile mills; industrialization, capitalist economies, and their social consequences will expand throughout much of the Western world over the next century.

1770 British explorer Captain James Cook arrives on the shores of Australia, a vast continent inhabited by diverse indigenous peoples.

1788 British colonists begin arriving in Australia and restrict the freedoms of the natives, whom they collectively refer to as Aborigines, by passing a series of Aboriginal Acts.

1808 The booming international slave trade is officially banned in the United States; since 1700 as many as fifteen million black African slaves had been transported across the Atlantic Ocean to the Americas.

July 1848 The first women's rights convention is held at Seneca Falls, New York, marking the beginning of an organized feminist movement.

Mid-1800s Chinese and Japanese begin immigrating to America finding work in mines and railroad construction in the western United States.

1865 Slavery ends in the United States with the South's defeat in the American Civil War (1861–65).

1867 Diamonds are discovered in Southern Africa followed by the discovery of gold in 1886; the newfound wealth draws broad international interest from foreign investors and lays the foundation for future racial segregation policies among the labor force.

1870s European countries rush to divide up Africa under their control, leading to German colonies in Southwest Africa, French control of Algeria, Italian control of Somaliland in Eastern Africa and later Ethiopia, and British control of Egypt and South Africa; the division of Africa is completed at the Berlin Conference of 1885.

1880s Southern and Eastern European immigrants began arriving in America in large numbers, increasing ethnic and racial prejudices in the United States.

1882 U.S. Congress passes the Chinese Exclusion Act, the first of various laws restricting foreign immigration.

1887 The U.S. government begins a major period of forced cultural assimilation with passage of the General Allotment Act, known as the

Dawes Act, authorizing the U.S. Bureau of Indian Affairs (BIA) to divide communal reservation lands into smaller, privately owned parcels.

1890s Jim Crow laws are introduced in the United States to legally enforce public racial segregation for the next half century.

1893 New Zealand becomes the first nation to establish universal suffrage, meaning voting rights for all adults.

1895 The Basque Nationalist Party led by Sabino Arana is established seeking a nation based on Basque racial purity with exclusion of what they consider racially inferior Spaniards.

1898 German doctor and scholar Magnus Hirschfeld forms the Scientific-Humanitarian Committee whose purpose is to oppose German laws outlawing sexual intercourse between men; later in 1919 Hirschfeld founds the Institute for Sexology to conduct research that promotes sexual reform, education, and women's rights.

1902 The First International Convention for Women meets in Washington, D.C., with representatives arriving from ten nations to plot an international strategy for gaining suffrage.

1905 Black American leaders meet in Niagara Falls, Canada, to develop a strategy to fight racial prejudice in America; it becomes known as the Niagara Movement.

1909 The National Association for the Advancement of Colored People (NAACP) is established to fight lynchings and other racist activities in the United States through legal action, educational programs, and encouraging voter participation.

1910 The National Urban League is founded to help black Americans adjust to city life as they move to the North seeking jobs in industry; through World War I (1914–18) hundreds of thousands of blacks leave the rural South in what becomes known as the Black Migration.

1910 The Mexican Revolution sends that country spiraling into political, economic, and social upheaval for a decade, and leads to over 680,000 Mexican citizens immigrating to the United States in search of jobs through the next twenty years.

1912 Hundreds of prominent Africans form the South African Native National Congress, later renamed the African National Congress (ANC), to protest racial segregation in South Africa.

1916 The Irish Republican Army (IRA) forms to fight a guerrilla war for Ireland's independence from England; the Irish Free State is formed five years later.

1918 Since 1889, 2,522 black Americans are lynched—hung, burned alive, or hacked to death—largely in the American South, as a result of extreme racial prejudice.

1918 Following World War I the Kingdom of the Serbs, Croats, and Slovenes is formed, later adopting the name Yugoslavia; it soon becomes apparent that the various ethnic groups are unwilling to blend together.

1918 Defeat of the Ottoman Empire in World War I leads the victors Britain and France to divide up the Middle East under their control with Britain forming a new country called Iraq and establishing rule over Arab Palestinian territory.

1919 Twenty-five race riots erupt across the United States leaving one hundred people dead and increasing membership in the Ku Klux Klan (KKK), a white supremacist hate group.

1920 The All India Home Rule League is formed, with Mahatma Gandhi as its president, to seek independence from British rule. It adopts anti-British measures including a boycott of British imported goods, refusing employment by the British, and refusing to pay taxes; these actions lead to the imprisonment of Gandhi.

1920 The United States passes the Nineteenth Amendment to the Constitution extending the right to vote to women.

1923 Forty states in the United States have institutions housing approximately forty-three thousand mentally defective persons.

1924 Congress passes the U.S. Immigration Act to limit all immigration to the United States, particularly immigration from Asia and eastern and southern Europe.

1928 The resistance movement for India's independence creates the Indian National Congress following a massive protest march that journeys over 250 miles.

1928 The Muslim Brotherhood is created in Egypt to resist European colonial powers controlling much of the Arab world in northern

Africa and the Middle East and promote a return to Islamic states of past centuries.

1929 To improve human genetic qualities, twenty-three states in the United States legalize sterilization of the mentally defective so they can not produce children.

1932 Soviet Union dictator Joseph Stalin allows seven million Ukrainians to starve to death during a harsh winter as a form of ethnic cleansing to provide room for Soviet expansion.

1933 Nazi Germany establishes its first concentration camps within Germany to hold political prisoners and those considered undesirable.

1933 The Holocaust, the most noted case of genocide in the twentieth century, lasts until 1945, during which the Nazi German government kills eleven million people including six million European Jews; other victims included Poles, Gypsies, Slavs, homosexuals, and various political opponents.

1934 The U.S. Congress passes the Indian Reorganization Act (IRA) providing opportunities for Native Americans to receive federal funds to purchase land, start businesses, and receive social services; tribes are to adopt written constitutions establishing democratic forms of government and forming federally chartered corporations.

November 9, 1938 Known as the Night of Broken Glass, the German government carefully orchestrates violence against Jews across Germany and German-controlled Austria for two days as rioters burn or damage over one thousand Jewish synagogues and damage almost eight thousand Jewish-owned businesses; some thirty thousand Jewish men are arrested and sent to concentration camps, the first mass arrest of Jews by Nazi Germany.

1940 The fourteenth Dalai Lama is installed as the religious leader of Tibet at the age of seven.

1941 For a four year period until the end of World War II in 1945, over 300,000 Serbs and Jews in Croatia are killed, disappear, or placed in concentration camps under the Croatian government led by Ante Pavelić.

1942 The United States and Mexico establish the Bracero Program that allows Mexican day laborers to legally enter the United States for seasonal work on farms and other jobs until 1964 when the program officially ends; almost five million workers journeyed from Mexico though working conditions were often harsh.

February 19, 1942 U.S. president Roosevelt signs Executive Order 9066 authorizing the removal of Japanese Americans from their homes in the West Coast to detention camps established by the War Relocation Authority (WRA).

July 19, 1942 Heinrich Himmler gives the order to begin deportation of Jews from the Polish ghettos, leading to the deaths of three million Jews, over 90 percent of the Jewish population in Poland.

December 1944 With the end of World War II in sight, the remaining forty-four thousand Japanese Americans being detained since 1942 are freed, although the last camp does not close until March 1946.

1945 The United Nations forms as an international world body to resolve international disputes; its membership includes fifty-one nations; among its branches is the Educational, Scientific, and Cultural Organization (UNESCO).

1945 Following World War II, the Federal Peoples Republic of Yugoslavia is established as a communist country under the control of the USSR, including the six states of Bosnia-Herzegovina, Croatia, Serbia, Slovenia, Montenegro, and Macedonia.

1946 Thousands of immigrants begin legally entering France from Northern Africa and Asia searching for work in rebuilding Europe from the ravages of World War II; by 1974 one million immigrants had entered France and by 1995 legal and illegal foreigners account for 25 percent of France's population.

1947 The Indian government stops legally enforcing the traditional caste system, establishes prohibitions against discrimination against members of former castes, and creates an aggressive affirmative action program to help those lower caste members historically discriminated against.

August 1947 Pakistan gains independence from India, leading to massive population displacements as an estimated ten million Hindus, Muslims, and Sikhs move from one country to the other.

1948 The Jewish state of Israel is formed within Palestinian Arab territory forcing thousands of Arabs from their homelands and leading to a long-standing conflict between Arabs and Jews over control of the region.

1948 The South African Nationalist Party, campaigning on its policy of apartheid, wins an election victory over the Unionist Party and immediately creates laws to impose racial segregation that remain in place for decades.

1948 Sri Lanka gains independence from Britain triggering long-standing ethnic conflict between the Tamils and Sinhalese.

December 1948 The United Nations adopts the Convention on the Prevention and Punishment of the Crime of Genocide in response to the Holocaust during World War II; the resulting trials continue through the remainder of the twentieth century setting precedents for future war crimes trials conducted by international tribunals.

April 18, 1949 The Republic of Ireland declares independence from Britain and pursues efforts to unite Protestant Northern Ireland with the Catholic Republic of Ireland.

1954 The U.S. Supreme Court rules in Brown v. Board of Education that racially segregated public schools are illegal marking a major legal victory for black Americans against Jim Crow laws.

June 1955 The South African Congress of the People, consisting of over three thousand delegates opposed to apartheid, assemble to draft the Freedom Charter for a future democratic South Africa.

October 29, 1956 Through November 6, Egypt nationalizes the Suez Canal blocking Israeli commercial ships from passing through the critical waterway and leading to a brief war in which Israel wins.

1957 For the first time an Aborigine is granted Australian citizenship; Aborigines finally gain the right to vote in national elections in 1962 and in 1967 they are finally included in the Australian national census.

1958 Racial violence breaks out in the Notting Hill district of London leading to calls for increased restrictions on immigration.

1959 Tibetan resistance to Chinese control and discrimination escalates into violence in Tibet's capital city of Lhasa causing the Dalai Lama and tens of thousands of Tibetans to seek exile in India while the Chinese systematically destroy Tibetan monasteries.

1960s Development of the oral contraception pill is one of the most significant steps in liberating women from traditional gender roles.

1961 Newly elected U.S. president John F. Kennedy forms the President's Commission on the Status of Women, chaired by former First Lady Eleanor Roosevelt; the resulting 1963 report identifies numerous national gender prejudice issues affecting women including discrimination at the workplace and unequal pay.

1962 The British Parliament passes the racially-prejudiced Commonwealth Immigrants Act increasing restrictions on immigration of blacks from Commonwealth nations to Britain.

July 1, 1962 The African state of Rwanda gains independence from Belgian rule.

1963 The U.S. Congress passes the Equal Pay Act addressing gender prejudice affecting equal pay for equal work.

August 28, 1963 Black leaders including Martin Luther King Jr. Philip Randolph, Roy Wilkins, James Farmer, and Whitney M. Young, Jr., lead a massive protest march on Washington, D.C., attracting over two hundred thousand people, both blacks and whites.

1964 The U.S. Congress passes the landmark Civil Rights Act prohibiting discrimination based on race and gender in public places and calling for equal opportunity in education and employment.

1964 Violence erupts in Northern Ireland as Catholics rebel against Protestant oppression, leading to a bloody terrorist campaign by the Irish Republican Army (IRA) leaving thousands dead.

1965 A gay rights march held outside Independence Hall in Philadelphia marks the beginning of the modern gay rights movement and formation of such groups as the Gay Liberation Front and Gay Activists Alliance.

1965 U.S. president Lyndon Johnson signs a presidential order establishing affirmative action programs to correct for past governmental injustices and end Jim Crow discriminatory social customs.

March 20, 1965 Martin Luther King Jr. leads a massive four-day march of thirty thousand protesters from Selma to the state capitol building in Montgomery protesting restrictions on voting rights of racial minorities, such as poll taxes.

August 6, 1965 The U.S. Congress passes the Voting Rights Act banning poll taxes as a voting requirement and placing close federal oversight over Southern voting practices such as voter registration.

1966 Two Mexican American farmworker unions merge to form the United Farm Workers and choose a Mexican Aztec eagle as its symbol; they begin nonviolent strikes against California grape growers to gain better working conditions.

June 1966 The National Organization for Women (NOW) is formed at the Third National Conference of the Commission on the Status of Women.

June 5, 1967 Israel goes to war against Syria, Egypt, and Jordan, referred to as the Six Day War because it ends on June 10 with another Israel victory.

1968 As part of the growth of Native American activism in the 1960s, the American Indian Movement (AIM) is created on the Pine Ridge Indian Reservation, an Indian community long known for its poverty and isolation.

February 1968 The Southwest Council of La Raza is formed in Phoenix, Arizona, that grows into a national organization known as the National Council of La Raza (NCLR) in 1972.

December 1968 Eunice Kennedy Shriver founds the Special Olympics dedicated to empowering persons with mental retardation through sports training and competition; the Special Olympics eventually spreads throughout the United States and over 150 countries.

1970 A loosely organized group of lesbians, referred as the Lavender Menace, becomes extremely frustrated with the leadership of the women's rights movement and protests against activities of the National Organization of Women (NOW) until their social issues finally gain acceptance by the organization.

1970 The Khmer Rouge, led by Cambodian communist leader Pol Pot, murder some two million Cambodians either by execution, starvation, or exhaustion resulting from forced hard labor.

1972 The French Front National (FN) political party organizes to promote anti-immigrant government policies and gains considerable popularity.

1972 Ed Roberts, a quadriplegic, forms the Center for Independent Living (CIL) to advocate for an end to discrimination against persons with disabilities and to instill pride and empowerment within the disabled community; numerous CIL branches open across the nation during the following years.

1972 The U.S. Congress passes Title IX as part of a national education bill that calls for equality in sports opportunities for women and men at most universities in America.

1972 A new magazine is founded by Gloria Steinem called *Ms. Magazine* to focus solely on second wave feminism issues.

March 1972 The U.S. Congress passes the Equal Rights Amendment (ERA) legislation that guarantees equal rights under the law regardless of sex and gives the state legislatures a seven-year deadline to ratify the amendment; by March 1979 thirty-five states have ratified the amendment, three short of the required number.

1973 The U.S. Congress passes the Rehabilitation Act, the first of three core laws created to give persons with disabilities legal access to life activities that are available to nondisabled Americans; the other two later acts are the Education for All Handicapped Children Act of 1974, that in 1990 is renamed the Individuals with Disabilities Education Act (IDEA), and the Americans with Disabilities Act (ADA) of 1990.

January 22, 1973 The U.S. Supreme Court issues the landmark decision on abortion rights in *Roe v. Wade* ruling that most laws prohibiting abortion, including many existing state laws, violate the constitutional right to privacy of women.

October 6, 1973 War again breaks out between Israelis and Arabs referred to as the Yom Kippur War after a very important Jewish holiday on which the war begins.

1975 In response to Mexican American strikes against California grape growers, the U.S. Congress passes the Agricultural Labor Relations Act that allows for collective bargaining by agricultural workers.

1975 In support of tribal sovereignty and economic self-sufficiency, the U.S. Congress passes the Indian Self-Determination and Education Assistance Act giving the Bureau of Indian Affairs (BIA) and other federal agencies authority to transfer responsibility for administering certain tribal programs to the tribes.

December 9, 1975 The United Nations General Assembly adopts the Declaration on the Rights of Disabled Persons declaring that disabled persons are entitled to the same rights as the nondisabled in all areas of life including rights to an education, medical services, employment, legal aid, to live with their families, and to be protected against abuse and discrimination.

1976 After monitoring racial discrimination in South Africa since 1946, the United Nations establishes apartheid as an international crime, imposes an oil and arms embargo against South Africa, and creates the International Criminal Court to discourage any other nation from adopting similar practices of racial domination and oppression as practiced in South Africa.

1979 Iranian Islamic fundamentalists led by Muslim cleric (religious leader) Ayatollah Ruhollah Khomeini overthrows the secular government of Mohammad Reza Shah Pahlavi, a close ally of the United States and Western Europe.

1979 The Rwandese Refugee Welfare Foundation (RRWF) is established to aid Rwandan refugees in exile; after several name changes the organization becomes the Rwandese Patriotic Front (RPF) in December 1987.

1980s Europe right-wing political parties gain increased support largely for their anti-immigration positions.

1980 The World Conference of United Nations Decade for Women held in Copenhagen attracts women from around the world and highlights the diverse goals and disagreements over priorities of the worldwide women's rights movement.

1980 A Miami, Florida, court acquits four police officers in the beating death of a black businessman leading to an eruption of violence as blacks attack whites on the streets, sometimes dragging them from cars, leading to the deaths of eighteen people and hundreds of millions of dollars of property damage.

1981 Members of the Egyptian Islamic Jihad, a violent wing of the Muslim Brotherhood, assassinate Egyptian President Mohamed Anwar Sadat for introducing Western ideas into Islamic societies.

1981 A wave of violence spreads through several major cities of Britain with minority youth, including blacks and Asians, clashing with police in reaction to charges of racial harassment by police authorities; over three thousand youth are arrested.

1983 Janjaweed militias with support of the Sudanese government begin systematically killing black Africans in the Darfur region of western Sudan leading to the murder of some two million people and displacement of another four million.

1984 For three years violence in Punjab orchestrated by Sikh separatists desiring independence from India leads to thousands of deaths with the majority of victims being innocent Sikh civilians due to military rule established in 1987 by the Indian government to stop the violence; the Sikhs claim extensive human rights violations.

1985 Violence erupts again in the major cities of Britain largely between black youth and police leading to the death of one police officer and injury to some 220 police.

1986 The U.S. Congress passes the Immigration Reform and Control Act, establishing crimes for American companies that hire illegal immigrants.

1988 Islamist rebels heavily funded by the United States successfully drive the armed forces of the Soviet Union out of Afghanistan after eight years of war.

1988 The U.S. Congress passes the Civil Liberties Act, symbolically named House Resolution 442 in honor of the U.S. Nisei battalion 442 of World War II, that awards each Japanese American who was interned during the war an apology and $20,000.

March 1988 Ali Hasan al-Majid, who becomes known as Chemical Ali, unleashes chemical weapons against the Kurdish populations of northern Iraq including residents of Halabja, a town of over forty thousand people.

1989 Newly elected South African president F.W. de Klerk announces he will seek to overturn all racial discriminatory laws, release political prisoners of apartheid including Nelson Mandela, and lift the ban on anti-Apartheid organizations such as the ANC.

1990s Accusations of discriminatory racial profiling escalate in various Western countries leading to the black community's frustration with alleged police harassment.

1991 Following the demise of the communist governments of Eastern Europe, a wave of nationalistic movements and their related prejudices sweeps the region leading to the formation of the Baltic States of

Lithuania, Estonia, and Latvia and the breakup of Yugoslavia; the ethnic struggles among the Serbs, Bosnian Muslims, and Croats of Serbia, Bosnia-Herzegovina, and Croatia leads to two hundred thousand Bosnian Muslims, Croats, and Serbs being killed and over one million being displaced from their homes.

June 25, 1991 Croatia and Slovenia declare independence from the Yugoslav federation followed by Bosnia-Herzegovina on April 6, 1992.

1992 The fight against prejudices leads the U.S. Congress to create a new type of crime category, the hate crime, described as acts committed against a person only because that person is considered to be a member of some social group that is devalued by society in general.

April 1992 A Los Angeles jury acquits police officers charged with assaulting Rodney King, triggering riots in Los Angeles and an outpouring of anger and loss of faith in the U.S. criminal justice system by blacks; the riots result in forty-four deaths, two thousand injured, and eleven hundred arrests.

1993 The UN Security Council establishes an international tribunal, known as the International Court Tribunal for the former Yugoslavia (ICTY), at The Hague, Netherlands, to prosecute war crimes allegedly committed during the conflict in Bosnia-Herzegovina since 1991.

1994 With the ANC winning all but two provinces, black African Nelson Mandela becomes the new president of South Africa.

1994 The UN Security Council establishes the International Criminal Tribunal for Rwanda (ICTR) to bring to trial those accused of genocide; by 2005 sixty-three individuals accused of being genocide leaders come under the ICTR process.

1994 During a one-hundred-day period the Hutus of Rwanda kill almost one million Tutsis and politically moderate Hutus.

November 8, 1994 California voters pass Proposition 187, the first of several propositions that directly discriminates against illegal immigrants.

July 1995 The Muslim community of Srebrenica in eastern Bosnia-Herzegovina falls to ethnic Serbs who perpetrate horrible crimes against the people of that town, including the murder of eight thousand men and boys.

December 14, 1995 The Dayton Peace Accords are signed, ending ethnic conflict in Bosnia but not before two hundred thousand Bosnian Muslims, Croats, and Serbs are killed and hundreds of thousands had fled their homes.

1996 The U.S. Congress passes the Defense of Marriage Act that denies same-sex couples federal benefits including Social Security pensions; survivor benefits for federal employees; Medicaid coverage; next-of-kin status for emergency medical situations; domestic violence protection orders; inheritance of property; and joint adoption and foster care benefits.

1996 The Taliban, an Islamist fundamentalist organization, gains power in Afghanistan.

1998 The FRY begins an ethnic cleansing of Albanians remaining in Kosovo, causing over 300,000 Albanians to flee Kosovo for Macedonia.

April 10, 1998 Violence in Northern Ireland finally ends as voters in Northern Ireland and the Republic of Ireland approve the Good Friday Agreement, or Belfast Agreement, by a large margin that provides for power sharing between Northern Ireland's Catholic and Protestant populations in an elected Northern Ireland Assembly and directs that the political status of Northern Ireland can only change with the approval of a majority of Northern Ireland voters.

March 18, 1999 Albanian, American, and British delegations sign the Rambouillet Accords calling for NATO to administer Kosovo as an autonomous province of Serbia.

March 24, 1999 Following the Rambouillet conference, the FRY intensifies a genocide campaign in Kosovo that lasts until June 20, 1999, with the murder of thousands of Albanians; NATO begins air strikes in Kosovo in late March.

2000 Studies estimate that domestic abuse affects 10 percent of the U.S. population, roughly thirty-two million Americans.

2000 The Leadership Conference on Civil Rights releases a report indicating that people of color in America are treated more harshly by police and the U.S. criminal justice system than whites.

2001 The U.S. Supreme Court rules that the Boy Scouts of America organization is not required to follow state anti-discrimination laws regarding sexual orientation and can exclude gays from membership.

September 11, 2001 Attention of the world is dramatically focused on the Islamic fundamentalist movement when Islamic extremists slam two fully fueled jetliners into the World Trade Center Towers in New York City and the Pentagon in Washington, D.C., killing some three thousand civilians and starting a strong wave of nationalistic fervor in the United States.

2003 U.S. forces invade Iraq and drive Saddam Hussein from power; religious hatred between Shiites and Sunni surfaces after decades of oppression under Hussein causing a deep divide in Iraq society.

2003 The Federal Marriage Amendment (FMA) bill that would ban same-sex marriages is introduced for the first time in U.S. Congress but fails to pass.

2003 The U.S. Supreme Court invalidates all state sodomy laws that restrict personal activity by ruling that a Texas state law criminalizing homosexual sodomy is unconstitutional; consensual sexual contact becomes a liberty protected by the U.S. Constitution.

2004 The Australian government begins providing assistance to Aborigines directly through the agencies that serve the general population and establishes the Office of Indigenous Policy Coordination within the Department of Immigration and Multicultural and Indigenous Affairs to coordinate the various programs for indigenous peoples.

2004 The Federal Bureau of Investigation (FBI) reports that over 15 percent of hate crimes committed in the United States are based upon the perceived sexual orientation of the victims.

November 2004 The question of gay marriage divides many Americans and becomes a major factor in the 2004 presidential election as socially conservative groups rally against the prospect of various states legalizing same-sex marriages.

2005 A study by the National Council on Disabilities indicates that while substantial gains against prejudice of the disabled have been made discrimination in housing is still a major problem.

2005 The United Nations High Commissioner for Refugees, established in December 1950, reports the existence of over nine million known refugees in the world not including four million Palestinian Arabs permanently displaced with creation of the state of Israel in 1948.

2005 In Egyptian parliamentary elections, members of the Muslim Brotherhood win 20 percent of the parliament seats even though the organization is still officially banned.

July 28, 2005 The IRA declares an end to its military campaign for independence for Northern Ireland and removes its store of weapons from service.

November 2005 Race riots across France increase fears of continued high immigration levels as anti-immigration feelings rise.

January 2006 The radical Palestinian group Hamas wins the majority of seats in Palestine's parliamentary elections, gaining a political victory over the PLO, the controlling political party in Palestine since 1967.

February 2006 The South Dakota legislature passes a bill making the performance of all abortions a felony crime.

Summer 2006 Israel launches a major offensive against Lebanon after Hezbollah militia kidnaps two Israeli soldiers and kills another.

Words to Know

A

affirmative action: A program to provide opportunities in education and employment long denied to minorities due to discriminatory social customs of the past.

alien: People who hold citizenship in a foreign country.

anti-Semitism: Prejudice against members of the Jewish faith.

apartheid: A government-enforced policy of racial separation and discrimination.

assimilate: Conforming to the cultural values of another social group and ultimately losing one's original ethnic identity to the new dominant culture.

asylum: A place of protection for those suffering from prejudice and discrimination.

autonomy: Freedom of a government to make its own decisions; also known as self-rule.

B

barrio: Spanish word referring to a neighborhood largely inhabited by people of Hispanic ancestry.

belief system: A set of values that guides peoples' lives.

bias: A personal judgment, often unreasoned; a prejudiced outlook.

bisexual: A person who participates in both heterosexual and homosexual relationships.

boycott: An organized effort to not buy certain products or use certain services in order to express disapproval with a person, store, or organization.

bracero program: A program to allow Mexican laborers to legally work on a temporary basis in the United States.

caste system: A rigid series of social classes allowing little opportunity for people to improve their individual standing in society.

civil rights: The protections and privileges that law gives to all citizens in a society, such as the right to a fair trial, freedom from discrimination, right to privacy, right to peaceful protest, right to vote, and freedom of movement.

civil union: A legal partnership between two people that confers many of the legal benefits of marriage.

classism: Prejudice against a social class.

colonization: One nation populating and gaining political and economic control of another, usually lesser developed, country and its resources.

Communism: A political and economic system in which a single political party controls all aspects of citizens' lives and private ownership of property is banned.

concentration camp: A guarded location set aside to hold detainees, usually prisoners of war, displaced peoples, or political prisoners.

conformity: A means of trying to avoid being a victim of prejudice and seeking acceptance by simply behaving within the traditions or norms of a society; it is also a means of perpetuating prejudices in the moral codes of the society or group.

crime against humanity: A criminal offense in international law that refers to murderous actions on such a large scale that it effects the global population as a whole.

cultural traits: Aspects of a society that include language, religion, marriage preferences, food preferences, music, dances, literature, games, and occupations.

D

decolonization: A nation withdrawing political and economic control from another, usually causing a major drop in income of those peoples previously colonized.

deportation: Lawful expulsion or removal of a person from a country.

diaspora: The dispersal of a population of people to other countries after being forced to live outside their traditional homeland.

discrimination: Treating some people differently than others or favoring one social group over another based on prejudice.

displaced persons: People forced to leave their homes, either entering other countries becoming refugees or remaining in their own country at some other safer location.

E

embargo: A ban on shipping of goods and trade, usually for the purpose of taking an action against a foreign nation in response to violated treaties or other undesired behavior.

enemy aliens: Noncitizens considered potential threats from a country at war with the host nation the foreigners are visiting.

ethnicity: Recognizing a group by certain traits such as a unique culture, common national origin or ancestral history, or certain physical traits.

ethnic cleansing: To eliminate the presence of a particular ethnic group from a region either through mass murder known as genocide, through displacement of the undesired population to another region or country, or placement in concentration camps.

ethnic prejudice: Holding negative opinions, beliefs, or attitudes about people for the simple reason that they belong to a specific ethnic group.

ethnocentrism: A group feeling superior to other groups because of physical trait or cultural differences including religious beliefs or other long-held traditions.

evangelical: Teaching a close personal relationship with God through rigorous faith in written passages of the Bible.

exile: Forced absence from one's own country due to consequences of prejudice or some other reasons.

exploitation: Making use of people without appropriate or just compensation, often based on prejudices such as through colonial rule.

extremist: One who takes a position on an issue that is beyond ordinary or moderate positions.

fascism: A strong central government usually run by a dictator.

federalist state: A national government system in which a central government shares power with provincial governments such as states.

feminism: A belief in the social equality of women.

fundamentalist movement: A movement stressing strict adherence to a basic set of religious beliefs and seeking to place a secular government with a sectarian one.

gay: A term used in referring to homosexuals.

gay bashing: Speaking hateful about homosexual people.

gender prejudice: Holding opinions about women or men, usually based on negative stereotypes; also referred to as sexism.

genocide: A deliberate destruction of a political or cultural social group.

ghetto: Small, run-down sections of cities where Jews were forced to live, usually behind stone walls or barbed-wire fences policed by armed guards.

guerrilla warfare: Irregular fighting by independent militant bands.

hate crime: A violent attack or verbal abuse against a person or group because of their race, ethnicity, religion, or gender.

heterosexual: A person who participates in sexual relations with, or is sexually attracted to, a person of the opposite gender.

Hispanic: A term referring to peoples of Spanish descent who settled various regions of the Western Hemisphere since the sixteenth century including Central America, Mexico, the American Southwest, parts of South America, and the Caribbean.

Holocaust: The program of genocide pursued by Nazi Germany during World War II to rid Europe of Jews leading to the murder of eleven million people overall including six million Jews; literally meaning a burnt sacrifice.

homophobia: An irrational fear of homosexuality or homosexual individuals.

homosexual: A person who participates in sexual relations with, or is sexually attracted to, an individual of the same gender.

human rights: Freedom from unlawful imprisonment, torture, or execution.

immigrant: A person who leaves his country of origin to reside permanently in another.

imperialism: One nation expanding its political control over other nations by force.

indigenous: The first or earliest inhabitants of a particular region.

industrialization: A change in the eighteenth and nineteenth centuries to a new economic system of mass producing large quantities of goods by wage-earning workers operating machines located in factories.

infanticide: A tradition in some cultures of selectively killing newborn infants, such as killing female infants while keeping males.

infrastructure: Public roads, power stations, and buildings necessary for a healthy economy.

internment: To confine or imprison a person without a trial.

isolationism: Opposition to foreign commitments or involvement in foreign disputes.

Issei: The first generation of immigrants moving from Japan to America.

Jim Crow laws: Legally enforced racial segregation in the American South during much of the twentieth century sustaining the racial dominance of white Americans from earlier days of slavery.

lesbian: A female homosexual person.

lynching: A violent crime of extreme racial hatred involving the murder of a minority person accused of wrongdoing by hanging or some other means often by a mob without giving the accused the benefit of a fair trial in a court of law.

marginalized: To be excluded from full participation in a society or fully enjoying the benefits of being a member of that society.

monarchy: A royalty line of kings and queens.

mosque: An Islamic place of worship.

nationalism: A belief that a particular nation and its culture, people, and values are superior to those of other nations, often leading to the promoting of one nation's interests over the interests of other nations; can also refer to promoting the creation of a new nation.

nation-state: A politically independent country, usually forming the basis of nationalistic prejudice.

naturalization: The process through which a citizen of one country becomes the citizen of another country, often requiring a certain length of residence.

Nisei: Japanese Americans born in the United States to Japanese immigrants known as Issei.

picket: An organized line of people in front of a business or organization holding signs protesting the policies of that organization with the purpose of discouraging others from using their services or buying their goods.

poll tax: A fee required to vote in a public election.

prejudice: A negative attitude, emotion, or behavior towards others based on a prejudgment about those individuals with no prior knowledge or experience.

racism: Prejudice against people of a particular physical trait, such as skin color, based on a belief that the physical trait primarily determines human behavior and individual capabilities; social and cultural meaning is given to skin color or whatever other trait is considered important.

refugee: A person seeking safety in a foreign country to escape prejudice or persecution.

repatriation: Sending an individual, usually a prisoner of war, immigrant, or refugee, back to his country of origin.

reservation: A tract of public land set aside for a special purpose, such as placement of an undesired social group away from mainstream society.

scapegoating: Shifting the blame for one's own difficulties, failures, and mistakes onto someone else, such as another ethnic group.

sectarian government: A government run by religious leaders of one religion.

secular government: A government run by nonreligious political leaders.

segregation: Using laws or social customs to separate certain social groups, such as whites and blacks or women and men.

separatism: The desire to form a new nation from a part of one currently existing.

sexism: A form of prejudice aimed at particular genders.

sit-in: The act of entering an establishment, such as a restaurant, and peacefully refusing to leave until the prejudicial policies of the establishment are changed.

socialization: The manner through which people learn, usually in their early youth, the proper social roles of their community, such as gender roles.

social class: Groups of people sharing similar wealth and social standing.

social codes: Patterns of expected behavior in society.

social hierarchy: The valuing of some social groups above others.

social mobility: The amount of opportunity a person has in a particular society to change their social standing from one social class to another.

sovereignty: A nation's ability to govern its own internal affairs.

stalking: To harass someone by relentlessly pursuing them, often driven by gender prejudice or some other form of prejudice.

stereotyping: An oversimplified prejudgment of others using physical or behavioral characteristics, usually exaggerated, that supposedly apply to every member of that group.

stigma: A person feeling shame or of lesser social value than others due to some form of prejudice aimed against them.

suffrage: The ability of all adult members of a society to vote regardless of gender or race or religious affiliation.

termination: The process adopted by the U.S. Congress in the 1950s in determining that certain Native American tribes no longer would enjoy a special tribal government legal status and, as a result, no longer qualify for certain government-funded social services.

Third World: Nations lagging in economic development and, as a result, facing impoverishment and the target of prejudice.

totalitarianism: Governments in which dictators hold absolute rule over a nation.

transgender: A person who appears as a member of the opposite gender.

xenophobia: A fear of people who are different.

Zionism: A movement that called for the reuniting of Jewish people and lobbied for the creation of a Jewish homeland in Palestine.

Research and Activity Ideas

The following research and activity ideas are intended to offer suggestions for complementing social studies and history curricula; to trigger additional ideas for enhancing learning; and to provide cross-disciplinary projects for library and classroom use.

- **Oral History Interviews:** Make a list of persons in your community, perhaps families of fellow students, of various ethnic and racial backgrounds and ancestry. Also, consider including people of different religious beliefs, the disabled, or families of mixed ethnic or religious backgrounds. Developing questions ahead of time, tape record interviews or take careful notes about the prejudices in society that one person you interview may have experienced. Transcribe the tapes or rewrite the notes into a clearly written story retelling the interview. This process is known as taking or recording an oral history. Share the oral history with the class.

- **Prejudice in Local Communities:** With the help of a librarian at your public library look into the history of your own hometown. How has your community been effected by prejudice and discrimination? Are their individual neighborhoods predominately reflecting different ethnic groups, races, or specific religious denominations? How did attitudes toward minorities in your community change through the twentieth century? Were there any community leaders who helped ease local prejudices? Looking at a map of your community, research what the race, gender, and social class of people for whom buildings, parks, and other public places are named for. If you find a pattern, what does it say about your community?

- **Student Support Organizations:** Do student organizations in your school exist to help students who face prejudice of some sort, such as racial, ethnic, religious, sexual orientation, or gender? Interview the student leader, sponsoring faculty, and perhaps some members of the organization about how they offer support. What kinds of prejudice are they concerned about? What rights do gay and lesbian students have in school? Are courses that strive to reduce classroom prejudice taught in your school? Do teachers respond to questions by students differently depending on their gender or race?

- **Employment Policies:** Visit a human resources department of prominent companies or government agencies in your city or community. Determine what personnel policies relate to employee diversity. How do the policies affect employees on the basis of race, gender, sexual orientation, and so on?

- **Write an Essay:** Selecting several students who have different race, gender, social class, and other factors interview them to determine how their life experiences differ from yours. Write an essay describing how their positions in society have helped or hindered their ability to attain what they want in life.

- **Local Anti-Discrimination Organizations:** Contact the local branch of a national organization dedicated to fighting prejudice and discrimination. Interview a representative about the kinds of prejudice they combat. What has it been like for people facing that particular prejudice at various times through the twentieth and early twenty-first centuries in your community and state? What progress has the organization seen in achieving greater equality and less prejudice for those people they represent? Have a class discussion how prejudice has changed through time.

- **Local Racial Prejudice Issue:** Contact the local branch of the National Association for the Advancement of Colored People (NAACP) and arrange to attend their next meeting. Identify the people who attend. What race and gender is most represented? What are the issues that are of current interest? What issues are the local branch currently working on?

- **Public Housing:** Does your community have public housing? If so, walk or drive around the area and determine what race and gender are predominant there. What is the condition of the housing and parks? Look at the parking lots, lawns, and playgrounds. If possible, ask residents about the quality of service they receive and the condition of their residential units.

- **School Survey About Prejudice:** Do a survey of students in your school. Ask students if they think prejudice is a problem in the United States in the twenty-first century. If so, rank the forms of prejudice in order of their severity—racism, sexism, and classism. Record the gender and race or ethnicity of the students. After gathering your survey information, analyze the data to determine which prejudice is considered the most threatening and who thinks so.

- **Personal Experiences in Prejudice:** Check your own prejudices in regard to gender and racial biases. Go to the *Beyond Prejudice* Web site and click on "Assessing Your Own Prejudices" (http://www.beyondprejudice.com). Do you agree with the results? Also, have a friend make a list of various occupations. Then have the friend read out the occupations one at a time and write down your initial response regarding the type of person you expect to fill that occupation. What does this say about your prejudices?

- **International Courts:** Explore information about the special war crimes tribunals established to prosecute people charged with war crimes. Visit the *International Criminal Tribunals and Special Courts* Web site (http://www.globalpolicy.org/intljustice/tri bindx.htm). Select one of the special courts and report on its successes in bringing alleged criminals to trial and conviction. Also explore the Web site of the *International Criminal Court (ICC)* (http://www.icc-cpi.int/home.html&l=en). Click on "Situations and Cases" to identify what issues have been related to prejudice. What was the prejudice?

- **Genocide in the World:** Make a chart with accompanying map noting the various occurrences of genocide that have occurred in the world since the beginning of the twentieth century. Note the number of people believed killed and the number of people displaced as refugees to escape death and oppression. Are there any patterns of occurrence, such as an increase or decrease through time? What does this say about efforts to eliminate prejudice in the world? What can be done to stop further genocides in the world?

- **Research a Country:** Using the *Human Rights Watch* Web site (http://hrw.org/wr2k5/) that contains their "2005 World Report" and the *Amnesty International* Web site that contains the "Countries and Regions" webpage (http://www.amnestyusa.org/countries/index.do), have each member of the class select a different country or region. Identify the key human rights issues for the selected country. Focus on prejudices and their consequences. You can also use the *Central Intelligence Agency's World Fact Book* Web site (https://www.cia.gov/cia/publications/factbook/index.html) to gain more information about the country and any other issues identified by the CIA.

- **First-Hand Accounts:** Many oral histories of people who experienced Jim Crow laws in the American South, apartheid racial segregation policies in South Africa, Japanese American internment in the American West, the Holocaust in Europe, ethnic conflict in former Yugoslavia, and Rwanda genocide in Africa have been published in the 1990s and early twenty-first century, such as *Remembering Manzanar: Life in a Japanese Relocation Camp* (2002) by Michael L. Cooper. Pick out two of the oral histories and identify the various feelings ranging from hope to despair as people faced the extreme consequences of prejudice. Consider how you would feel if in their place. What would you consider doing to ease the oppression?

- **The Holocaust:** Over a half century after the end of World War II the United States Holocaust Memorial Museum (http://www.ushmm.org) was completed. Located on the Washington, D.C., mall, the memorial serves as a lasting reminder of the most horrible results of prejudice. Research the issues surrounding the memorial's development. Visit the "Holocaust Encyclopedia" on its Web site (http://www.ushmm.org/wlc/en/) to explore other aspects of the Holocaust. Also visit the *Anti-Defamation League* Web site (http://www.adl.org/backgrounders/Anti_Semitism_us.asp) to find out more about the prejudice against Jews in the world.

- **United Nations Declarations:** Go to the *United Nations* Web site and lookup the "Declaration of Human Rights" (http://www.un.org/Overview/rights.html). List the rights that are recognized by the international organization. Do you think they have been effective in combating prejudice?

- **Human Rights Watch Groups:** Explore the Web sites of Amnesty International and Human Rights Watch. What situations are they currently monitoring? Select a study and report to the class what current issues are involved. What prejudices are driving the issues?

- **Middle East Class Debate:** Have the class divide into two groups to discuss the Arab-Israeli conflict. One side present the arguments of the displaced Palestinian Arabs and the other side defend the existence of the state of Israel. What solutions can the class come up with to reach a peaceful co-existence of both?

- **Gender Discrimination:** Show the class a videotape or CD of *The Fairer Sex* (Primetime Live, Oct. 7, 1993), a film that explores the world of gender discrimination in various facets of life. After watching the film, have the class consider whether the discrimination shown is common in their community. If not, why would that be? How is gender discrimination similar to other forms of discrimination, such as racial discrimination? Do the students feel they experience less gender discrimination than shown in the film? Why do they think that is?

- **Gender and the Media:** What gender roles do you see portrayed in popular television programs? How much variation in gender roles do you see? Are there any consistent role models you can identify? How are people portrayed who do not conform to standard gender roles in television programs?

- **Sexual Orientation Prejudice:** Because of the prejudice they face, gays and lesbians often hide their true sexual identity individually and as a group. To gain a better understanding of this segment of society, obtain a list of gay and lesbian groups in your state from the *National Gay and Lesbian Task Force* Web site (http://thetask force.org/). Make a list of the issues currently of concern to gays, lesbians, and transgender groups at http://thetaskforce.org/issues.

- **Gays and the Courts:** Visit the *American Civil Liberties Union (ACLU)* Web site to see how they fight sexual orientation prejudice in the criminal justice system (http://www.aclu.org/lgbt/crimjustice/index.html). To explore further the legal issues facing gays, lesbians, and transgenders, visit the Web site of the *Lamda Legal Defense and Education Fund* (http://www.lamdalegal.org). To learn more about violence against gays and lesbians, see the *New York City Gay and Lesbian Anti-Violence Project* Web site (http://www.avp.org).

- **Government Policies Toward Gays and Lesbians:** In what ways do laws discriminate against gays and lesbians? How are federal employees who are gays or lesbians treated differently than others regarding employment benefits? How do the different legal standards applied to gays and lesbians correspond to the equal protection under the law guaranteed by the U.S. Constitution?

- **The Military and Gays:** What are the military policies toward gays and lesbians? What kind of prejudice from others do gays and lesbians experience in the military?

- **Prejudice in Democracies:** How have prejudices affected representative, democratic governments, such as in the United States? Are the working and lower classes underrepresented among those who vote, donate monies to candidates for public office, and hold office? Can a system be developed that makes access to political power less dependent on wealth? What legislative changes might occur if more women or minorities become members of Congress? How does the percentage of people in different ethnic and gender categories in the last U.S. census compare to percentage of women and minorities in elected offices?

- **Enemy Aliens:** At the beginning of the U.S. involvement in World War II 112,000 Japanese Americans were rounded up by U.S. authorities along the West Coast and placed in remote detention camps. Many were kept there for three years. Sixty years later following the September 11, 2001, terrorist attacks on New York City and Washington, D.C., Arab Americans became highly suspected by the U.S. government and the general public. What similarities and differences to you see between the two periods? How has prejudice played a role in the treatment of people suspected of being enemy aliens? Divide the class into two groups. First discuss the earlier time period from the perspectives of Japanese Americans and general public. Then discuss the later time period from the perspective of Arab Americans and the general public.

- **Race Riots:** Race riots have erupted in various countries throughout the twentieth and early twenty-first centuries, including in France, the United States, South Africa, and Britain. Select a country and write down what factors contributed to its riots. Consider relations between minorities and police departments, treatment of minorities in the criminal justice system, availability of jobs and a good education, and other social factors. See if there was a specific incident that sparked the riots. Compare in class the information gathered on various countries.

- **Racial Profiling:** Examine the issues surrounding racial profiling. Visit the *American Civil Liberties Union* Web site at http://www.aclu.org/profiling. Contact the local police department and see if you can ride along with a police officer on his or her shift. Discuss how the officer keeps alert toward possible crimes. What characteristics of people does the police officer pay attention to? Observe who is stopped and how they are treated.

- **Discussing Racism in Groups:** Examine among class members recent current events that involve racism. How do reactions vary among class members of different racial or ethnic backgrounds? Is the discussion relaxed, or more tense than other kinds of discussions?

- **Crime Statistics:** Annual publications reporting crime statistics in the United States can be found either online or in the reference section of local libraries. They include the Federal Bureau of Investigation's *Uniform Crime Reporting Program (UCR)* yearly report (http://www.fbi.gov/ucr/ucr.htm) or the *National Crime Victimization Survey (NCVS)* by the Bureau of Justice Statistics, an agency in the U.S. Department of Justice (http://www.ojp.us doj.gov/bjs/cvict.htm). Information is provided about both offenders and victims. Look up and report to the class on various statistics reported in the publications relating to different racial groups and each gender. What trends do you detect in homicide victims and offenders by race and gender? What patterns are evident in those who are executed or sentenced to death? How do the statistics reflecting race compare to the overall percentage of minorities in the general population?

- **Prejudice in Advertising:** Advertisements placed in popular magazines through the twentieth century provide a unique look at everyday American life. Not only did companies promote sales of their products in these advertisements, but they eagerly demonstrated expected gender and social role models of the types of people expected to use their products. Magazines that had many full-page advertisements included *Life, Ladies Home Journal, Woman's Home Companion, Good Housekeeping, House & Garden, The Saturday Evening Post, McCall's,* and *Business Week.* At a public or college library request a few issues printed from the early and mid-twentieth century and look at the many advertisements. See if you can detect a gradual change in the ads that reflect changes in society and broader acceptance of people with different backgrounds.

- **Native American Marginalization:** Visit a nearby American Indian reservation or community. If a cultural center exists, visit it and explore the history of that particular tribe and of Native Americans in general. What prejudices had they experienced in life? How did government policies influence Indian marginalization? If there is not a reservation nearby, research if there ever had been one in your area and if so, what happened to it.

- **Hate Crime:** Divide the class into five groups and assign each group to learn about one type of hate crime: (1) racial, (2) gender, (3) religious, (4) sexual orientation, or (5) religion. Find actual high profile examples of hate crime incidents. Each group explain their type of hate crime so the rest of the class can readily understand what is involved.

- **School Violence:** Research, then have a class discussion about what possible prejudices might push a young person to acts of violence ranging from vandalism to shooting his teachers and classmates. What is your school doing to combat acts of prejudice and discrimination, such as bullying?

- **Hate Web sites:** Cyberspace is full of what are referred to as hate Web sites promoting various forms of prejudice, such as neo-Nazis posting anti-minority and anti-Semitic prejudices. Gather information from the *Anti-Defamation League* Web site in regard to hate crimes (http://www.adl.org/hate-patrol/main.asp). What kind of effect do these Web sites pose for society? What leads people to be attracted to such Web sites? What should be done about them while still protecting people's freedom of speech?

- **Social Class Prejudice:** Are social classes in the United States organized groups or simply collections of individuals who happen to have similar incomes and lifestyles? How is the nature of jobs and social classes changing with the loss of higher paying jobs from the United States to other nations in the global economy? Will it continue to change over the next decade or two? How?

- **Employment Trends:** Using *America's Career InfoNet* Web site (http://www.acinet.org/acinet), identify what occupations are growing fastest in your state? Which ones are declining? What do these patterns suggest about opportunities for minorities or women to improve their social status? Visit the *AFL-CIO* union site (http://www.aflcio.org/home.htm) to see what labor issues are most important to workers at present.

Prejudice in the Modern World

Almanac VOLUME 2

12

Genocide in Rwanda

Genocide is an end result of extreme prejudice (a negative attitude towards others based on a prejudgment about those individuals based on little prior knowledge or experience). Genocide is a planned, systematic attempt to eliminate an entire targeted population by murdering all members of that group. In the late 1930s and during World War II (1939–45), the Nazi army, under Germany's dictator, or ruler, Adolf Hitler (1889–1945), methodically rounded up and murdered over six million European Jews. This horrific episode in world history was a genocide known as the Holocaust. Nazis also targeted two other groups, gypsies and homosexuals, for elimination.

Polish lawyer Raphael Lemkin (1900–1959) coined the term "genocide" in the early 1940s. *Genos* is a Greek word meaning race or tribe. The ending *cide* means "to kill." Lemkin, a Jew, fled the Nazi occupation of his homeland Poland in World War II but lost family members in the genocide.

Each genocide that occurs in the world results from issues and difficulties specific to the country where it takes place. However, all genocides have several characteristics in common: (1) racial hatred or long-standing prejudice against a particular group; (2) scapegoating, which means blaming a minority faction, or section, in a society for all of that society's problems; (3) characterization of a minority people as subhuman, unworthy of living; (4) an organized killing plan developed by officials within the country; (5) the means to carry out massive killings, usually involving the country's military; and (6) in the twentieth and twenty-first centuries, an international community that turns away and does not intervene.

Beginning on April 6, 1994, and continuing through June of that year, a genocide took place in a small country in central Africa called Rwanda. Best estimates place the number of people murdered during that period at 800,000 to 850,000. The total population of Rwanda in 1994 was between 7.5 and 8 million people. The Rwandan genocide was aimed at the

WORDS TO KNOW

colonizer: A country that establishes political and economic control over another country and sends citizens to settle in the new country.

extremist: One who takes a position on an issue that is beyond ordinary or moderate positions.

genocide: The deliberate destruction of a racial, religious, or cultural group.

ingrained: A deep-rooted quality.

prejudice: A negative attitude towards others based on a prejudgment about those individuals based on little prior knowledge or experience.

race: A group of people who share a distinctive physical trait.

refugee: A person who flees in search of protection or shelter.

---

elimination of a group of people known as Tutsi, who made up about 14 percent of the country's population. Organized by factions within the Rwandan government, the attempted extermination of the Tutsi was carried out by a group of people called Hutu. Hutu comprised 85 percent of Rwanda's population and controlled the government. Individual Tutsi were not killed because they were poor or wealthy, criminal or law abiding, political or nonpolitical, lazy or hardworking, man, woman, or child, but because they were Tutsi. The international community labeled the turmoil a civil war and chose not to step in until it was too late.

For centuries in Rwanda, Tutsi and Hutu had lived side by side, often intermarrying. Yet in 1994 one group of ordinary poor people, the Hutu, were willing to exterminate their innocent neighbors and family members merely because they were Tutsi. Neighbors killed neighbors, teachers killed their students, and husbands killed their wives. The Rwandan genocide is partly traceable to issues of poverty, land scarcity, and over-population. Most importantly, deeply ingrained ideas of racial differences based on physical characteristics and long-standing bitter prejudice led a frustrated and desperate Hutu people, manipulated by their Hutu leaders, to murder hundreds of thousands of their Tutsi neighbors. This chapter describes how such prejudice took root and grew.

Rwanda: land of a thousand hills

Known as the land of a thousand hills, Rwanda is neither a desert nor a teeming jungle, but a hilly country that lies entirely above 3,280 feet

Bodies of Rwandan genocide victims lie on a mound, while a front-end loader prepares to bury them in a mass grave in July 1994.
AP IMAGES.

(1,000 meters). For centuries it had been protected from hostile tribes and slave traders by mountains, lakes, and marshes. Its temperature, rainfall, and soil were favorable to human habitation and farming. Rwanda resembled a giant garden. The fertile land supported high densities of people. Hutu and Tutsi lived side by side on the same hills. The dense population required a centralized, controlled social structure in order to organize and carry out everyday activities, such as farming, cattle grazing, and keeping order for the benefit of all.

The highly structured society had been headed by a king beginning at some point during the sixteenth or seventeenth centuries. In the late nineteenth century just before European colonizers settled in Rwanda, the king was Tutsi leader Kigeri IV Rwabugiri (d. 1895). Although Rwandan kings were of Tutsi lineage, they did not force Hutu into a slave-like feudal system, a misconception commonly held in history. Instead, they oversaw a complex arrangement where Tutsi and Hutu worked together to sustain a livelihood based on farming and cattle grazing. The king appointed three chiefs for each hill. The chief of landholdings oversaw distribution of land, food production, and taxation. The chief of pastures oversaw cattle and grazing. The chief of men kept a watchful eye on relationships and recruited men for the king's army. Most chiefs were Tutsi but Hutu were also represented among the chiefs. Sometimes one chief might have certain responsibilities on more than one hill. The end goal of the complex system was to sustain all Rwandan families on each hill. Perhaps because it was the only way to maintain order in the densely populated land, the people for centuries had unquestioningly obeyed the king and their chiefs. This habit of strict obedience would play a large part in the 1994 genocide.

Three groups of people—the Hutu, Tutsi, and the Twa—lived in Rwanda. Hutu made up about 85 percent of the population and farmed the land. Tutsi made up about 14 percent of the population and were predominantly cattle herders. In the twenty-first century, most think Tutsi moved into the Rwanda hills sometime during the fifteenth century, most likely to escape famine. Historians and anthropologists (scientists who study human origins) have never reached agreement on the Tutsi's place of origin. The Twa, less than 1 percent of the population, lived by hunting and gathering natural foodstuffs such as roots, or worked in servitude for the king. The three were not separate tribes but shared the same language, worshipped the same gods, and shared the same culture. Intermarriage was common between the Hutu and Tutsi.

Germans arrive in Rwanda

On May 4, 1894, the first European, German count Gustav Adolf von Gotzen, came into the Rwandan kingdom. Rwanda had been previously shut off from the outside world by its landlocked remoteness. At the Berlin Conference of 1885, control of the African continent was divided among European powers so its natural resources could be developed to bring increased wealth to the European countries. Tiny, beautiful Rwanda was claimed by Germany to be part of its colonial empire. Germans knew nothing of Rwanda and sent von Gotzen on an information-gathering mission.

When von Gotzen arrived he found the Hutu, Tutsi, and Twa. He quickly observed that the three differed significantly in physical characteristics. The Twa were pygmies, very small, muscular, and hairy. The Hutu were generally short, but not pygmies. They had thick bodies with big heads, wide noses, and prominent lips. But the Tutsi were different. Tutsi were tall and thin with fine facial features, thin noses and lips, and straight, white teeth.

Manufacturing the great myth

Prior to 1894 the only Europeans to have ventured near Rwanda were British explorers John Hanning Speke (1827–1864) and Sir Richard Francis Burton (1821–1890). They were partners in a 1857–58 expedition to explore the lakes of central Africa, hopefully find the source of the River Nile, and to study local tribes. They never entered Rwanda but located Lake Tanganyika southwest of Rwanda in February 1858. Speke then ventured east of Rwanda to Lake Victoria, which he believed was the source of the Nile. While trekking toward Lake Victoria, Speke encountered black people that he noted had a thin graceful stature. These were most likely Tutsi. In his 1863 report, *Journal of the Discovery of the Source of the Nile,* he presented his theory that the people he encountered were a superior ruling race that had conquered other inferior races living in the area. Speke merely made up his theory as it had no factual basis.

British explorer John Hanning Speke, who encountered people who were likely Tutsi during the 1857–58 expedition he made with Sir Richard Francis Burton. © HULTON-DEUTSCH COLLECTION/CORBIS.

Late-nineteenth-century European anthropologists—along with most all Europeans—were very aware, even obsessed, with racial differences. They considered Caucasians (people of light skin color, commonly from European and Middle East ancestry) superior to any black-skinned group. German colonists who arrived in Rwanda were amazed at the kingdom's sophisticated organization. They believed blacks were savages and never could have produced such an organized society.

Expanding on Speke's thinking, the Germans and other Europeans who learned of Rwanda in the 1890s began building a variety of illogical theories that the fine-featured Tutsi were a superior race that invaded Rwanda in earlier times, conquered the Hutu and Twa, and were the people responsible for Rwanda's organized society. They spoke of the Tutsi as a worthy race that, aside from being black, had none of the Negroid features of the Hutu or Twa. Various theories claimed the Tutsi descended from superior stock in southern Ethiopia, or from the ancient Egyptians, or even from Tibet. The made-up theories became more bizarre, such as Tutsi came from the Garden of Eden (home of Adam and Eve in the Bible), or the fabled lost continent of Atlantis, said to have sunk beneath the sea during an earthquake.

Such theories resulted in the myth of Tutsi superiority. German colonizers stated that Tutsi were gifted with intelligence, boundless energy, natural leadership abilities, refinement in speech manners, and capable of self-control and feelings of love and goodwill. Hutu and Twa were both considered inferior races.

Due to intermarriage, not all Rwandans exhibited precise Tutsi or Hutu physical characteristics, but a mixture of both. Therefore, the German colonists set up physical standards to determine who was a superior Tutsi and who was an inferior Hutu. Their standards were based on nose width and length, height and weight, head width and height, and the shape of their eyes. The colonists manufactured two racial groups in a country that had never before recognized differences. Few in number and pygmies, Twa were ignored.

German placement of Tutsi and Hutu into the mythical categories was the first step, however unintentional, on the path to genocide one hundred years later. The myth became accepted as scientific truth. It greatly influenced both German and later Belgian views toward Tutsi and Hutu.

The myth had a major effect on Rwandan society. For the next sixty years, the Tutsi believed themselves physically and mentally superior, and racial prejudice against the Hutu was extreme. Hutu were deprived of all political and economic power and told they deserved their fate because of their alleged inferiority. This served to frustrate and quietly infuriate the Hutu. A social time bomb had begun ticking.

German colonizers instituted a system called indirect rule. The minority Tutsi were given most chief positions, educated and trained to privileged positions. Germans ruled through the Tutsi. Any punishment to keep Hutu in line was carried out by Tutsi, not the white colonizers. Hutu resented Tutsi, not the Germans who remained in the background.

Belgian colonial domination

Following the defeat of Germany by the Allied powers of Britain, France, Italy, Russia, and the United States in World War I (1914–18), Germany's colonies in Africa were divided between Britain, France, and other countries. Control of Rwanda went to Belgium. The Belgians began to further empower the Tutsi over the Hutu by putting only Tutsi into government jobs. The remaining few Hutu chiefs were replaced with Tutsi chiefs.

The Belgians introduced a forced labor system where every man, woman, and child had to volunteer a specific number of days each week to public projects. Public projects included building permanent structures, such as buildings and bridges, digging anti-erosion terraces, and maintaining roads. The Hutu despised the system; they were often forced to devote over 50 percent of their work time to public projects, taking away from time to grow food for their family. Tutsi were in charge of forcing Hutu to cooperate. Hutu strongly resented Tutsi treatment.

Becoming Christian

In the late 1920s, Tutsi realized that to be on best terms with the white men they had to become Christians, the main religion of the Belgians. Tutsi rejected their native worship practices called kubandwa and flocked to the Catholic Church, newly established in Rwanda by missionary European priests. Destruction of the native religion further destroyed existing cultural ties and connections with Hutu.

The Church immediately supported the Tutsi and from then on played an important part of Rwandan society and politics. The Church provided the only education in the country, and Tutsi were given priority.

Deep-rooted racial prejudice

Racial prejudice had become firmly established in Rwandan society. Most Tutsi were still poor peasants like their Hutu neighbors. However, they too believed the Tutsi/Hutu myth. No matter what the real characteristics of each and every individual, if a person was Hutu he was considered to be stupid, lazy, and dishonest. By merely being Tutsi, an individual was smart, hardworking, and trustworthy.

A clear social order of superior to inferior developed. At the top were the white colonizers: Belgium government officials and Catholic priests. Next in line were the Tutsi elite, then poor Tutsi, and finally all Hutus at the bottom. Few Tutsi had actually become part of the Tutsi elite. Elites are influential and powerful members of the highest social class. As such, they receive the best educations and accrue the most wealth.

After at least four hundred years of Rwandan history in which Tutsi and Hutu lived in equality, the European colonizers had successfully changed the course of the future by altering relations between the two groups. Rwandans had not always lived in peace before colonization; there were kingdom and family battles. But never were the battles simply between Tutsi and Hutu. By the late 1950s, that was the only way struggles were defined.

Hutu's rise

By the early 1950s, the Catholic Church had as many black priests, mostly Tutsi, as white priests. The educated black priests began challenging the European priests for leadership of Rwanda's Catholic Church. Likewise, the Tutsi elite in government leadership roles were challenging the white Belgian colonialists who still held top leadership positions in the country. These Tutsi elite wanted the whites out of Rwanda's government and church so they could declare Rwanda an independent country and rule without oversight of the Europeans. Both Belgian government administrators and the European priests felt their power threatened.

Fearing the Tutsi elite were about to take over control of the Church and government, the European priests and Belgian colonizers decided to raise the status of the Hutu that made up the majority of Rwanda's population. They then planned to use them to suppress and defeat the Tutsi elite. Once the Tutsi elite were removed from leadership roles in the government and Church, the colonizers and European priests intended to install Hutu into those roles. Uneducated and grateful to those in power for their rise in status, Hutu could easily be controlled so that colonizers and European priests would retain all real power in the country.

Carrying out their plan, the colonizers and priests began to incite Hutu against Tutsi elite by claiming they (Tutsi) were responsible for the miserable conditions in which the Hutu lived. With clear moral support and organizational help from the whites, Hutu in the late 1950s established groups for security and for economic and cultural advancement. World coffee prices were strong and Hutu's average family income rose. (Economically the country depended on its export crop, coffee, plus growing subsistence food for the population.) Hutu leaders emerged and the majority Hutu race began to revel in its newfound self-esteem and improved economic situation.

The 1959 revolution of the Hutu began in earnest when a Hutu chief was attacked and severely beaten by Tutsi on November 1. The situation exploded and fierce fighting between Hutu and Tutsi followed. Since Hutu and Tutsi had thought solely in racial terms for about sixty years since the European colonizers made up the Tutsi superiority myth, Hutu indiscriminately lashed out at all Tutsi, including the poor. Just like the Tutsi elite, they were hunted down and killed by the Hutu. Sixty years of Hutu racial hatred towards Tutsi suppression boiled over.

By mid-November amid the violence, Belgian government officials had lost control of the situation and began talking of self-government for Rwanda. Sporadic fighting went on as Hutus continued to hunt down and kill Tutsi. Hutu emerged as clear victors poised to take over the Rwandan government.

In 1960, Hutu began replacing Tutsi chiefs with new Hutu authorities called bourgmestres (legislators). Belgian authorities and Catholic priests supported the Hutu bourgmestres and helped them set up a provisional (transition) government. Bourgmestres formed the Parmehutu Party led by Grégoire Kayibanda (1924–1976). On January 28, 1961, over three thousand bourgmestres, almost all Hutu, declared the creation of the Republic of Rwanda. In September 1961 bourgmestres elected Kayibanda president of Rwanda. On July 1, 1962, Rwanda became formally independent, separate from Belgium.

Although European government control of Rwanda ended, the Catholic Church remained under the leadership of white European priests. The priests no longer supported Tutsi but instead supported and educated the Hutu, who posed no threat to their leadership. Rather than challenging the white priests, Hutu praised whites as their liberators from Tutsi.

Republic of Rwanda

In 1961, the Republic of Rwanda's population was approximately 2.8 million. About 15 percent, or 420,000, were Tutsi. Of those Tutsi, about 120,000 fled to refugee (person who flees in search of protection or shelter) camps in the neighboring countries of Uganda, Burundi, Tanzania, and Zaire (Congo). From both Uganda and Burundi, Tutsi tried to reorganize and periodically launched attacks into Rwanda. For revenge, Hutu officials ordered the slaughter of all remaining Tutsi leaders plus at least ten thousand other Tutsi still living in Rwanda. The violence finally slowed, then ended in 1964.

Kayibanda held power from 1961 until 1973. The president was responsible for the appointment of all leaders, even those at very low levels of local government. He, of course, appointed Hutus, who gradually became the new elites.

The government constantly promoted ideas consisting of three themes: the lofty human worth of being Hutu; the importance of following a moral Christian lifestyle as instructed by the Catholic Church; and the importance of hard work to better the country.

The overwhelming majority of the population worked long hours on the land and lived in poverty, yet never questioned the leadership of the Hutu government or the Catholic Church. Poor but proud, Hutu peasants were content with the idea that they were, each and every one, superior over any Tutsi. Most Tutsi who held positions of power prior to 1959 had fled to neighboring countries. The most wealthy had immigrated to European countries and the United States. Tutsi who remained in the country were poor farmers just like the Hutu peasants. The old way of unquestionable obedience to the local authority predominated and would be a major influence in the genocide to come.

Habyarimana regime (1973–94)

In the early 1970s, as Kayibanda began to age, calls for his replacement mounted among Hutu politicians. In a military coup, the Rwandan army overthrew the Kayibanda government in July 1973. Rwandan army commander Major-General Juvenal Habyarimana (1937–1994) took over the presidency on July 5, 1973. Habyarimana did not allow political parties but in 1974 created his own single party, the Movement Revolutionnaire National pour le Developpement (MRND). Every Rwandan citizen was required to be a member of MRND and to carry a residence identification card. On the ID card was printed where the person lived and whether he or she was Hutu or Tutsi. There were MRND leaders on every hill.

The first ten years of Habyarimana's regime appeared peaceful. However, there was strong ingrained racial prejudice against the Tutsi. Members of the Rwandan army were forbidden to marry Tutsi women. In the government, there were only two Tutsi parliament members out of seventy-one and one Tutsi government agency minister out of about thirty.

Hutu manipulation of foreign aid

In the 1970s, Rwanda's main source of income was from coffee exports. In addition to coffee income, foreign aid that had been nonexistent in the 1960s began increasing as the wealthier countries began programs of providing development aid to poor nations. While the country's economy appeared significantly improved, most of the incoming monies were controlled by the Hutu elite, including Habyarimana, his wife, her family, and close colleagues. They used the money to support extravagant lifestyles—expensive cars, travel, and land purchases from the poor peasants. The Hutu elite grew greedier and greedier while the poor grew more despondent.

It was difficult to recognize what was actually happening in the country. The World Bank and International Monetary Fund (IMF) (international organizations providing money to developing countries), called Habyarimana's regime highly efficient and a model of development in Africa. With coffee export money and developmental aid increasing, the economic picture appeared greatly improved. The international organizations did not look beneath the surface. If they had, they would have found that almost all income went to Habyarimana's inner circle. The World Bank and the IMF granted more and more loans and grants to Rwanda.

By the mid-1980s, developmental aid from foreign countries and international agencies like the World Bank and IMF made up 70 percent of the Rwandan government's budget. Chief donor countries were Belgium and France. The United States was Rwanda's third-largest donor. Switzerland, Germany, and Canada also contributed. The money supposedly went to agricultural development projects to benefit all the people, most of whom were farmers. However, Rwandan government policy actually excluded peasants from economic benefit and favored the Hutu elite and foreign European assistants sent to help with projects. Throughout the 1970s and 1980s, only 4 to 6 percent of aid was spent on rural development, even though 95 percent of the population lived in rural areas. Most development aid money went to the construction of elaborate houses and offices for the Hutu elite and their friends in the capital city, Kigali. The few development projects in rural areas began with big expensive houses for the foreign technical assistants.

Coffee crisis

In 1987 the International Coffee Organization (ICO), an international organization that fixed prices paid for coffee worldwide, began to dissolve as member countries began to not honor their commitments. World prices fell sharply. In June 1989 Rwanda's coffee income and, as a result, its economy was dealt a fatal blow. Under intense pressure from U.S. coffee traders who wanted to pay much less for coffee on the world market, the ICO became deadlocked and lost all control of world prices. By the end of 1989 coffee prices had dropped 50 percent. Retail prices for coffee were more than twenty times the price paid to African farmers as a tremendous amount of coffee wealth went to rich countries.

Since a large percentage of Rwanda's land had been planted in coffee, food for the people to live on was purchased from other countries. With substantially less income, Rwanda could not purchase enough food for its population. By 1990, 50 percent of the population was malnourished.

The Hutu elite, unwilling to give up their fancy lifestyles, cornered what export monies that did come in plus development aid monies. Within the Habyarimana regime there was bickering and in-fighting over money, while the majority of Rwandans sunk more deeply into poverty and hunger.

By the summer of 1990, the Habyarimana regime was being challenged by a number of factions. An increasing number of moderate Hutus in Kigali were unhappy with the greedy, corrupt Habyarimana government. They wanted to overthrow Habyarimana and install an honest Hutu leader who would look after the people. More radical Hutus, mostly within the Hutu elite group, wanted more and more of a share of monies and were angry that Habyarimana even listened to the moderate Hutu. It appeared the Hutu political system was about to collapse. Such a situation was just what Tutsi refugees whose families had fled Rwanda in the early 1960s were waiting for.

Tutsi refugees

In 1964 there were roughly 336,000 Tutsi refugees. They lived in Burundi (about 200,000), Uganda (78,000), Tanzania (36,000), and Zaire (Congo, 22,000). The total number of refugees by 1990 was between 600,000 and 700,000, increased by births and further migration out of Rwanda. Tutsi refugees reminisced about the Rwanda they remembered as a land of prosperity and hoped to return.

In 1979, the refugees had established the Rwandese Refugee Welfare Foundation (RRWF) to aid those in exile. The organization's name was changed several times and in December 1987 it became the Rwandese Patriotic Front (RPF). The RPF was by then a Tutsi military organization intent on returning to and retaking Rwanda. Well-supplied with money from Rwandan Tutsi exiles that had reestablished themselves in successful careers in European countries and the United States, the RPF purchased weapons, planned multiple invasions from Uganda, and waited for the right moment to make a move.

A member of the Rwandese Patriotic Front (RPF) loads a mortar as crowds watch in Kigali, Rwanda, in 1994. © BACI/CORBIS.

Tutsi RPF advance

When it appeared the Hutu political system was about to collapse in 1990, about 2,500 RPF forces moved in. The RPF attacked on October 1, 1990, from Uganda. Kigali residents were terrified and convinced that the Tutsi RPF was ready to launch a full attack on the city. Over national radio the Minister of Defense told the general population to track down and arrest Tutsi infiltrators. In reality, this was an order to track down and kill any Tutsi.

The conflict appeared to have ended by October 30, 1990. Rwanda's regular army, the Forces Armées Rwandaises (FAR), beat back the RPF and they retreated to their Ugandan strongholds. Contrary to appearances, the Tutsi RPF advance into Rwanda was the beginning of a four-year conflict.

Arusha Peace Accords

By 1992, President Habyarimana believed the only way to retain any power was to negotiate some sort of settlement with the RPF. Habyarimana decided to support a ceasefire and began negotiations in Arusha, Tanzania.

The peace agreement signed in Arusha on August 4, 1993, between Habyarimana and the RPF disbanded both the RPF and FAR armies, allowed the return of the Tutsi refugees, and agreed on government power sharing between the Habyarimana government and the RPF. Back in Kigali, many of the Hutu elite had no intention of abiding by the Arusha Accords and were planning their own extremist solution.

Planning of the genocide

The Hutu elite within the Habyarimana regime had benefited from forty years of controlling the government and incoming money from both coffee and foreign aid. Those same Hutu had no intention of allowing President Habyarimana to begin a real democratic process of sharing power with Tutsi.

The Hutu extremists believed they could carry out a scheme to take absolute control of the country. They planned to expel Habyarimana, murder moderate Hutu, defeat the RPF, and kill all Tutsi so as never to be challenged for power by the Tutsi again. They began by organizing anti-Tutsi extremists. In 1992, they formed the radical anti-Habyarimana, anti-Tutsi group, Coalition pour la Defense de la Republique (CDR). The CDR established a fiery radio station and several radical publications, which helped to incite the Hutu masses against all Tutsi.

By the early 1990s, the Hutu peasants had slid from poverty into misery. They were easily manipulated with racist hate propaganda to see the Tutsi as the source of all their problems. During 1992, not only did CDR membership grow but the numbers of anti-Tutsi extremists within the MRND and FAR increased by thousands. The FAR extremists established secret death squads made up of both soldiers and civilians ready and able to kill at a moment's notice when commanded to do so.

Using foreign development aid money, FAR, CDR, and MRND extremists established armed local militias of volunteer citizens, mostly poor, illiterate Hutu peasants. The militias were known as Interhamwe and Impuzamugambi. Both obeyed orders from leaders without questioning. Total acceptance of authority had been the nature of Rwandans in general for centuries. A process known as "Sensibilisation" became commonplace.

"Sensibilisation"

With each new RPF raid into northern Rwanda in 1992 and 1993, the increasingly organized extremist Hutu carried out retaliation by killing Tutsi civilians. To motivate local Hutu peasants to kill Tutsi, the local Hutu officials followed a set pattern known as sensibilisation.

Extremist authorities came to a village and told ridiculous tales that Tutsi were evil beings with horns, tails, hooves, pointed ears, and red eyes that glowed in the dark. Although hard for Americans to understand how, the Hutu peasants were long conditioned to believe what authorities said. Authorities also told Hutu peasants to fear all Tutsi, not just those connected with the RPF. Generally, an extremist official from Kigali came along to lend an air of importance and respectability to the meeting. The killing plan would be approached as if it was just another community work project, a job to do for the good of the people. Since calling the project a bloody massacre would be too harsh, the project was generally called "bush clearing." When the order to go to work came, the peasants carried out the killings as they would any other work order.

Genocide begins

On April 6, 1994, Habyarimana was returning to Kigali airport on his private airplane when two missiles were launched from just outside the airport. Directly hit, the plane crashed into Habyarimana's garden. All aboard were killed. The genocide started in Kigali within the hour.

The identity of Habyarimana's killer is not known. However, the president's assassination and organized start of the genocide within forty-five minutes of it strongly suggested the president's murder was planned by some faction of the Hutu extremists, perhaps extremists in the inner core of his regime. By 9:15 PM, the Interahamwe had set up roadblocks to prevent various Tutsi from fleeing their homes. Impazamugamhi search teams systematically searched Tutsi houses and killed all occupants. Hutu extremists had devised a systematic genocide plan as early as late 1992, complete with names and addresses of proposed victims. In the first hours of the genocide, well-known moderate Hutu in Kigali were murdered along with Kigali Tutsi. At the same time, the radical radio station was pleading for the Hutu population throughout Rwanda to avenge the president's death and kill the Tutsi before the Tutsi could kill them. The genocide had begun.

The final solution

For the Tutsi victims, there were no places to hide. The country was densely populated, leaving no wild country into which one could flee. Neighbors hunted down neighbors. One of the few hiding places was between the ceiling and roof of a house, but soon this became the first place to be checked. Churches proved poor hiding places and turned into death traps. The wounded in hospitals were lined up and killed. It was presumed if individuals were already wounded, they must be Tutsi. Victims were shot or, more often, hacked to death. Victims would sometimes offer their killers money to use bullets rather than machetes.

Eighty percent of deaths occurred between the second week of April and third week of May. Approximately 7,776,000 people lived in Rwanda. On April 6, 1994, approximately 930,000, 12 percent of the population, were Tutsi. By late July, only about 130,000 Tutsi survived—105,000 in refugee camps in Rwanda and neighboring Burundi and 25,000 still in Rwanda but not in camps. It is impossible to determine a precise number of persons killed in the 1994 Rwandan genocide. The United Nations (UN; an international organization created to resolve conflicts in the world and provide humanitarian aid where needed) estimated between 500,000 and 1,000,000 people died in October 1994. In its November 1994 *Final Report* the UN backed off to the more conservative number of 500,000 killed. Within a few years further calculations by researcher Gerard Prunier published in his 1998 book *The Rwanda Crisis: History of a Genocide* taken from the Rwandan census put the number between 800,000 and 850,000 killed. This estimate has been more universally accepted. These number included moderate Hutu killed during the genocide; however, their numbers varied wildly from 10,000 to 30,000.

RPF advance What the Hutu extremists did not count on was the strength of the RPF. While Hutu militias occupied all their time murdering innocent and unarmed Tutsi, the determined, well-armed, and disciplined Tutsi RPF marched into Kigali by April 11 and began a month-long battle to take the city. RPF cut off roads to Kigali and on May 22 took over the airport. The RPF had taken Rwanda.

The RPF swore in their new Tutsi government July 19, 1994. The figurehead president was a Hutu but had supported the RPF. The real man in power was Tutsi RPF leader General Paul Kagame (1957–) who took the title of vice president. The combination of genocide and war had killed 10 percent of the population, left 30 percent in refugee camps, and the rest of the population in complete disarray.

Rwandan refugees. It has been estimated that over 800,000 people were killed in the 1994 Rwandan genocide. © HOWARD DAVIES/
CORBIS.

International community's indifference

During the early 1990, Western powers remained almost entirely passive toward Rwanda's deteriorating human rights record and violent racism. From late 1993 onward, the governments of Western powers and the UN possessed information about an impending genocide.

Arms distributions to the Hutu populations, extremist anti-Tutsi propaganda, violent actions of militia groups, and government-supported massacres of Tutsi all increased. In January 1994, a high-ranking official of the anti-Tutsi Interahamwe militia informed the UN of plans to exterminate all Tutsi. The informant bragged his Interahamwe troops could kill one thousand Tutsi in twenty minutes. He also reported a plan to kill Belgian peacekeepers, hoping their deaths would result in withdrawal of any remaining foreign peacekeepers.

On October 5, 1993, the UN secretary general created the United Nations' Assistance Mission to Rwanda (UNAMIR) to monitor the

French troops offering humanitarian intervention. ©PETER TURNLEY/CORBIS.

situation and protect civilians. UNAMIR had first been proposed by the Arusha Peace Accords. However, UN member countries revealed an unwillingness to send troops or provide resources to give UNAMIR muscle. Rwanda was not politically or economically important enough to any other country to justify the expenditure of sending in assistance.

UNAMIR troops, numbering only 2,548, began arriving in Rwanda in November 1993 but were virtually powerless. The troops witnessed and reported that the Rwandan government was arming Hutu peasants throughout the country. As the genocide began in April 1994, ten Belgian peacekeepers were killed as predicted in January. Belgian and French governments withdrew all their troops participating in UNAMIR by April 14. Western powers still refused to distinguish between a genocide and a civil war. As long as the action in Rwanda was considered a civil war, the foreign powers could ignore the slaughter (see box).

When the UN secretary general received reports on April 29 that 200,000 people had already been massacred, he asked for UNAMIR

Convention on the Prevention and Punishment of Genocide

The General Assembly of the United Nations presented the first international human rights treaty to the world in December 1948. The Convention on the Prevention and Punishment of the Crime of Genocide was the United Nations's answer to the Nazi Holocaust in which six million European Jews and other targeted groups were murdered during World War II (1939–45). In signing the treaty, a nation declared it would cooperate with other nations to ensure genocide never happened again.

The treaty's fundamental intent was to make clear that if the threat of genocide loomed over a people, that threat concerned all humanity. The articles of the treaty defined genocide, listed punishable acts, stated that private individuals as well as rulers and officials could be tried, and declared that trials would be held within the country where the genocide took place or in an international court. As the 1994 Rwandan genocide began, nations of the international community, including the United States, refused to call the unfolding horror a genocide. Instead it was labeled a civil war so the 1948 treaty would not have to be invoked.

In a visit to Rwanda in March 1998, Democratic president Bill Clinton (1946–; 1993–2001) apologized for the United States and world community's lack of help in the crisis. Later, after he left office, Clinton remarked his biggest regret of his presidential years was not acting to prevent the Rwandan genocide.

reinforcements. The United States blocked the reinforcements. With the recent U.S. military disaster in Somalia in October 1993 in which U.S. soldiers were brutally killed by Somalia militia in the Battle of Mogadishu, President Bill Clinton (1946–; served 1993–2001) argued that the UN could not become involved in every conflict in the world. The United States had no pressing national interest to be involved in Rwanda. The United States sent no help until July 1994 when President Clinton directed a humanitarian airdrop of life sustaining supplies and troops to distribute them.

International criminal tribunal for Rwanda

Following the genocide, the UN Security Council established the International Criminal Tribunal for Rwanda (ICTR) to bring to trial those most responsible for the genocide. The ICTR moved slowly and inefficiently in bringing suspects to trial. The ICTR had only a handful of judges and the appeals court was far away in The Hague, Netherlands. In Rwanda the ICTR worked under primitive conditions frequently with no electricity. The Rwandan government was in constant conflict with the

The UN Security Council established the International Criminal Tribunal for Rwanda (ICTR) to bring to trial those most responsible for the genocide. © LANGEVIN JACQUES/CORBIS SYGMA.

ICTR over who would try defendants, Rwandan courts or ICTR, and the death penalty, which ICTR refused to support. Between 1994 and the end of 2004, about sixty-three people, individuals who were accused of being genocide leaders, came under the ICTR process.

Despite inefficiency, the ICTR actions have had a few significant results. Over one hundred genocide leaders, including at least fourteen high-level suspects, remain free as of late 2004. Nevertheless, the international court prosecutors made it extremely difficult for them to reorganize. The ICTR obtained the first-ever international convictions of genocide and the first international conviction for rape (forcing another person to submit to sexual acts) as a war crime (any of various crimes committed during war and considered in violation of the rules of warfare). Furthermore, the ICTR judges and prosecutors are piecing together a factual historical record of the genocide. The successes came at a high cost, about $1.2 billion by 2005, with 872 paid staff members.

The UN Security Council gave the ICTR a deadline of 2008 to complete trials and 2010 to complete appeals.

Aftermath in Rwanda

Shortly after the genocide, Kagame's government detained about 135,000 to 140,000 Hutu in Rwanda and accused them of participation in the genocide. The regular Rwandan courts were in disarray following the genocide. Kagame attempted to reorganize the judicial system so it could handle the thousands of detained Hutu. Still, the number of detainees overwhelmed the Rwandan courts and jails. Between 1997 and June 2002, the courts tried 7,211 persons. These trials resulted in 1,386 acquittals, or releases, and 689 death sentences. However, no executions occurred after 1998.

Ten years after the genocide, Kagame remained in control of the government, a Tutsi government. Of the approximately seven million Rwandans, one million were Tutsi. In 2004, Amnesty International, an international human rights watch group, reported that Rwanda was a tightly controlled country where opposition to the Kagame government was suppressed. Political opposition leaders faced harassment and arrest. There was no freedom of the press. Journalists criticizing the government were harassed, threatened, and detained.

Both Tutsi and Hutu were traumatized people. Whether an individual was a Tutsi survivor or Hutu who carried out horrible acts, all had been severely damaged by the genocide. In the end, both would have to come together as one people to heal the nation. By 2006 it was uncertain if this would be possible. Rwanda remained a very traumatized country in a very unstable part of the world.

For More Information

BOOKS

Berry, John A., and Carol Pott Berry, eds. *Genocide in Rwanda: A Collective Memory.* Washington, DC: Howard University Press, 1999.

Human Rights Watch. *Rwanda: The Search for Security and Human Rights Abuses.* April 2000, Vol. 12(1). Also can be found online at http://www.hrw.org/reports/2000/rwanda/ (accessed on November 7, 2006).

Kim, Sungmin. *Genocide in Rwanda and External Influences: The Intermeshing of Colonial Racism, Development Aid, and Western Powers' Calculated Apathy.* M.A. Thesis, University of Oregon, 2002.

Melvern, Linda. *A People Betrayed: The Role of the West in Rwanda's Genocide.* New York: Zed Books, 2000.

Prunier, Gerard. *The Rwanda Crisis: History of a Genocide.* London: Hurst & Company, 1998.

Scherrer, Christian P. *Genocide and Crisis in Central Africa: Conflict Roots, Mass Violence, and Regional War.* Westport, CT: Praeger, 2002.

Twagilimana, Aimable. *The Debris of Ham: Ethnicity, Regionalism, and the 1994 Rwandan Genocide.* Lanham, MD: University Press of America, 2003.

United Nations Commission of Experts Established Pursuant to Security Council Resolution 935 (1994) on Rwanda. *Final Report.* Geneva, Switzerland: United Nations, 1994.

WEB SITES

International Campaign to End Genocide. http://www.genocidewatch.org (accessed on November 22, 2006).

PBS, and Helen Cobban. "Rwanda Today: The International Criminal Tribunal and the Prospects for Peace and Reconciliation." *Frontline: Ghosts of Rwanda.* http://www.pbs.org/wgbh/pages/frontline/shows/ghosts/today (accessed on November 22, 2006).

"Rwanda." *Amnesty International.* http://web.amnesty.org/report2005/rwa-summary-eng (accessed on November 22, 2006).

"Rwanda." *Central Intelligence Agency (CIA) World Fact Book.* https://www.cia.gov/cia/publications/factbook/geos/rw.html (accessed on November 22, 2006).

"Rwanda." *Human Rights Watch.* http://www.hrw.org/doc?t=africa&c=rwanda (accessed on November 22, 2006).

13

Japanese Internment in America

From 1942 to 1944, over one hundred and twenty thousand Japanese Americans living along the Pacific Coast were detained in internment camps (places in which people are confined in wartime) by the United States government. In Canada, about twenty-three thousand people of Japanese descent were removed from their homes in British Columbia and moved to camps further inland. Both governments' actions were defended as a military necessity after the Japanese bombed Pearl Harbor, Hawaii, on December 7, 1941.

Immigration from Japan to North America began during the late nineteenth century. By 1900 there were over twenty-five thousand Issei (first-generation immigrants from Japan; pronounced "EE-say"), or Japanese citizens, living in the United States. Most settled along the West Coast, where they experienced economic success, especially in agriculture since a large part of the Pacific Coast's economy was built on agriculture and they could bring with them farming skills. However, they did not find social acceptance because of public prejudice against Asian immigrants. By 1940, about one hundred and twenty-seven thousand Japanese Americans lived in the United States. Approximately one-third of these were Issei and the remaining two-thirds were their children and grandchildren, who had been born in the United States and were U.S. citizens.

After the United States entered World War II (1939–45) in 1941, American citizens and government officials assumed Japan would attack the West Coast. In a striking overreaction based on fear and prejudice, Japanese Americans and Japanese aliens were regarded as potential enemy agents. Despite questions from government lawyers about the violation of citizens' constitutional civil rights, the government passed legislation allowing the U.S. Army to detain Japanese Americans based solely on their race. Those living in California, Oregon, Washington, and Arizona were removed from their homes and placed in one of ten internment camps throughout the United States.

WORDS TO KNOW

alien: People who hold citizenship in a foreign country.

detainee: A person held in custody, often for political reasons.

internment camp: A place in which people are confined in wartime.

isolationism: Opposition to foreign commitments or involvement in foreign disputes.

Issei: The first generation of immigrants from Japan to America.

naturalization: The process through which a citizen of one country becomes the citizen of another country, often requiring a certain length of residence.

Nisei: Children of Issei born in the United States.

Thirty-three thousand Japanese Americans served with distinction in the U.S. armed forces, even though many of their family and friends were detained throughout the war years. Prejudice against Asian Americans had been well established during the early years of the nineteenth century in North America. Restricted immigration, laws, and outright hostility set the stage for detaining an entire class of people based on race.

Japanese immigration into the United States

The United States opened Japan to world trade in the mid-nineteenth century when U.S. commodore Matthew C. Perry (1794–1858) sailed into Tokyo Harbor. Japan strove to meet the new challenges of trade and industrialization. Leaders worked to build a powerful nation that would not fall under the domination of any foreign power. The heavy taxes imposed to fund this drive fell mostly on the Japanese farming class. Under the burden of taxation, young males began to leave Japan to look for work as laborers in the independent monarchy, or realm, of Hawaii. Hearing about the new possibilities in America with rapid growth of industry and agriculture in the American West, Japanese began to arrive in the United States by the 1890s. This first generation of immigrants from Japan to America was called Issei.

Issei drew the anger of Americans, who saw the alien Japanese as a competitive threat to their own livelihoods. Alien is a term used to describe people who hold citizenship in a foreign country. Under U.S. immigration law that was strongly prejudiced against Asian immigrants, the Issei were aliens not eligible for citizenship. In contrast, other immigrants arriving from Europe could obtain citizenship. Therefore, they were not able to vote and held no political power among politicians to see that their needs and wants were recognized by the government.

Objecting to the presence of the Japanese on racial and economic grounds, a group of American labor unions formed the Asiatic Exclusion League in 1905 in San Francisco. The League gathered in California in May 1905 to protest the immigration of all Asians into the United States. Various organizations, primarily labor unions, proposed laws and resolutions that encouraged prejudice against the Japanese. In 1906, heightened racism resulted in Japanese children being segregated (separated) from American students in the public school system in California. The move sparked a diplomatic crisis between the two countries. The following year, the United States and Japan reached the Gentleman's Agreement. Japanese children would be integrated back into the public schools, and Japan would not issue any more passports to Japanese wanting to immigrate to the United States to find work.

An unanticipated result of the Gentleman's Agreement was that tens of thousands of Japanese women began to immigrate to the United States. They came in order to participate in arranged marriages with the Issei who desired to create Japanese American families and remain in the United States. The sentiment on the West Coast among the predominantly white public remained one of suspicion against the Japanese, and this new development in immigration only heightened the uneasiness.

While the Japanese were recognized as good laborers with a strong work ethic, they were viewed as competitors for jobs and not welcomed as fellow citizens. This prejudice existed despite the Japanese willingness to take physically difficult and exhausting work that few Americans were willing to take at low pay. They differed in appearance and customs, including clothing and religion, and they experienced limited interaction on a social level with their white neighbors, who were mostly of northern and western European descent. However, the services provided by the Issei became more and more important to the West Coast economy as Japanese small businesses expanded to include everything from produce houses and laundries to hotels and restaurants.

In 1913 and 1920, the California legislature passed the Alien Land Acts which made owning land illegal if the owner was ineligible to apply for citizenship. Some Issei dealt with the problem by setting up corporations to hold title to the land they had accumulated. Others registered their holdings in the names of their children, the Nisei (pronounced

"NEE-say"), who had been born in the United States. Anyone born in the United States, even if parents were aliens, was a U.S. citizen. Both attempts to evade the intent of the law were closed by an amendment to the Alien Land Law in 1923.

Like other immigrant groups who had difficulty integrating into U.S. society in large part due to racial and ethnic discrimination, the Issei tended to gather together in isolated communities such as "Little Tokyo" in Los Angeles and "Little Osaka" in San Francisco. These communities provided educational and religious organizations that strengthened the security of the immigrants' position in their adopted country. On the other hand, it set the largely self-sufficient Japanese apart from the larger community and increased the sense of suspicion and discrimination against them. Initiatives and legislation to restrict or prohibit Japanese immigration, land ownership, and U.S. citizenship would continue for decades to come.

Acting on the public prejudices, Congress passed the Immigration Act of 1924 in order to limit immigration to the United States. Immigrants from Asia and eastern and southern Europe were particularly restricted. Asian immigrants were entirely banned. Americans were greatly prejudiced against eastern and southern European immigrants, who had begun arriving in the United States in large numbers in the 1890s. They were darker skinned and had different cultural traditions than western and northern Europeans who had largely settled North America and many of the southern and eastern Europeans were Catholics, a religion much disdained by the general public in the United States. Life became especially difficult and complicated for children of Issei—the Nisei—who, although they were American citizens, were caught between two countries and two identities. The Issei criticized their own children for being too American while American society viewed them as too Japanese. Despite high expectations from their parents, the Nisei faced limited employment opportunities outside their community.

In the late 1920s, the Nisei organized the Japanese American Citizens League (JACL) in order to increase their involvement in American politics. Membership was extended only to those who possessed U.S. citizenship. One hundred and two registered delegates attended the first convention in Seattle, Washington, on August 29, 1930. The JACL creed, adopted in 1940, declared "I'm proud I'm an American citizen of Japanese ancestry. I pledge myself to do honor to her [America] at all times and places; to defend her against all enemies, foreign and domestic;

to actively assume my duties and obligations as a citizen, cheerfully and without any reservation whatsoever, in the hope that I may become a better American in a greater America."

By 1940, about 127,000 Japanese Americans lived in the United States, approximately 112,000 of them in California and along the Pacific Coast. Less than 50,000 were Issei and the majority were Nisei or their children, called Sansei or "third generation," who were also U.S. citizens.

United States enters World War II

Germany, Italy, and Japan formed an alliance in the late 1930s with the mutual goal of acquiring additional territory for each nation. The three together were known as the Axis Powers. The Japanese leaders believed boundary expansion was necessary to gain control of natural resources for the Japanese people to remain economically competitive with the West and assure Japan's future existence as a strong nation. By the early twentieth century, Japan had already developed an aggressive plan to increase its hold on the territory and natural resources of southern Asia. By 1940, Japan's stated goal was to construct a Japanese Empire that would extend from Manchuria (in Northeastern China) to Thailand.

In 1939, German troops invaded Poland to further expand Germany's growing military domination of Europe. Through a secret agreement with the Soviet Union, Germany divided Poland between itself and the Soviets. As a result of the invasion, Great Britain and France declared war on Germany on September 3, 1939, marking the beginning of World War II. The United States maintained a position of neutrality (not taking sides).

When France was defeated by Germany in June 1940, the United States changed from a policy of neutrality to supporting Great Britain, the chief country opposing Germany. War strategists concluded that the security of the United States depended on the continued existence of the Great Britain. The American government chose to avoid an outright declaration of war because the general public and Congress favored a policy of isolationism (staying out of foreign commitments or involvement in foreign disputes). Instead, the United States planned to provide the British with war materials while maintaining a defensive position against Japan in the Pacific. In July 1940, President Franklin D. Roosevelt (1882–1945; served 1933–45) froze all Japanese assets, or possessions, in the United States and later established a commercial blockade (shutting off a seaport entrance to prevent ships from entering

The Japanese attacked Pearl Harbor on December 7, 1941, with devastating success. GETTY IMAGES.

or leaving) against Japan. This political action greatly increased tensions between Japan and the United States.

In December 1941, Prime Minister Hideki Tojo (1884–1948) began Japan's move toward expansion in the Pacific with an attack on the U.S. naval fleet at Pearl Harbor, Hawaii. Japan's goal was to cripple the U.S. fleet. Tojo reasoned if the United States was unable to resist at sea, Japanese forces would be able to complete their expansion into Southeast Asia and protect their growing empire. The Japanese attacked Pearl Harbor on December 7 with devastating success. On December 8, President Roosevelt asked Congress to declare a state of war against the Empire of Japan. Following declarations of war against the United States by Japan's allies, Germany and Italy, the United States also officially entered World War II in Europe.

The final days of 1941 and early months of 1942 were marked by U.S. preparations for war and fear of further attacks, most likely on the West Coast. Reports of successive Japanese victories throughout Southeast Asia filled the news media. Rumors that Japanese Hawaiians had aided the attack on Pearl Harbor were reported in the U.S. press. Statements by government officials as well as newspaper editors added to the public's fears that a West Coast invasion was at hand.

Threat of a Japanese invasion, often referred to as the "yellow peril" in a derogatory reference to skin color, loomed in the minds of Americans living on the shores of the Pacific Ocean. The shores were patrolled constantly in search of the enemy. Because of the perceived threat to national security, the U.S. and Canadian governments began an intense campaign to remove persons of Japanese ancestry, both U.S. and Canadian citizens and non-citizens, from the Pacific Coast. From 1942 to 1944, the U.S. government evacuated over one hundred and twenty thousand Japanese Americans from their homes and transferred them to detention camps because of fears about their loyalty.

Executive Order 9066

After the Japanese attacked Pearl Harbor, all Japanese living in North America were regarded as potential enemy agents. There was a great deal of pressure to remove them from their West Coast homes. In Canada, there were about 23,000 people of Japanese descent living in the west, mostly in British Colombia. As a member of the British Commonwealth, Canada had been involved in the war since it began in 1939. Following the attack on Pearl Harbor the Canadian government began to move Japanese men of military age to inland work camps. In February 1942, those Japanese Canadians remaining in British Colombia were relocated to camps farther east. Most of their property was confiscated and they lived under stark conditions with poor protection from harsh winter conditions.

Despite warnings from U.S. attorney general Francis Biddle (1886–1968) that the forced removal of U.S. citizens was unconstitutional, President Roosevelt signed Executive Order 9066 on February 19, 1942. Order 9066 authorized the evacuation of selected persons from certain military areas in the country and established curfews and evacuation directives. Congress quickly passed Public Law No. 503, which put Order 9066 into U.S. law.

All Japanese Americans—Issei, Nisei, and even those with only one grandparent of Japanese ancestry—were affected. With the United States

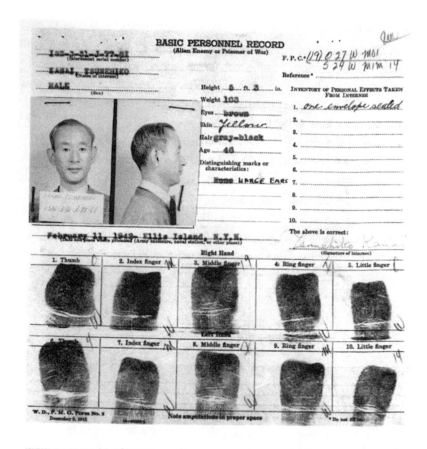

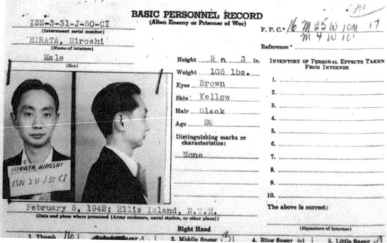

Identification records of Japanese Americans, who during World War II were designated enemy aliens.
AP IMAGES.

at war with Germany and its ally Italy, German and Italian citizens who lived in the United States, and greatly outnumbered the Japanese people living in the designated areas, were also affected by the order. However, those Germans and Italians who were considered suspect would be allowed individual hearings, while the Japanese were not treated as individuals but as an enemy race. All Japanese, Italian, and German aliens in the United States were designated "enemy aliens" and were required to carry special identification or run the risk of being detained or deported. Besides being restricted from traveling near important defense installations such as military bases and shipyards, enemy aliens could not possess short-wave radios or cameras. The government did not want them potentially communicating with Japanese officials overseas or taking pictures of prospective military targets.

The signing of Order 9066 set in motion the steps leading up to the relocation of Japanese Americans on the West Coast. President Roosevelt established the War Relocation Authority (WRA) to oversee their removal. Milton Eisenhower (1899–1985), brother of famous American general Dwight D. Eisenhower (1890–1969), headed the WRA for its first three months to get the program established. He then left to help lead the Office of War Information. Dillon S. Meyer replaced him.

In early 1942 U.S. Army lieutenant general John L. DeWitt (1880–1962), commanding general of the Army's Western Defense Command, ordered the removal of two thousand Japanese living on Terminal Island in Los Angeles, California. They were given twenty-four hours to sell their homes and businesses. DeWitt then declared the western half of California, Oregon, and Washington to be military zones but allowed for voluntary evacuation. Despite selling their property as directed, most Japanese at this time remained where they were as they had no where else to go.

On March 24, 1942, another military order established a nighttime curfew and a five-mile travel restriction on persons of Japanese ancestry. That same day, a removal order was issued on Bainbridge Island, Washington, where military operations were located. Japanese Americans were given twenty-four hours to evacuate. Attempts to resettle outside the military zones were complicated by the five-mile travel restriction. There was uncertainty and confusion over where the Japanese could evacuate to. The general public's threatening attitude frightened the Japanese Americans trying to comply with the military order. The evacuation was initially very chaotic.

In 1942, Japanese Americans were given twenty-four hours to sell their homes and businesses. COURTESY OF THE LIBRARY OF CONGRESS.

By early spring of 1942, the American government solved the evacuation confusion. Officials posted orders in Japanese communities directing all persons of Japanese ancestry to report to assembly points. Each family was issued a number and a list of approved baggage. They could bring only what they could carry and pets were not allowed. With only days to prepare, the Japanese were forced to sell their homes, cars, and businesses at prices far below their market value. Neighbors and others took advantage of the evacuees' situation by buying their possessions and businesses for very little money. Some welcomed the elimination of Japanese Americans as competitors in agriculture and small business. The U.S. government also began legal proceedings to gain control of the evacuees' farmland and other properties.

Relocation centers and internment camps

By June 1942, all Japanese Americans living in California, Oregon, Washington and Arizona had been removed from their homes. The WRA was placed in charge of overseeing the resettlement process for over one hundred thousand people. Some of the detainees had little awareness of their Japanese ancestry, as they were American citizens with as little as one-sixteenth Japanese blood.

Because the evacuation had been hastily arranged, no facilities for detaining the evacuees existed when the order to relocate was given. The WRA used existing structures such as abandoned stockyards, off-season racetracks, and unused fairgrounds to temporarily house the detainees. Having recently left comfortable houses with every modern convenience, the Japanese Americans often found themselves now calling a horse stall their home. Freedom was eliminated and privacy was minimal. Government officials at the centers administered tests to determine each person's level of loyalty to the United States. Among the numerous questions, they were asked whether they wanted to renounce their U.S. citizenship. Feeling great pressure, almost six thousand did. Families stayed an average of one hundred days at an assembly center before being transported to a detention camp.

The first permanent internment facilities were located at Manzanar, California, and Poston, Arizona. They were army reception centers that had been turned over to the WRA to house the detainees. Other camps were hastily built in remote areas inland because many communities were unwilling to accept the detainees in their neighborhoods. Additional camps were built in Tule Lake, California; Gila River, Arizona; Topaz, Utah; Minidoka, Idaho; Amache, Colorado; Heart Mountain, Wyoming; Rohwer, Arkansas; and Jerome, Arkansas. By the first anniversary of the Pearl Harbor attack, over one hundred and ten thousand people of Japanese descent had been placed in a WRA camp. Under the direction of a manager appointed by the army, several hundred white staff members and soldiers managed each camp. Amache was the smallest camp, housing seventy-three hundred detainees, and Tule Lake, holding about eighteen thousand, was the largest.

Early on there was a drive to separate loyal Japanese Americans from the threat of pro-Japanese agitators who considered themselves to be prisoners of war because of their internment by the United States. By 1943, most of the openly defiant detainees who professed to be anti-American had been transferred to the camp at Tule Lake in California where they were under heavy guard.

By June 1942, all Japanese Americans living in California, Oregon, Washington and Arizona had been removed from their homes. AP IMAGES.

The U.S. military commanders in Hawaii were less prejudiced against the 150,000 Japanese Americans living there, about one-third of the island's population. Therefore, people of Japanese ancestry living in the Hawaiian Islands were not sent to relocation camps. Japanese people were the largest single ethnic group in Hawaii at the beginning of World War II and their businesses were an essential part of the economy. As a result, they were not affected except for a few hundred whose loyalty to the United States was suspect. Those were sent to the U.S. mainland for detention.

Creating a life within camps The WRA camps were built in remote parts of the country that few other Americans found habitable. Summer temperatures were often suffocating and winter temperatures sometimes dipped below zero degrees Fahrenheit. Each camp consisted of hundreds of wooden barracks covered with tar paper. A single building housed up to three hundred Japanese Americans. Within each building a family's one-room living quarters measured twenty feet wide by twenty-five feet long. Walls were paper thin and families could hear all that went on within their barracks. WRA officials planned for a family of four to live in each unit but as many as ten people often crowded together in order to keep their extended family together. The residents went to work making furniture and sewing curtains to add personality and privacy to their small homes.

The embarrassing lack of privacy in the barracks was overshadowed by the complete lack of privacy in the public showers and toilets in the camp. Women wore swimsuits to take showers in the crowded facilities and the men gathered scrap lumber to build screens for the men's and women's latrines to allow each individual some privacy.

The barracks were not equipped for each family to cook their own meals and so detainees ate in a common dining hall. A recreation hall housed numerous activities in the camps. For recreation, the Issei made traditional Japanese crafts and artwork from whatever materials they could scrape together. For games, the Nisei used whatever equipment the evacuees had brought with them. Ping pong, badminton, and cards were common indoor games in the recreation halls that were much larger than any of the housing. Basketball, football, golf, and tennis were also options, but everything took second place to the favored American sport of baseball. The detainees, using seeds provided by the government, also tended small "victory gardens" that contained lettuce and various vegetable. These gardens were widely promoted by the government to encourage all Americans, even detained Japanese Americans, to add to the nation's production of food.

The camps developed a sense of routine, and each fall nearly thirty thousand Nisei children were prepared to start school in makeshift classrooms set up by the WRA in one of the barracks. The schools lacked textbooks and laboratory equipment. Often each student's only school supplies were a small blackboard and chalk or writing tablet and pencil. The schools were staffed by white teachers as well as teachers selected from among the detainees.

There was plenty of work for the adults in the camps. Many worked in the kitchens, laundries, or administrative offices while others worked

Japanese Americans line up for a meal at the internment camp in Washington. © SEATTLE POST-INTELLIGENCER COLLECTION; MUSEUM OF HISTORY & INDUSTRY/CORBIS.

in any available fields or orchards. Detainees from the medical professions staffed small hospitals to provide medical care for other residents. Over time, people established churches, post offices, fire departments, and newspapers in order to make life more tolerable in the camps. They made great use of the scant supplies provided them by camp guards or could be salvaged within the camp.

Japanese Americans also willingly worked to do their part for the war effort. Some made huge camouflage nets for the Army to hide military equipment on the battlefield. Where the land allowed, sugar beets were grown to provide sugar for overseas as well as the homefront. Because there was a nationwide shortage of rubber, farmers grew guayule, a plant that contains rubber. It was used to make tires for military vehicles and airplanes necessary for the war. In general, interned Japanese Americans tried to keep up the same homefront activities that all Americans

The Ringle Report

The curfews, evacuations, and detentions of Japanese Americans were all legally challenged in the U.S. courts throughout the war. Over one hundred individuals attempted to challenge the government's orders and a few cases even reached the Supreme Court. These included *Yasui v. United States* (1943), *Hirabayashi v. United States* (1943), and *Korematsu v. United States* (1944). Although Gordon Hirabayashi was convicted of curfew violation, his case did cause the Court to consider the constitutional question of whether the curfew orders issued by U.S. Army Lieutenant General John L. DeWitt could be applied selectively on the basis of race. The Court declared that military necessity required Japanese Americans to be selectively subject to the curfew order because their racial group constituted a greater source of danger to military efforts. Fred Korematsu's case forced the Court to rule on the constitutionality of evacuation and internment. The Court sided with the federal government in stating that the detention was a military necessity and Korematsu's conviction was upheld.

Decades later, a 1983 report by the Commission on Wartime Relocation and Internment of Civilians concluded that Executive Order 9066 was not justified by military necessity. The Commission's findings allowed the courts to reopen the *Korematsu, Yasui,* and *Hirabayashi* cases. It stated that the policies of detention and exclusion were the result of racism, war hysteria, and a failure of political leadership. The commission found that the U.S. government had suppressed important information in a report known as the Ringle Report.

Lieutenant Commander Kenneth D. Ringle, of the Office of Naval Intelligence, had questioned the validity of interning Japanese Americans in a memorandum written in February 1942. The Ringle Report estimated that the number of Japanese Americans who could be considered enemy agents of Japan was less than 3 percent of the total, or about 3,500 Japanese Americans in the United States. The most dangerous of these were already in custodial detention or were well known to the authorities. Ringle concluded that the "Japanese Problem" was greatly distorted and cases should be handled individually and not based on race.

De Witt was aware of the Ringle Report and therefore knew that, according to Naval Intelligence estimates, 90 percent of the Army's evacuation of Japanese Americans was unnecessary. When the Department of Justice filed government briefs in the *Hirabayashi* and *Korematsu* cases it chose not to mention the Ringle Report. Instead it asserted that Japanese Americans must be evacuated as an entire class. The Ringle Report held key evidence that the court could have used in determining the critical question of military necessity. When the cases were reopened, all three convictions were overturned (decision of lower court reversed). It was determined that the government's suppression of evidence resulted in a miscarriage of justice.

participated in across the nation such as Red Cross blood drives, war bond (government certificates sold to individuals and corporations to raise money to finance war with the purchaser receiving their money back plus interest at a future time) sales, and scrap-metal drives. Scrap-metal drives gathered discarded or unused items made of metal, such as metal pots and pans and car parts, that were needed by the defense industry.

Japanese in the U.S. military

Late in 1942, the WRA distributed a form titled "Application for Leave Clearance" for detainees to fill out. The WRA explained that the form would help administrators determine the loyalty of those interned. Japanese Americans who gave acceptable answers would be allowed to leave the camps and move to cities in the eastern and midwestern parts of the country. It was determined there were fewer prejudices against the Japanese in these cities and there were also many war-industry jobs available. U.S. farms were suffering from a labor shortage and many detainees left to return to jobs in agriculture. Anyone who could prove he had employment outside the camp was permitted to leave. Between 1943 and 1944, many thousands of the detainees left for jobs in government departments, defense plants, agriculture, and the military.

The "Application for Leave Clearance" contained twenty-eight questions. The last two questions initially caused a sharp division among those living in the camps. The applicant was asked to swear unqualified allegiance to the United States of America and be prepared to serve in the Armed Forces. Many Issei believed renouncing their Japanese citizenship while not being allowed to become U.S. citizens would leave them without a country. There was also a strong negative reaction to sending young men to war to fight for freedom, liberty and justice while it was denied to their families because of their race.

Nevertheless, despite their internment some Nisei believed that joining the military was their opportunity to finally demonstrate the loyalty that they had always sworn to have for the United States. There were twenty-three thousand men of military age in the camps and the Army initially received about twelve hundred volunteer applications for basic training. Of these, approximately eight hundred passed their physicals and were inducted.

Early in 1943, Nisei recruits left the internment camps for basic training at Camp Shelby, near Hattiesburg, Mississippi. They joined a group of Hawaiian soldiers who made up the 100th Infantry Battalion. Once basic training was completed, the Army shipped the Hawaiian 100th and the all-Japanese American 442nd Regimental Combat Team overseas for combat duty. Over twenty-five thousand Japanese Americans served with distinction in the U.S. armed forces, but the 442nd became the most decorated, or honored with awards, army unit of World War II. The 100th Battalion compiled such an impressive war record that it earned the nickname "the Purple Heart Battalion."

In January 1944, Nisei became eligible for the military draft. They participated in all major campaigns in the Pacific. Several hundred Nisei women also joined the Army. In the war against Japan, Japanese Americans also served in Military Intelligence where they translated captured documents, interrogated prisoners of war, worked with signal intelligence intercepting enemy electronic communications, and issued war propaganda (spreading information, often misinformation, to persuade people to adopt a certain viewpoint). The names of former residents serving in the military were proudly displayed as an honor roll on a billboard in each camp.

Resettlement

While Japanese Americans fought and died for their country, many of their friends and families still lived in internment camps. Angry about their continuing confinement, several thousand Japanese Americans renounced their U.S. citizenship while in camp. Those considered by U.S. officials as greater threats to the United States had been sent to other camps with higher security. Some who renounced their citizenship were repatriated back to Japan; however, most had their U.S. citizenship reinstated when it was ruled that their renunciation occurred under coercion.

By December 1944, the end of the war was in sight with a probable Allied victory. The U.S. Supreme Court ruled in *Korematsu v. United States* that the forced internments were a military necessity and therefore did not violate the U.S. constitutional principles. Nonetheless, the war was winding down and the remaining forty-four thousand Japanese Americans being detained were freed. Many had nowhere to go and lingered at the camps. As a result, the last camp did not actually close until March 1946.

Japanese Americans were allowed to move anywhere in the United States except to the West Coast. Reports of cruelty and inhumane acts by the Japanese military during the war overshadowed the acts of bravery by the Nisei soldiers for many Americans. A great deal of hatred for people of Japanese heritage still existed in the Pacific states. This sentiment is reflected in a quote from a union leader of a central California agricultural association. As reprinted in Michael Cooper's 2000 book *Fighting for Honor: Japanese Americans and World War II,* it reads: "We're charged with wanting to get rid of the Japs for selfish reasons. We might as well be honest. We do. It's a question of whether the white man lives on the Pacific Coast or the brown men. They came into this valley to work, and they stayed to take over."

The Civil Liberties Act

The economic losses suffered by Japanese American internment amounted to more than $400 million in property and income. The psychological stress of confinement and the humiliation of being regarded as traitors to their country cannot be calculated. After the war, some Japanese Americans began to seek financial compensation for the losses they had suffered. The American government passed the Japanese American Evacuation Claims Act of 1948 to compensate evacuees for property damage. The McCarran-Walter Act of 1952 removed the ethnic and racial bars to immigration and naturalization (the process through which a citizen of one country becomes the citizen of another country, often requiring a certain length of residence). Japanese immigrants, as well as resident aliens who had lived in the United States for many years, were allowed to become naturalized citizens. In 1959, U.S. citizenship was restored to Japanese Americans who had renounced it in protest during their confinement.

The extreme ethnic and racial discrimination against Japanese Americans during World War II was long overlooked or ignored by the American public. Finally, in 1976 President Gerald R. Ford (1913–; served 1974–77) formally revoked Executive Order 9066 and issued a statement declaring that the evacuation was wrong. In 1980, Congress established the Commission on Wartime Relocation and Internment of Civilians. The Commission's report, issued in 1983, concluded that 9066 was not justified by military necessity and the government withheld information in the Ringle Report. Congress passed the Civil Liberties Act of 1988 and symbolically named the bill House Resolution 442, in honor of the Nisei battalion 442 of World War II. President Ronald Reagan (1911–2004; served 1981–89) signed the bill, which awarded each person who had been interned an apology and $20,000.

Forty years after the bombing of Pearl Harbor by Japanese, the United States was faced with fear of another ethnic group, Arab Americans. On September 11, 2001, almost three thousand civilians died when terrorists from the Middle East attacked the U.S. mainland. As a result, the U.S.

General hostility made some Japanese Americans fearful of returning to U.S. society at all. In November 1945, fifteen hundred renounced their U.S. citizenship and boarded a ship bound for Japan.

Although some community leaders resisted having Japanese Americans settle in their cities, most of the violence against them occurred in rural farming communities. Stores displayed signs stating Japanese would not be served and town buildings were marked with graffiti bearing racial slurs and threatening physical harm. Just as much as anger over the war, the hostilities were believed to be rooted in the fear of economic competition from the Japanese Americans.

The government offered little assistance for Japanese Americans in their efforts to resettle. The loss of property and income left most with government investigated and deported many Middle Eastern people who were staying in the country illegally. However, the Civil Liberties Act guaranteed that the government would never again incarcerate a group of its own citizens without due process of law (treated fairly and their civil liberties respected). They could not be detained solely on the basis of race Because of that bill, the government did not round up and detain American citizens of Middle Eastern descent or Middle Easterners who were legally in the country as it had with Japanese Americans during World War II.

Ronald Reagan after signing the Civil Liberties Act of 1988. © WALLY MCNAMEE/CORBIS.

little to return to and the additional challenge of starting over. Those who had managed to store some of their property often found it had been stolen or vandalized during their three-year absence. Complicating the struggle to resettle was a housing shortage in many U.S. cities. The severe shortage was caused by American workers who had moved into cities to take advantage of the high wages of war-industry jobs plus the return of millions of veterans. To alleviate the situation, Japanese American churches organized hostels, or inns, for those returning from the camps while others settled into old Army barracks or trailers. Many Japanese Americans were able to integrate back into mainstream society but they carried with them a fear that their ancestry, rather than their actions, would always determine how they would be treated.

For More Information

BOOKS

Conrat, Richard, and Maisie Conrat. *Executive Order 9066.* Los Angeles: California Historical Society, 1972.

Cooper, Michael L. *Fighting for Honor: Japanese Americans and World War II.* New York: Clarion Books, 2000.

Fugita, Stephen S., and Marilyn Fernandez. *Altered Lives, Enduring Community.* Seattle: University of Washington Press, 2004.

Lehman, Jeffrey, and Shirelle Phelps, eds. *West's Encyclopedia of American Law.* 2nd ed. Detroit: Thomson Gale, 2005.

Wells, Anne Sharp. *Historical Dictionary of World War II: The War Against Japan.* Lanham, MD: Scarecrow Press, 1999.

WEB SITES

Japanese American Citizens League. http://www.jacl.org/ (accessed on November 22, 2006).

Japanese American National Museum. http://www.janm.org (accessed on November 22, 2006).

National Japanese American Historical Society. http://www.nikkeiheritage.org/ (accessed on November 22, 2006).

"The War Relocation Authority and The Incarceration of Japanese-Americans During World War II." *Truman Presidential Museum and Library.* http://www.trumanlibrary.org/whistlestop/study_collections/japanese_internment/background.htm (accessed on November 22, 2006).

14

Prejudice in Iraq: Shiítes, Sunni, and Kurds

The modern nation of Iraq (in the Middle East) is home to twenty-six million people. Of those, 97 percent are followers of the religion known as Islam. People who adhere to Islam are called Muslims. Almost all Muslims belong to the two major sects or branches of Islam: Sunni and Shiítes. While worldwide 85 to 90 percent of Muslims are Sunni, in Iraq and neighboring Iran Shiítes are in the majority. Shiíte Arabs make up 60 to 65 percent of the Iraqi population, or about 15.6 to 17 million people. Sunni Arabs represent 32 to 37 percent, about 8.3 to 9.6 million people. People of Arab ethnicity originated in Southwest Asia on the Arabian Peninsula.

Kurds are also Muslims, the majority of whom are Sunni. However, they identify themselves as only the Kurdish people. Kurds make up 15 to 20 percent of Iraq's population, between four and five million people. Kurds descend from Indo-European tribes.

Iraqi Shiítes live primarily in central and southern Iraq, from Baghdad south between the Tigris and Euphrates Rivers to the city of Basra and the Persian Gulf. The Sunni live from Baghdad north along the Tigris and Euphrates Rivers. The entire area of the Tigris and Euphrates River was commonly known as Mesopotamia from ancient times until the end of World War I (1914–18) when the country of Iraq was created. Kurds live in mountainous northeastern Iraq. Kurdish areas in Iraq are bordered on the east by Iran and the north by Turkey.

During the twentieth century, the story of Iraq was one of prejudice, discrimination, and persecution—Sunni against Shiíte, Shiíte against Sunni, and the Sunni-controlled Iraqi government against the Kurds. Taught in early childhood, any Iraqi can relate the story of the separation of Shiíte and Sunni that occurred during the seventh century. The separation left a legacy of prejudice, hatred, and violence among Shiíte and Sunni that spanned fourteen centuries.

WORDS TO KNOW

Kurds: An ethnic group native to a region that includes parts of Syria, Iraq, Iran, and Turkey.

Muslim: A follower of the Islam religion; the two main branches of Muslims are the Sunni and Shiite.

sectarian: A government run by religious leaders of one religion.

secular: A government run by political leaders rather than by leaders of a certain religion.

Sunni-Shiite separation

Sunnis and Shiites originally split over who should rightfully succeed the prophet Muhammad at his death in 632 CE. Sunni followed Abu Bakr (c. 573–634), who was Muhammad's closest companion and a member of Muhammad's tribe, but not his family. Others believed Muhammad wished his son-in-law Ali to succeed him. Ali's followers became known as the Party of Ali or Shi'at Ali.

Over the next twenty-four years, the number of Muslims who followed Ali increased to, eventually, some 160 million followers in 2006. Ali became the fourth Islamic spiritual leader known as a caliph. After only five years as caliph, Ali was assassinated in 661. Devastated followers granted Ali's last wish. They tied his lifeless body to a camel and sent the camel off. Where the camel stopped they built a shrine to Ali and a mosque for worship. The camel stopped at Najaf, located about 100 miles south of Baghdad, near the Euphrates River.

A few decades later in 680, Ali followers—then known as Shiites—urged Ali's son Husayn to challenge the then seventh caliph, a Sunni. However, at the town of Karbala, roughly halfway between Najaf and Baghdad, Husayn, his family, and companions were ambushed and killed by the caliph's men. Both Najaf and Karbala became holy sites to Shiites. The roots of Shiite hatred for Sunni and Sunni for Shiite were firmly rooted.

Shiite Muslims remained a small minority living in the region along the Euphrates River near Najaf and Karbala. Just as the Shiites living in modern day Iran, they were predominantly of Persian ancestry rather than Arab ancestry. Persians descend from various peoples in history, including Arabs, Turks, and Mongolians who settled primarily in Iran.

Shiite population increases

In the nineteenth century, the Iraqi Shiite population dramatically increased with the agricultural improvements that included irrigating

Islamism

Two major groups of Islam worshippers were Sunni and Shiite Muslims. Muslim fundamentalists (religious followers who strictly interpret religious guidance) of both Islamic sects held a set of political beliefs in the early twenty-first century that Islam is not only a religion, but a political system as well. This belief was known as Islamism. The fundamentalists believed that the increasing influences from Western society in the Arab world—including an emphasis on wealth and individualism, as well as Western entertainment— were evil for Islamic societies. Their unhappiness also targeted other Muslims, including leaders of Arab countries who were deemphasizing the role of Islamic religion in government.

In the 1960s, such movements as pan-Arabism (a desire to politically unite all Arab populations in the Middle East and Northern Africa and become free of Western influences) and Arab nationalism (the belief that a particular nation and its culture, people, and values are superior to those of other nations) focused more on cultural similarities among Arab states and favored governments that were more secular in nature. Influenced by the Soviet Union, the more liberal and moderate Arab countries adopted socialist (economic production is controlled by the government for the benefit of all the citizens) forms of government. Islamists opposed this type of government. They wanted a society and legal system strictly based on Islamic codes. During the 1980s, Islamist rebels joined together to challenge the Soviet army in Afghanistan. Heavily funded by the United States, they successfully drove the Soviets out.

Dismay over continued poverty in the Arab states led more Muslims to join in the support of Islamism, and it became a growing influence in Arab countries. Israeli occupation of parts of Palestinian Arab territories in the West Bank and Gaza Strip in the Middle East further fueled the popularity of Islamism and disdain of the United States, which supported Israeli activities. Islamism was carried forward by various organizations, such as the Muslim Brotherhood, in the late twentieth century. During the 1990s, Islamist conflicts occurred in Algeria, Sudan, and Nigeria. In 1996, the Islamist organization known as the Taliban gained power in Afghanistan. Fundamentalists also gained control of Pakistan.

Though Islamism—led by such groups as the Muslim Brotherhood—developed in the early twentieth century, the movement did not become internationally active until the 1980s. It gained considerably more worldwide recognition in the 1990s in reaction to increased U.S. and European military presence in the Middle East triggered by the Persian Gulf War of 1990. In Saudi Arabia, an Islamic group known as the Wahhabi increased its following during this time. Saudi resident and future Al-Qaeda leader Osama bin Laden (1957–) was greatly influenced by the Wahhabi. This gain in support was in reaction to the friendly relations of the Saudi government with the United States during the 1991 Gulf War allowing establishment of permanent U.S. military bases. A coalition force led by the United States repelled Iraqi forces following their invasion of Iraq, and a permanent U.S. military presence was established in Saudi Arabia. Iraqi leader Saddam Hussein took advantage of the Islamists' sentiments by charging that Saudi Arabia had sold out Islamic interests to the West.

The terrorist attack in New York City and Washington, D.C., on September 11, 2001, was attributed to Muslims from Saudi Arabia. The attack, which killed more three thousand civilians, brought the world's attention to Islamism. The Islamist movement in the early twenty-first century remained strong, driven still by U.S. support of Israel, strong U.S. presence in Saudi Arabia, and the U.S.–led war against Muslims in Iraq since 2003. Many Muslims continued to believe the West was prejudiced against them and persecuting them.

the southern desert with a canal from the Euphrates River that was completed. The irrigated land supported dates, rice, and grain. Many Sunni Arabs moved into the region to farm. Being close to the holy places of Najaf and Karbala, the Sunni assimilated and gradually became members of the Shiíte sect. Hence these new Shiítes were of Arab origin, and soon Shiíte Arabs greatly outnumbered Persian Shiítes.

When Shiítes died, they wanted their bodies buried near Ali's at Najaf or Husayn's at Karbala. Cemeteries around the towns grew large. Shiítes made pilgrimages (journeys to a sacred place) to both Najaf and Karbala to pray at the mosques (Muslim houses of worship) and shrines of their ancient leaders.

Iraq is created

Modern Iraq history began in 1920. The Middle East, including Mesopotamia, had been part of the Ottoman Empire (Turkish Empire) since 1534. With the defeat of the Ottoman Empire at the end of World War I, the British and French, both victors, divided the Middle East. Mesopotamia came under British control. Britain arbitrarily (randomly, without apparent logic) created a country out of three former Ottoman provinces: Basra, the Shiíte-dominated land in the south of the Tigris and Euphrates Rivers; Baghdad, the Sunni area to the north; and Mosul, the oil-rich northeastern Kurdish region. This new country was called Iraq. Both Shiíte and Sunni revolted, but the British quickly squashed the uprisings. Britain appointed as king a Sunni Muslim named Faisal I (1885–1933). Britain's move to install a Sunni king led to eight decades of Sunni rule.

King Faisal I died in 1933. His son, Ghazi, took over but was killed in an automobile accident in 1939. Prince Abdul Ilah, Ghazi's brother, led the country until 1953, when Ghazi's son became King Faisal II (1935–1958) at the age of eighteen.

Shiítes, led by their clerics (religious leaders), resisted Sunni rule. Sunni rule was staunchly secular, not run by religious leaders. The Sunni government acted continuously to suppress the Shiítes, whom they considered uneducated radicals.

Constantly denied representation in the government, Shiítes revolted in 1935, but the Faisal monarchy, or realm, easily put down the revolt. Sunnis were favored over the Shiítes for positions in government employment and education. Nevertheless, some Shiítes migrated to Baghdad, Iraq's capital and largest city, and within the city tried to lose their Shiíte identity. Some managed to obtain an education while others became successful shop owners.

Baáth Party rises to power

In the early 1950s, the Iraqi government established oil agreements with foreign companies, and money soon poured into the country. Young educated Sunnis, tired of being under a monarchy and wanting a share of power and oversight in the increasingly prosperous government, moved to overthrow King Faisal II. In 1958, Sunni rebels and army officers overthrew the monarchy, killing both the king and Prince Abdul Ilah. Ten years of political instability followed that included two violent changes in government leadership in 1963, the first as a result of an assassination of the president and the second from a military coup. Through the power struggles the Sunni political party known as the Baáth grew in strength. The Baáth party took control of the government in 1968 and a member, Saddam Hussein (1937–2006), began

King Faisal II was killed and his monarchy was overthrown in 1958. AP IMAGES.

his rise to power. The Baáth party was overwhelmingly Sunni and remained rigorously secular. Baáthist viewed the Shiítes as religious fanatics.

In 1971, the Baáth government completed a takeover of all Iraqi oil facilities from foreign control, a process that had begun in 1961. Many Sunni became wealthy, and Sunni communities prospered. Many Sunni also became prosperous landowners, especially north of Baghdad. Shiítes moved north to work on the Sunni land and some found ways to acquire their own property. However, most Shiítes struggled and lived in poverty.

Shiítes, to combat Sunni dominance, established a political party—al-Dawa—that called for an Islam government run by clerics. The same movement to establish an Islamic state (one run by clerics) was taking place in neighboring Iran but there the Shiítes were in the overwhelming majority, comprising about 90 percent of the population.

Sunni Saddam Hussein takes control

Baáthists' discrimination against and oppression of Shiítes turned deadly. Between 1974 and 1977, thirteen Shiíte clerics were murdered and fifteen others were sent to prison for life. Members of al-Dawa responded with attacks on Baáth offices. The Baáth Party outlawed al-Dawa. Sunni

Muslim Brotherhood

Weary of European colonial powers controlling much of the Arab world in northern Africa and the Middle East, a movement known as the Muslim Brotherhood was created in Egypt in 1928. The Brotherhood opposed Western influences in Arab societies and promoted a return to Islamic states of past centuries. Believing Muslim lands had been trampled over by foreign influences, they also sought to rid Arab nations of leaders who were friendly to Western powers. Branches of the Muslim Brotherhood grew in other Arab states, including Syria and Jordan and, though officially banned, gained political influence. The Brotherhood was not only a religious movement, but a social movement as well. Their goal was to protect workers from unfair treatment by Western companies operating in Arab country. They also promoted construction of hospitals, schools, and other social institutions. By 1948, the Muslim Brotherhood had half a million members, and Cairo was a central meeting place for Muslims.

Anwar Sadat. COURTESY OF THE LIBRARY OF CONGRESS.

The assassination of Egyptian president Anwar Sadat (1918–1981) in 1981 was attributed to the Egyptian Islamic Jihad (a military religious war), a violent wing of the Muslim Brotherhood. They believed Sadat was responsible for introducing Western ideas into Islamic societies. Another violent wing of the Brotherhood was the Islamic Jihad in Palestine to combat the presence of the state of Israel. They also opposed the moderate political policies of the Palestine Liberation Organization (PLO), led by Yasser Arafat (1929–2004). The Brotherhood's popularity continued into the twenty-first century as they continued insisting that Muslims should live according to strict Islamic codes and reject Western ideas and innovations. Another armed wing of the Brotherhood was Hamas, which formed in Gaza in 1987. In the 2005 Egyptian parliamentary elections, though the organization was still officially banned, Brotherhood members won 20 percent of the parliament seats. They largely ran as independent candidates. The Brotherhood was also believed to be influential with insurgents fighting in Iraq against U.S. occupational forces and Iraqis friendly with the Western powers.

Saddam Hussein, by then a Baáthist leader, took control of the Iraqi government in 1979.

At the same time Hussein came to power, the Iranian Shiíte majority overthrew the leader of Iran, Mohammad Reza Pahlavi Shah (1919–1980), and installed a sectarian (religious led) Shiite government with cleric Seyyed Ruhollah Khomeini (c. 1900–1989) as its leader. From that time on, Iraqi Shiites were treated with brutal oppression. Hussein, determined to prevent a Shiite power shift in Iraq as happened in Iran, used his Sunni army and security forces to round up and execute al-Dawa members as well as persons known to aid or sympathize with the party. Tens of thousands of Shiites were kidnapped from their families and never seen again.

Hussein started his brutal hunt of Shiites a year before he began a war with Iran in 1980. Tensions between Iraq and Iran had increased greatly following the Iranian Revolution the previous year in 1979. The Ayatollah Ruhollah Khomeini overthrew the existing Iranian government and established the Islamic Republic of Iran. He called for Islamic revolutionaries across the Muslim world to follow Iran's example. Tensions across the Middle East escalated including a border dispute between Iran and Iraqi. Hussein finally launched an attack on the oil-rich, Iranian-held land of Khuzestan in southwest Iraq, along the Persian Gulf, in September 1980. The very costly war lasted eight years and, all the while, Hussein's forces continued to abduct Shiites and demand proof that they did not sympathize with Iranian Shiites. If their claims were unsatisfactory, they were either executed or forced out of the country. In reality, many Iraqi Shiites fought for Iraq against Iranian Shiites during the war.

Hussein forbade Shiites from public religious rituals and from displaying pictures of Shiite leaders, especially those of Ali and Husayn. He also banned Shiite pilgrimages to Najaf and Karbala. People were threatened to never speak against Hussein. The penalty was death.

The 1991 Shiite uprising

The Iraq-Iran war wound down by 1989 with no significant victories or change of borders but with perhaps as many as nine hundred thousand Iraqis and Iranians killed and injured. The war ended with a ceasefire negotiated under international pressure. In 1990, Hussein directed his forces to invade oil-rich Kuwait, a small Middle East country on the coast of the Persian Gulf between Iraq to the north and Saudi Arabia to the south. Fearful of further expansion by Iraq troops across Kuwait toward the border of Saudi Arabia, a U.S.–led coalition force (made up of many nations) repelled Iraqi forces. U.S. Republican president George H. W. Bush (1924–; served 1989–93) encouraged Iraqi Shiite to rebel and overthrow Hussein.

Out of Iraqi's eighteen provinces, fourteen experienced Shiíte uprisings. However, the United States decided not to lend military support and Hussein brutally halted the rebellion. He bombed Shiíte shrines, houses, and bazaars (marketplaces). His forces terrorized the country slaughtering tens of thousands of Shiítes.

United States invades Iraq, 2003

The United Nations, an organization of the world's nations created to resolve conflicts in the world and provide humanitarian aid where needed, passed resolutions throughout the 1990s demanding Hussein halt any productions of weapons of mass destruction (nuclear and biological weapons capable of killing large numbers of people). Hussein continued to terrorize the Kurdish and Shiíte populations as the United States carried out numerous bombing missions against Iraqi military installations including Operation Desert Strike that lasted several weeks in October 1996 and Operation Desert Fox in December 1998. The resolutions seemingly went unheeded and U.S. forces invaded Iraq in the spring of 2003 amid an international controversy over whether any weapons of mass destruction actually existed. Hussein's government fell on April 9, 2003, and Hussein was captured on December 13, 2003. Shiítes for the first time in eighty years were no longer under Sunni rule. However the Iraq war continued even though U.S. president George W. Bush (1946–; served 2001–) had declared it over in 2003. By 2006 a civil war had developed between the Sunnis and Shiítes.

Shiítes embraced their newfound freedom enthusiastically. They immediately renamed streets, bridges, and public gathering areas after Shiíte leaders and heroes. All likenesses and representations of Hussein were destroyed. Pilgrimages to Najaf and Karbala began again and crowded those cities. Merchants sold prayer beads, rugs, and clogs of earth from the holy cities to the faithful.

Shiítes again performed public religious rituals once banned under Hussein. For example, Shiíte men paraded through streets beating their backs with chains. The ritual symbolized Ali's suffering. The Shiítes again publicly commemorated their holiest day of the year, Ashoura, marking the death of Husyn in Karbala in BCE 680.

The already vast cemeteries around Najaf and Karbala grew dramatically as Shiítes brought back corpses of loved ones they had sought and found. Human rights groups estimated anywhere from three hundred thousand people to seven million, mostly Shiítes, were murdered under

Shiítes again perform public religious rituals once banned under Saddam Hussein. AP IMAGES.

Hussein's rule. At the end of 2003, two large issues loomed. Iraqi Shiítes would have great difficulty putting aside grievances and deep hurt. They, along with the Sunni, would need to carve out a new Iraqi self-image as one people, which would require Sunnis to accept not being in total control of the country.

By early 2006, Iraqis had freely elected a permanent government. Reflecting the Iraqi population makeup, Shiítes won a clear majority, but about 20 percent of representatives were Sunni. A new constitution had been completed and approved by the people in October 2005. The constitution provided several basic principles: a democratic (power of government held by the people through election of political leaders) form of government; freedom of religion though Islam is identified as the national religion; and, the right to assemble. Whether the new Iraq would actually work was uncertain because of the sectarian (religious) strife that steadily worsened through 2006.

The United States still maintained an occupation force of about 150,000 troops in Iraq to attempt to keep order. However, daily violence continued claimed the lives of Iraqi civilians, police, and military, as well as American soldiers. By late 2005 and early 2006, Iraqis were segregating into Shiite and Sunni enclaves. By late 2006 some 53,000 Iraqi civilians had been killed and over 3,000 U.S. and other coalition soldiers including over 2,700 U.S. soldiers after the war was declared over by American leaders.

Deep division

Two and half years after the U.S. invasion, the deep divisions and hatred between Shiite and Sunni surfaced. The most violent areas in late 2005 and early 2006 were in a large circle around Baghdad. The U.S. military estimated 85 percent of violent attacks were occurring in Baghdad and in communities to the north, west, and south.

The belt around Baghdad, including the city and at least forty outlying towns, had until the last few years been mixed with Sunni and Shiite residents. Since the U.S. invasion, families seeking safety from violent prejudicial acts had been packing up and moving where their sect predominated. The movement resulted in segregation of areas in Baghdad and of whole towns. In Baghdad, as in towns around the city, entire sections were becoming Sunni only or Shiite only.

In 2006, violence continued to escalate in the Baghdad belt. Contributing to the violence were the Iraqi security forces who were supposed to maintain peace. Although the United States trained a new Iraqi army and police force, it appeared the new Iraqi battalions were not mixed. Instead, men in battalions in the northeast were overwhelming Kurdish, battalions to the south were Shiite, and battalions in the belt were largely segregated into either Shiite or Sunni. According to news reports, some Shiite young men openly declare that they joined a security force to make their revenge-taking against Sunni appear lawful.

Sunni leaders claimed daily harassment, seizure, and executions of Sunnis by Shiite-dominated security forces. According to these leaders, the Shiite forces who were under command of the Iraqi Interior Ministry canvassed neighborhoods, arresting and allegedly assassinating Sunni. Shiites, on the other hand, claimed they were targeted by Sunnis in killings, often by suicide bombings. Threatening letters, hate graffiti on walls, individual murders, and suicide bombers at funerals, mosques, and most any public place all are part of dangerous daily life in Iraq.

The Shiíte families who lived in the predominantly Sunni towns of Samarra and Tarmiya north of Baghdad constantly received death threats. By 2005 and 2006, they were unable to leave the walls of their homes. Most moved from Sunni to Shiíte communities within Baghdad or to towns to the south such as Madaen, Hilla, and Hut. Conversely, Sunni families of those same towns moved to Sunni neighborhoods in Baghdad or towns to the north such as Samarra and Tarmiya. Such scenarios were playing out throughout the Baghdad belt. Those who remained in mixed neighborhoods were keenly aware of their surroundings and lived in fear with threats and violence. Violence and counterviolence (violence in response to violence) made the old hatreds only more bitter and lessened the likelihood of a united Iraq.

Kurds in Iraq

Kurds numbered twenty-five to thirty million worldwide in the early 2000s. The majority lived in a mountainous area of about 230,000 square miles that is located in four countries, Iraq, Turkey, Iran, and Syria. For over a millennium this area was called Kurdistan. There were approximately four to five million Kurds in Iraq, 13.5 million in Turkey, 6.5 million in Iran, and a little over one million in Syria. Several million more lived in various countries in Asia. Kurds are not Arabs; instead, their ancestors are Indo-European tribes that inhabited the mountainous regions for as long as four thousand years. Arabs conquered these mountain people in the seventh century and Islamicized them, meaning they made them followers of Islam. In modern times Kurds like other Muslims were either Sunni or Shiíte. The majority were Sunni. However, the hatred that separated Sunni Arabs from Shiíte Arabs did not exist among Kurds.

The Kurds were the world's largest ethnic group without their own country. Their desire for a Kurdish nation led to uprisings in all four countries of Iraq, Iran, Syria, and Turkey comprising ancient Kurdistan. In modern times, the Kurdish lack of an independent homeland became known as the Kurdish problem.

Following World War I and the breakup of the Ottoman Empire (1299–1922), the 1920 Treaty of Sevres called for a country for Kurds. However, the subsequent Treaty of Lausanne, signed in 1923, failed to fulfill that promise of a Kurdish homeland. Uprisings among the Kurdish in Iraq, Iran, Turkey, and Syria resulted.

Prejudice Suffered by Kurds in Turkey, Syria, and Iran

Prejudice (a negative attitude towards others based on a prejudgment about those individuals with no prior knowledge or experience) against Kurds in countries bordering Iraq—Turkey, Syria, and Iran—is ongoing even in the twenty-first century. Kurds experience prejudice and discrimination (treating some differently than others or favoring one social group over another based on prejudices) culturally, socially, politically, including the banning of their language.

Following World War I, Article 62 of the Treaty of Sèvres signed in 1920 allowed for self-rule, called autonomous rule, in areas predominantly populated by Kurds. Article 64 suggested independence for the Kurdish people. However, the subsequent Treaty of Lausanne signed in Switzerland in 1923 made no provision for Kurdish independence.

With no hope for a homeland, Kurds in Turkey rebelled in three violent uprisings in 1925, 1930, and 1936-38. Movement for Kurdish autonomy arose in the 1960s, 1970s, and 1980 but was harshly repressed by Turkish military.

As a result, Turkey attempted to abolish any Kurdish identity. Through the 1980s, the Turkish constitution banned the use of the Kurdish language in both speech and written word. Someone overheard using Kurdish words were subject to police surveillance or arrest. During the 1980s, Turkish troops destroyed thousands of Kurdish villages, just as Saddam Hussein destroyed Kurdish towns in Iraq.

Turkey. Referred to as animals, microbes, or worthless, Kurds in Turkey were subjected to dehumanizing speech. Kurdish political parties were systematically restricted and shut down. Those Kurdish leaders who spoke of a separatist movement (separating from Turkey and claiming independent rule) were imprisoned. The most famous jailed political leader was Leyla Zana

(1961–), the first Kurdish woman elected to Turkey's parliament (government) in 1991. When taking the oath for her seat in parliament, Zana spoke in Kurdish and wore the colors representing the Kurdish flag, yellow, green, and red. Her language and clothing outraged the other members of parliament. The Kurd areas of southeastern Turkey are the most economically underdeveloped in the country. While other areas of Turkey had greatly modernized with industrial growth, Kurdish areas lagged far behind since the Turkish government withheld resources from the area.

Syria. Amnesty International, a worldwide human rights organization, reported in 2005 that Kurds, although the second largest ethnic group in Syria, were routinely victims of prejudice and discrimination. Kurds were barred from many professions, not allowed to own property, and refused admission to study at the university. No published materials in Kurdish were allowed. When Kurds attempted to protest the discrimination, they faced arrest, torture, and unfair trials.

Iran. Since World War I, the Kurds were in constant revolt against the Iranian government. They actually managed to establish in December 1945 the only Kurdish independent nation, the Mahabad Republic of Kurdistan. The Mahabad Republic came to a quick end in December 1946 when the Iranian army easily defeated the Kurds. Subsequent revolts by Kurds—the largest occurring from 1979 to 1984, when the Ayatollah Khomeini established religious rule in Iran—were met with suppression of Kurdish activities, including arrests, and executions. One tactic used by Iranian governments to end revolts was the assassination of Kurdish leaders. At the beginning of the twenty-first century, Kurds in Iran continued as a discriminated minority.

In Iraq, most Kurds lived in the northeast in an area about the size of Austria. The land they occupied held about two-thirds of the oil production and reserves of Iraq. For this reason, the Iraqi government long feared Kurdish separation and the loss of most of its wealth. Furthermore, the Iraqi government believed if the Kurds gained independence, then Shiítes in the southern regions might also demand independence, likely meaning an end to modern Iraq. Since the establishment of the Iraqi state in 1932, succeeding Iraqi regimes have kept Kurdish separation movements suppressed. Kurds have suffered cultural and political discrimination, destruction of entire towns, and, in the late 1980s, genocide. Genocide is a planned systematic attempt to eliminate a whole targeted group of people by exterminating all members of that group.

Kurdish and Iraqi militaries engaged in fighting in the 1960s, conflict that ended with sixty thousand deaths and hundreds of thousands of displaced persons when hundreds of villages were destroyed. Fighting again broke out in 1978 and 1979 with Iraqi government forces soundly defeating Kurdish guerilla fighters (small groups of combatants). Six hundred Kurdish villages were destroyed and 200,000 Kurds displaced to other parts of Iraq.

Chemical attacks wipe out thousands Determined to halt the Kurd rebellions, the Baáth Party in the 1960s began severe oppression of Kurds, murdering many. When Saddam Hussein took power in 1979, he continued the campaign. However, in the 1980s, Kurds attempted to take advantage of situations when Iraqi forces were busy warring with neighboring Iran. Hussein's response culminated in a Kurdish genocide in 1987-88. Al-Anfal (anfal means spoils) was the codename for the genocide, a planned military operation directed by Hussein's cousin Ali Hasan al-Majid. Al-Majid became known as "Chemical Ali" because he unleashed chemical weapons against Kurds.

During the genocide, rebel villages were identified as "prohibited" areas where the Iraqi military were told to kill every living thing, humans and animals alike. In many villages, men fifteen to seventy were separated from children, women, and elderly men and either killed or taken to detention camps (a large center created to hold members of an undesirable peoples, such as political prisoners or members of an ethnic group).

In March 1988, Chemical Ali used lethal chemicals on the residents of Halabja, a town of forty to fifty thousand people. The attack on Halabja took place on March 16. Within hours, five thousand innocent

Ali Hassan al-Majid, Iraqi president Saddam Hussein's cousin, became known as "Chemical Ali" because he unleashed chemical weapons against Kurds. ROBERT NICKELSBERG/TIME LIFE PICTURES/GETTY IMAGES.

people (75 percent of them women and children) were dead and another ten thousand maimed, disabled, or disfigured. The other days were spent attacking other of the forty cities and towns. The attack on Halabja was the worst chemical attack in modern times. The chemicals used included mustard gas, cyanide, and the nerve agents Sarin, Tabun, and VX. Most victims are believed to have died instantly when the chemical agents destroyed their body or paralyzed them. Conventional weapons such as bombs and artillery shells also were used to bombard the town. Over the course of three days, about twelve thousand innocent people died.

The fighting continues The embittered Kurds again rose up against Hussein in 1991 when his forces were involved in the invasion of Kuwait. When the United States military, with help from forces of many nations, repelled the Iraqi forces from Kuwait, a safe haven was set up in northern Iraqi Kurdistan for Kurds. Under the direction of the

Two million Kurds flee Iraq, settling at camps on the border to wait for humanitarian aid. © DANIEL LAINÉ/CORBIS.

United Nations, humanitarian aid reached the Kurds located along the Iraq-Turkey border. A northern no-fly zone was established to prevent the Iraqi air force from carrying out bombing raids on the Kurds.

From October 1991 until the overthrow of the Iraqi government by U.S. forces in 2003, the Kurdish people in the safe haven were left to govern themselves. The area became a place of freedom. Thousands of Iraqi refugees seeking freedom and a more peaceful existence went to the no-fly zone. Basic rights of the people—including those other than Kurds—were protected by the Kurdish leadership.

Thousands of destroyed villages and towns in Iraq were rebuilt, and families returned. Following the U.S. invasion of Iraq in 2003 and the fall of Saddam Hussein, the Kurdish region was the most stable of the entire country. Kurds participated in the democratic election of government officials and voted approval of the Iraqi constitution that protected their rights. In 2006, as Sunni Arabs and Shiíte Arabs carried out violent actions against one another elsewhere in Iraq, Iraqi Kurdistan remained stable and relatively free of violence.

Building a unified Iraq continued to prove difficult. Kurds, Sunnis, and Shiites, though all Muslim, had far different goals. In federal government elections Shiite Arabs voted overwhelmingly for candidates of religious parties. If their votes were the only votes, a sectarian (ruled by religious leaders) or theocratic government, such as that of neighboring Iran, would no doubt be established in Iraq. Sunni Arabs had no desire for a sectarian government and were anti-Iranian. Sunni strongly opposed and feared the establishment of a sectarian Shiite government in Iraq. Kurds also desired a secular (non-religious) government. However, Iraqi Kurds ideally preferred to be separated from Iraq so that they might establish their own nation: Kurdistan.

The newly approved constitution actually protected all three groups, allowing each to partially achieve their goals for governance. All three received a share of Iraq's oil revenue (income). When Sunni dictators were in power they used oil revenues to finance their own development and the destruction of the northern Kurdish region and the Shiite south. Kurds remained secular in their region; the Shiites created a sectarian region in southern Iraq if they desired. Sunnis were to be protected from Shiite domination. Whether the newly elected representative government and the constitution could hold the country together remained in question in late 2006.

For More Information

BOOKS

Esposito, John L. *Oxford History of Islam.* New York: Oxford University Press, 1999.

Kepel, Gilles. *Jihad: The Trail of Political Islam.* Cambridge, MA: Harvard University Press, 2002.

Lapidus, Ira M. *A History of Islamic Societies.* New York: Cambridge University Press, 2002.

Peters, Francis E. *Muhammad and the Origins of Islam.* Albany: State University of New York Press, 1994.

PERIODICALS

Di Giovanni, Janine. "Reaching For Power." *National Geographic,* June 2004, pp. 2–35.

Tavernise, Sabrina. "Sectarian Hatred Pulls Apart Iraq's Mixed Towns." *New York Times,* November 20, 2005.

WEB SITES

"Iraq." *CIA World Factbook.* https://www.cia.gov/cia/publications/factbook/geos/iz.html (accessed on November 22, 2006).

"Saddam's Chemical Weapons Campaign: Halabja, March 16, 1988." *U.S. Department of State.* http://www.state.gov/r/pa/ei/rls/18714.htm (accessed on November 22, 2006).

15

Multi-Ethnic Conflict: Yugoslavia

At the end of the twentieth century no region of the world better illustrated ethnic conflict than that of the Balkan countries formerly united as Yugoslavia. The term ethnic refers to a group of people recognized by certain characteristics, such as culture, national origin, ancestral history, or certain physical traits. Ethnic prejudice and violence became so dramatic in the region that the term ethnic cleansing was commonly used for the first time. It was used widely by the news media reporting on the conflict. Ethnic cleansing means the deliberate attempt to eliminate an entire ethnic group. Ethnic cleansing is a particular form of genocide (the deliberate destruction of a racial, religious, or cultural group) based on ethnic prejudice.

The violence erupted in Yugoslavia following the breakup of the Soviet Union in 1991. The former world superpower had controlled Yugoslavia for more than forty-five years following World War II (1939–45), a war in which the Allied forces including the United States, Britain, and the Soviet Union defeated Germany. Turmoil in the region lasted through much of the 1990s based on long-standing ethnic tensions within the former Yugoslavia. It led to mass killing among ethnic Serbs, Croats, Bosnian Muslims, and Kosovo Albanians as Yugoslavia broke apart. Western nations from Europe and North America responded with force after numerous rounds of peace negotiations failed. The ethnic violence was associated with the rise and fall of Serbian leader Slobodan Milosevic (1941–2006). For many around the world Milosevic became the human face of ethnic cleansing and violence.

Early ethnic tensions

Immediately following World War I (1914–18) in 1918 the Kingdom of the Serbs, Croats, and Slovenes was established. They adopted the name Yugoslavia in 1929. During the 1930s it became apparent that the ethnic

WORDS TO KNOW

autonomy: Freedom of a government to make its own decisions known as self-rule.

crime against humanity: A criminal offense in international law that refers to murderous actions on such a large scale that it affects the global population as a whole.

embargo: A ban on shipping of goods and trade; usually an action taken against a foreign

nation for violating treaties or other undesired activities.

federalist state: A national government system in which a central government shares power with provincial governments such as states.

genocide: The deliberate mass destruction of a racial, religious, or cultural group.

groups were unwilling to blend and merge together. The Serbs who made up about 40 percent of the population dominated politics. The Croats and Slovenes resented Serbian aggressiveness. These ethnic groups lived an uneasy coexistence each distrustful of the other. Political assassinations were not unusual.

World War II and ethnic violence

Yugoslavia witnessed bitter ethnic relationships and rivalries during World War II. At the beginning of World War II, the Yugoslav leadership formed a military alliance with Nazi Germany. However, political upheaval followed and German dictator, or tyrannical ruler, Adolf Hitler (1889–1945) ordered air attacks on Belgrade. German ground troops arrived on April 6, 1941. The Yugoslav army was defeated in eleven days by forces from Germany and its allies including Italy, Albania, Bulgaria, Romania, and Hungary. They were known as the Axis Powers in addition to Japan.

Following the German arrival, Yugoslavia was no longer a single, independent state. Instead, its land was parceled among its conquerors. For example, Italy and Germany shared Slovenia, Italy controlled various other areas including Albania and the Kosovo region of southern Serbia, and Germany and Bulgaria controlled parts of Serbia and Macedonia. Croatia declared itself an independent state and incorporated large sections of Bosnia-Herzegovina with the help of Nazi troops.

The Croat leadership, sharing a belief in the fascist (a political system in which a strong central government, usually run by a dictator, controls the nation) Nazi vision of ethnic purity, set out to rid Croatia of Serbs. From 1941 to 1945, the regime of Ante Pavelić (1889–1959) expelled

Serbs from Croatia and Bosnia-Herzegovina, forced Orthodox Serbs to convert to Catholicism, and placed Serbs in concentration camps just as Germany was doing to Jews. Over 300,000 Serbs and Jews in Croatia were killed or disappeared.

Meanwhile violence and murder accompanied the German occupation of northern Slovenia. Slovenes were forcibly removed from their farms and homes and placed in Serbia. Slovene culture was banished and German colonists claimed the land and dwellings left behind by the forced relocation.

Various resistance movements formed in the areas occupied by the Axis powers, most notably led by Communist activist Josip Broz Tito (1892–1980), a Croat-Slovenian. (Communism is a political and economic system where a single party controls all aspects of citizens' lives and private ownership of property is banned.) In July 1941, after the Germans launched a surprise attack on the Soviet Union, armed Communist supporters in the Yugoslav region launched

Communist activist Josip Tito.
GETTY IMAGES.

attacks against their German occupiers. They succeeded in holding parts of western Serbia. In December 1943 the Allied forces held a conference at Tehran, Iran, and decided to support Tito's resistance movement. They provided weapons and supplies. After all enemy armies were driven out of Yugoslavia, Tito became prime minister of a newly reunified government of Yugoslavia and the Communists had positioned themselves to rule.

In November 1945 the Communist Party captured 90 percent of the vote for the nation's legislature. The next year, Yugoslavia adopted a constitution modeled upon the Soviet Constitution of 1936. Yugoslavia was a federation (sharing power between a central government and various states) called the Federal Peoples Republic of Yugoslavia comprised of six states or provinces: Bosnia-Herzegovina, Croatia, Macedonia, Montenegro, Serbia, and Slovenia.

Bosnia-Herzegovina's population included the ethnic groups of Bosnian Muslims, Serbs, and Croatians. Ethnically, Bosnian Muslims were originally the same as Serbs many centuries ago. However, they converted to Islam in the fifteenth century. Bosnian Muslims traditionally

Bosnian Muslims

Under Yugoslav dictator Josip Tito, Muslims in Bosnia gained status and were eventually accorded equal footing with the other five peoples of Yugoslavia—Serbs, Croats, Slovenes, Montenegrins, and Macedonians. In the 1970s many Islamic places of worship, known as mosques, were built in Bosnia and many Bosnians made the annual religious pilgrimage to Mecca. Following World War II, intermarriage between Muslims and non-Muslims increased, as did secularism (non-religious political leadership) within Bosnia. When Sarajevo was awarded the 1984 Winter Olympic Games by the International Olympic Committee, it was a recognition from the international community of the tolerant and cosmopolitan (worldly) atmosphere that flourished in Bosnia.

Bosnian Muslim woman praying. AP IMAGES.

lived in cities working as professionals and in government. Serbs predominantly populated Serbia with Albanians in its southern region known as Kosovo. The majority of Croatia's population was Croatian, Slovenia's population was overwhelmingly Slovene, Montenegro's was predominately of Montenegrins, and Macedonia was dominated by Macedonians.

Despite the language of the constitution and the appearance of Western-style federalism, the government of Yugoslavia was totally controlled by the central Yugoslav Communist Party led by Tito and it was under the direction of the Soviet Union leadership. The party leaders dictated the policies and laws of the nation. Yugoslavia would be controlled by Communists until 1991.

Stirrings of ethnic conflict and the rise of Milosevic

Tito ruled until his death on May 4, 1980. His final years were marked with economic, agricultural, and most notably ethnic difficulty. Tito's death was followed by a decade of attempts to hold the multi-ethnic

Serbs, Croats, Bosnia, and Kosovo Albanians

The people known as Serbs, Bosnian Muslims, and Croats belong to three distinct ethnic groups. All three speak their own dialect of the Serbo-Croatian language. Originally farmers, after World War II Serbs increasingly migrated to cities where they became wage earners. Serbs are strongly influenced by Eastern European culture. Their religion is Eastern Orthodox.

Bosnian Muslims, sometimes referred to as Turks, were originally ethnically the same as Serbs, but converted to the Muslim religion in the fifteenth century. Bosnian Muslims live mostly in cities and are professionals, business owners, and government workers.

Croats are predominantly rural farmers, but many live in cities of southern Croatia. Croats are strongly influenced by the Western European culture in literature, art, science, and education. They are geographically located near the Italian cities of Genoa and Venice. Croatian culture reflects Italian culture. Croats are Roman Catholic.

country together. While the Slovenians and Croats sought increasing independence in economic policies and political decisions, the Serbs supported a stronger federal government. In addition, Albanians in Kosovo voiced demands for greater autonomy (freedom to self-rule). A movement for recognition as a republic began in Kosovo. Slavic Muslims in Bosnia-Herzegovina also asserted their vision of a distinct nation.

In March 1981 Albanian students demonstrated in protest of their poor living conditions at the University of Priština. This protest gained the support of fellow Albanians in Kosovo who made greater demands for republican (a country governed by the consent of the people and for the benefit of the people through elected representatives) government in place of Communist rule. The protests also increased anti-Serb sentiment. The Serbs, who numbered far fewer than the Albanians, countered with accusations of discrimination, terror, and genocide. The Albanian revolt was eventually stopped by the Yugoslav army, but ethnic relations in Kosovo continued to grow more contentious.

The need for police action in Kosovo and the resulting rising costs for that action paid by the citizens of Slovenia and Croatia created resentment. Slovenia became the center of non-Communist political groups. They campaigned for nuclear disarmament of the world's superpowers, feminism (a belief in the social equality of women), and rights for minority groups. Slovenian politicians blamed Serbs for standing in the way of political and economic reform. Moderate Communist leaders tried to lessen the tension between Serbs and Slovenes.

Into the growing chaos and tension stepped Slobodan Milosevic (1941–2006), an ambitious Communist party activist. A Serb, Milosevic emerged as Serbia's leader in 1989 and began pushing to expand Serbia's borders wherever Serbs lived. Milosevic began to violently enforce his dream of a greater Serbia. First focusing within Serbia, he used the Albanian conflicts in Kosovo and the grievances of the Serbs as excuses to remove the former supporters of Tito from the Serbian Communist Party. He assumed its top leadership position. Milosevic persuaded many that Serbs had been the victims of discrimination at the hands of the Tito supporters and that the time had come to assert control over Kosovo and Vojvodina, the northern-most province of Serbia. In 1989 Milosevic and his supporters crafted a new Serbian constitution that eliminated any autonomy enjoyed by Kosovo and Vojvodina. In addition, a new established pro-Milosevic government in Montenegro expanded his control over four of the eight seats in the collective presidency of Yugoslavia that was created following Tito's death.

The breakup of Yugoslavia

In 1990 with the demise of the Soviet Union and its influence, Yugoslavia began to break apart.

Ethnic war begins

Serbs within the province of Croatia, armed and financed by the Serbian-dominated Yugoslav National Army, revolted in August 1990. They blockaded roads and train tracks. Order quickly dissolved as the local Croatian government began trying to disarm the Serb population and dismiss them from employment. In January 1991 the Yugoslav National Army started arresting Croat officials for their anti-Serbian actions while talks aimed at avoiding civil war broke down. Armed conflicts increased as more talks between Croat leaders and Milosevic only further empha-sized their differing points of view.

Finally, Croatia along with Slovenia declared independence from the Yugoslav federation on June 25, 1991. Though the Croat leaders prom-ised equal rights for Serbs within the country, conflicts immediately broke out in Croatia. Serbs living in Croatia, about 12 percent of the population, joined with the nearby Serbian military to halt the indepen-dence move by the Croats. Serbs from Serbia and Croatia immediately began attacking Croatian targets with weapons while the Yugoslav National Army provided air support. Able to fend off the Serb forces through the rest of 1991, Croatia received official recognition as an independent nation by other European nations on January 15, 1992.

Following the path of Croatia and Slovenia, Bosnia-Herzegovina led by the Bosnian Muslims and Croats living in Bosnia and Macedonia also announced in late 1991 their intention to break from the Yugoslav federation. As a result, the war expanded to Bosnia-Herzegovina when Bosnian Serbs joined with the Serbian military to halt the move toward independence.

After engineering the control of Kosovo, Milosevic used his appeal to Serbian nationalism (a belief that a particular nation is superior to other nations) to attract support of Serbs in Croatia and Bosnia-Herzegovina. Croatian Serbs attempted to establish an autonomous (the right to political independence) Serbian cultural society in Croatia. However, this effort only served to increase public support for a Croatian nationalist government that reaffirmed the sovereignty of Croatia.

As a result, the long history of ethnic differences among the Serbs, Bosnian Muslims, and Croats exploded into ethnic war over who would govern whom and what territory would be controlled. All three feared dominance by the other. They believed that dominance by one of the others would mean forced changes in their ethnic traditions.

During the winter of 1991-92, the Yugoslav National Army built artillery camps around Bosnian government-controlled areas, including the city of Sarajevo. The Serbian leader put in place by Milosevic created a Serbian national assembly in place of the Bosnian parliament. Bosnian leaders held free elections in their controlled areas. The vote was nearly unanimous for independence from Yugoslavia. In response, Serbian paramilitary groups began setting up barricades in Sarajevo and taking control of sections of Bosnia. The Yugoslav National Army also began using Bosnian territory to conduct offensive operations against Croatia, while secretly arming Bosnia Serbs and disarming the local Bosnian defense forces.

The resulting war was brutal on all sides. Serbian forces tortured, raped, and murdered Croats and Bosnian Muslims in Serb-controlled regions. Croats and Bosnian Muslims fought back with equal brutality. Homes and businesses were looted and destroyed. Churches including hundreds of mosques, museums, public buildings, architectural and historical landmarks, and cemeteries, all symbols of ethnic identity, were destroyed. Included was the Oriental Institute in Sarajevo, which had housed and preserved thousands of valuable documents and artifacts chronicling the Ottoman history of Bosnia.

On April 6, 1992, Bosnia-Herzegovina joined Croatia and Slovenia in gaining international recognition. The total disintegration of the

The once beautiful city of Sarajevo, which hosted the televised 1984 Winter Olympics, was reduced to a death trap with residents living in basements. MR. TEUN VOETEN.

former Yugoslav federation was nearly complete. In only one year after the fall of Soviet influence the previous six Yugoslav states became five independent countries. Only Serbia and Montenegro remained together as one nation called Serbia. The new nations of Slovenia and Macedonia proved somewhat stable, but conflict raged among the Serbs, Bosnians, and Croats in the other three nations of Serbia, Bosnia-Herzegovina, and Croatia. The ethnic war would eventually be the bloodiest war in Europe since World War II.

During the following three years of war the fighting grew more unpredictable. Local paramilitary bands formed, some no more than groups of thugs, and fought neighborhood to neighborhood. It was frequently difficult to tell who—Serb, Croat, or Bosnian—was fighting whom. The once beautiful city of Sarajevo, which hosted the televised 1984 Winter Olympics, was reduced to a death trap with residents living in basements. It was destroyed. After two years of the fighting that began in Bosnia in 1992, more than two hundred thousand Bosnians died and two million more became refugees.

The West steps in

During the rise in tensions in 1991, Western nations began looking upon the chaotic situation in Yugoslavia with increasing concern. In June 1991 U.S. secretary of state James A. Baker (1930–) visited the region and declared U.S. support for a unified Yugoslav federation. At that time, Baker stated that the United States would not recognize an independent Croatia or Slovenia. However, the United States would also oppose any use of force to prevent their secession (withdrawal from political control).

Months prior to the recognition of these independent states, in September 1991 a conference of European nations fashioned a plan for peace and presented it to the various combatants. The plan was called the Caringon-Cutiliero Plan after its authors, Lord Carrington (1919–) of Great Britain and Portuguese ambassador Jose Cutiliero. The specific aim of the conference was to prevent Bosnia-Herzegovina from slipping into violent conflict already involving Croatia. The proposed plan offered a revised system of government in which power was shared among ethnic groups. It eliminated a Yugoslav centralized government. The local ethnic communities would self-govern. For example, Bosnia-Herzegovina's districts would be classified according to ethnicity. The various groups initially accepted the plan, but before long Bosnian Muslim leader Alija Izetbegovic (1925–2003) decided to withdraw his support and the plan died.

United Nations' involvement

Despite attempting to stay personally removed from involvement in the fighting in early 1992, Milosevic was still seen as the culprit. Many in the West began placing blame for the fighting and violence on Milosevic. He was described as a modern-day Hitler in pursuit of creating what was called greater Serbia, just as Hitler sought an expansion of Germany across Europe. In response to the violence, the United Nations (UN; an international organization founded in 1945 composed of most of the countries in the world) imposed a full-scale embargo (a government order preventing trade of goods with a particular foreign country) upon Yugoslavia. Troops under the flag of the United Nations enforced the embargo.

After the first fighting that took place in Bosnia in the spring of 1992, the frontlines became relatively fixed though the continued fighting was very bloody. In 1993 the United Nations established clearly marked locations under its protection called safe havens. The UN established these places near the cities of Sarajevo, Goržade, and Srebencia.

Two more peace plans

In early 1993 UN special envoy Cyrus Vance (1917–2002), who had earlier served as U.S. secretary of state in the late 1970s, and European Community leader Lord Owen (1938–) began peace negotiations with the warring sides in Bosnia. Vance and Owen proposed dividing Bosnia into ten semi-autonomous (partially independent) regions. The UN supported the plan, but the Serb-dominated Bosnian assembly totally rejected it. This plan was the last peace proposal calling for a united, ethnically mixed Bosnia-Herzegovina.

A later plan fashioned by Lord Owen and Vance's replacement, Norwegian foreign minister Thorvald Stoltenberg (1931–), called for dividing Bosnia into three separate independent states. This proposal allotted to Bosnian Serbs 52 percent of the land, 30 percent to Muslims, and 18 percent to Bosnian Croats. This alternative, offered in late July 1993, was also rejected.

NATO military arrives

With all peace negotiations failing, in 1994 the North Atlantic Treaty Organization (NATO) became involved in the conflict. NATO is a military defense alliance established in April 1949 among Western European and North American nations. Showing its resolve to keep Serbian forces out of Bosnia, NATO jets shot down four Serb aircraft when the Serb planes violated airspace that the UN had identified as off-limits to warring aircraft, known as a "no fly zone."

Despite the NATO presence, the Serbs continued their offensive and began air attacks in November 1994 against Bosnian government installations and areas that the UN had earlier declared as safe. Following a NATO air raid on a Serb air base in Croatia, Bosnian Serbs seized nearly 450 UN peacekeepers as hostages. They also fired missiles at two British aircraft patrolling under the command of NATO. Despite these Serbian actions, UN undersecretary Kofi Annan (1938–) refused a request from NATO to intensify air attacks.

A short-lived ceasefire

In December 1994 the warring factions in Bosnia agreed to a temporary ceasefire. Bosnian Serb leader Radovan Karadzic (1945–) invited former U.S. president Jimmy Carter (1920–; served 1977–81) to meet with leaders of the warring sides. Carter agreed to attend as a private citizen, not as a representative of the U.S. government. Bosnian president Alija Izetbegovic announced that Bosnia would agree only to a short ceasefire. A longer ceasefire agreement would appear as if his government was accepting the territorial gains made by the Serbs.

During the ceasefire in February 1995 a group of five nations proposed another peace plan for Bosnia. The group consisted of France, Germany, Great Britain, Russia, and the United States. They requested that Milosevic recognize the international borders of Bosnia and Croatia and accept a division within Bosnia that would give 49 percent of Bosnia's territory to Bosnian Serbs. At that time, the Serbs held 70 percent of the country's land. In return for his cooperation, the group of nations assured Milosevic that international sanctions (formal restrictions) against Yugoslavia would be lifted. Milosevic rejected the offer.

Ethnic violence escalates

After lasting only four months the ceasefire negotiated by Carter was abruptly broken in March 1995 when the army of Bosnia and Herzegovina launched an offensive against Serb forces. Later that month, American newspapers revealed the contents of a report made by the Central Intelligence Agency (CIA). The report concluded that 90 percent of the ethnic cleansing taking place in Bosnia was by the Serbs. Later that spring, Bosnian Serbs began seizing weapons from UN safe areas and once again taking peacekeepers as hostages.

In July 1995 the Muslim community of Srebrenica in eastern Bosnia-Herzegovina fell to the Serbs who then perpetrated horrible crimes against the people of that town. Nearly eight thousand men and boys were separated from their wives, sisters, daughters, and mothers and killed by Serb soldiers. Following the executions, the dead were buried in mass graves and later dug up and reburied in other graves in a futile attempt to cover up the crime. Even into the twenty-first century many Serb groups continued to deny this act of genocide ever took place.

Another bloody event also soon took place that summer in Croatia. In August 1995 Croats attacked the Serb-held Krajina region inside Croatia. They drove out approximately 170,000 Serbs in just three days. This action was said to be the greatest act of ethnic cleansing during the fighting in the former Yugoslavia at that time.

Violence continued. On August 28 a Sarajevo marketplace was the target of a bomb, killing thirty-seven people. In reaction to the bombing, on September 1 General Bernard Janiver of France, commander of UN forces

A Muslim woman cries in front of her destroyed house in a villager near Srebenica in 2002. © REUTERS/CORBIS.

in the former Yugoslavia, told the head of the Bosnian Serb military, General Ratko Mladic (1943–), that the Serbs must stop any further attacks and withdraw from Sarajevo. NATO declared this same order as an ultimatum (a final demand followed by a penalty if not met) and announced a deadline of September 4. On September 5, supported by an order from the UN Security Council, NATO planes began bombing Serbian-held positions. With this air cover, Bosnian Croat, Croatian, and Bosnian Muslim forces captured large areas of land previously held by Serbs.

Dayton Peace Accords

With the more intensive NATO air strikes, the Bosnian-Serb leadership quickly decided to give Milosevic authority to negotiate on their behalf at peace talks held in Dayton, Ohio, at the Wright-Patterson Air Force Base in November 1995. Serbs, Bosnian Muslims, and Croats were all represented at the talks. Croatian president Franjo Tudjman (1922–1999) and Bosnian president Izetbegovic represented their interests. Assistant

Secretary of State Richard Holbrooke (1941–) represented the United States. The conference lasted three weeks.

The resulting Dayton Peace Accords led to an agreement on Bosnia and eastern Slovenia, and the remaining Serb holdings in Croatia. The borders of Bosnia were not changed. However, the republic was formally recognized as consisting of two parts—a Muslim-Croat federation and a Serbian republic.

The terms of the agreement called for peace to be enforced by sixty thousand NATO troops, known as IFOR (Implementation Force). The Dayton Peace Accords were initially agreed to on November 21 and the full, formal agreement was signed on December 14. The agreement formally ended the conflict in Bosnia.

War crimes tribunal

Ultimately two hundred thousand Bosnian Muslims, Croats, and Serbs were killed during these several years of ethnic conflict. Over one million had fled their homes. The world was dismayed to see a seemingly civilized region transformed into a bloody ethnic battlefield. The United Nations responded by establishing the first international tribunal or court in 1995 to prosecute war crimes. The UN War Crime tribunal was permanently located in The Hague, Netherlands. The tribunal indicted twenty-one Serbs for crimes against humanity for actions taken in the war in Bosnia. Only one of the twenty-one individuals indicted was then in custody. One of the accused faced an additional charge. Zeljko Meakic (1964–), a former commander of a concentration camp (large prison camp run by the Nazis where prisoners endured overcrowding, malnutrition, disease, and brutality), was accused of genocide in connection with the mass killing of Muslims and Croats during the war. This was the first time an international war crimes tribunal had formally charged an individual with genocide.

Because the Serbians agreed so quickly to peace terms after NATO air strikes, many in the West now saw Milosevic as a figure who would stabilize the region. U.S. president Bill Clinton (1946–; served 1993–2001) even supported Milosevic's presidency of Serbia despite a growing resistance in the general region to Milosevic's leadership. The reaction of Milosevic and the Serbs to peace also caused Western nations to wrongly assume that the reaction of Serbs would be the same when the powder keg that was Kosovo exploded in 1999.

Developing ethnic conflict in Kosovo

Serbia includes the once independent region called Kosovo. In Serbia's southwestern corner two million Albanians called Kosovo home in the 1990s. Serbs made up 10 to 15 percent of Kosovo's population. Immediately southwest of Kosovo is the independent country of Albania. Both Serbs and Albanians claimed ancestral rights to Kosovo. They each claimed their ancestors were the first to settle the area.

In the mid-1980s Albanians in Kosovo began a separatist (seeking to form a new nation from one currently existing) movement in response to growing religious and ethnic tension between Christian Serbs and Albanian Muslims. In 1989 Albanians tried to win greater governing rights of Kosovo. Milosevic, who had just risen to power as president of Yugoslavia of which Serbia was a member state, denounced these efforts. In retaliation he announced changes in the Kosovo government in March 1989. Most state employees who were Albanian were removed from their jobs. Approximately 115,000 Albanians were displaced from employment and replaced by Serbs.

After political changes proposed by the Serbs were ratified (formally approved) in a public referendum across the republic of Serbia, Kosovo's political institutions were disbanded altogether by Milosevic. In 1990 Milosevic completely abolished the autonomy of Kosovo. Milosevic ordered the Serbian military to close down Albanian businesses, hospitals, schools, and newspapers. The Albanian-language newspaper was banned from publishing, and television and radio broadcasts in Albanian were shut down. The university in Kosovo was purged (eliminated) of Albanian professors and Albanian students were expelled. He also imposed a curfew and declared a state of emergency due to violent demonstrations and the deaths of twenty-four people.

Resistance to Serb dominance grows in Kosovo

Resistance to Milosevic's actions grew in Kosovo. The Democratic League of Kosovo led by writer Ibrahim Rugova (1944–2006) advocated peaceful resistance to the disappearance of Kosovo autonomy. Rugova called for the boycott of public elections, resistance to the compulsory (required acceptance) Yugoslav military draft, refusal to pay taxes, and establishment of separate schools and other institutions for Albanians in Kosovo. A shadow Kosovo government (a government waiting to take over control from another government) was established and in a Kosovo referendum held in late 1991 Rugova was elected its president. Serbia declared the election illegal and voided the result.

Largely thanks to the civil disobedience practiced by Rugova's followers, Kosovo avoided the violence that at the time characterized Croatia and Bosnia-Herzegovina even though many Albanians within Kosovo were extremely frustrated. Frustration increased when the 1995 Dayton Accords, which ended the war in Bosnia-Herzegovina, did not address the political status of Kosovo. Rugova had lobbied the United Nations and the West for a peacekeeping force in Kosovo, but was largely ignored.

The Kosovo Liberation Army

Continuing ethnic repression and systematic violence at the hands of Serbs motivated many Albanians to conclude that armed resistance was necessary to change the situation. In 1993 Kosovo Albanians formed the Kosovo Liberation Army (KLA). KLA members began attacks against the Serbian police called the Federal Republic of Yugoslavia police (FRY). KLA activities continued through the following years including four attacks against Serbian civilians in April 1996. Serbs accused the KLA of terrorism. Despite the growing violence, nations outside of the region remained little concerned and did not come to the aid of the ethnically oppressed Albanians. The notion that the Dayton Accords had solved the region's problems was widespread and believed by many foreign governments in the West.

Kosovo's president, Ibrahim Rugova. AP IMAGES.

The situation grew dire in 1997 as both sides became embroiled in what amounted to a guerilla war (irregular hostilities) against one another. Serbian authorities decided to deploy Serb armed forces against not only the KLA, but Albanian citizens. The result was more bloodshed and continuous reprisals. By the summer of 1998 over 300,000 Albanians had fled Kosovo for Macedonia. This threatened Macedonia's tranquility and the peace of its surrounding neighbors. A ceasefire was attempted in Kosovo, but it failed as Serbs ignored international pleas to stop the violence. The FRY had begun an ethnic cleansing of Albanians remaining in Kosovo.

Prejudice in the Modern World: Almanac

NATO forces take action again

NATO decided to take action in 1999 when it became clear that genocide and other atrocities were being committed in Kosovo. The organization attempted to set up a military peacekeeping force to forcibly contain both sides while scheduling a peace treaty conference at Rambouillet outside of Paris. NATO also threatened to launch air strikes should the Serb forces continue their violence against Albanians. The talks at Rambouillet saw little success. On March 18, 1999, the Albanian, American, and British delegations signed the Rambouillet Accords. This agreement called for NATO to administer Kosovo as an autonomous province of Serbia, place thirty thousand troops on the ground, and operate with immunity (protected from legal requirements) from Serbian law. Serbia and Russia, which also participated in the international conference, refused to sign the accords.

Following the Rambouillet conference, the genocide campaign in Kosovo intensified. From March 24 to June 20, 1999, the FRY murdered thousands of Albanians. The precise number may never be known; however, 3,000 Albanians were still missing in 2006. Thousands more Albanians fled to Macedonia and Albania. By April 1999 it was estimated that over 800,000 people had left Kosovo.

In reaction to the violence, NATO began air strikes in Kosovo in late March targeting Serb encampments in Kosovo and other strategic locations. The United States was the primary member of the NATO air force. Some 38,000 combat missions were flown by mid-June. The goal of the air strikes was to remove the Serb forces from Kosovo and make it possible for the displaced Albanians to return.

Kosovo fighting ends

By early April Milosevic saw that NATO air power was too much to overcome. In addition, the nations of NATO began seriously contemplating a ground invasion of Kosovo to finish the campaign. Finally, Finnish and Russian peace negotiators convinced Milosevic to end the violence and accept a military presence in Kosovo under UN leadership but administered by NATO.

NATO casualties during the campaign were extraordinarily limited. No deaths were recorded as a result of combat operations. The alliance lost only three helicopters, thirty-two unmanned vehicles, and five aircraft, all of them American. Similarly, the Serbian armed forces sustained few deaths and loss of vehicles and planes. However, around 1,500 civilians were killed during the NATO air raids and other operations.

By the end of 1999 nearly all of the over 800,000 Albanian refugees (people who flee in search of protection or shelter) had returned to Kosovo. However, much of the Serb population fled in fear of reprisal attacks. The number of Albanians killed by the Serbs remained unknown. Apparent mass graves were found on Serbian military bases. Many bodies were also found in the Danube River. The largest mass grave was found in the nearby Bulgarian village of Dragodan. It became evident that many of the bodies in the mass graves were earlier removed in an attempt to cover up the atrocities.

International tribunal at The Hague formed

In 1993 the UN Security Council established an international tribunal at The Hague in the Netherlands to prosecute war crimes allegedly committed during the conflict in Bosnia-Herzegovina. The tribunal was known as the International Court Tribunal for the former Yugoslavia (ICTY). It had jurisdiction (legal authority) over crimes committed in Yugoslavia since 1991. The maximum sentence the court could impose was life imprisonment.

The court began its operation on November 7, 1993. It first indicted (formal criminal charges) a former Serb commander of a detention camp located in Bosnia. The commander was indicted for crimes against humanity. Milosevic was indicted in May 1999 for crimes against humanity in Kosovo. He was the first sitting head of state in history to be indicted for war crimes. Milosevic's Bosnian Serb army commander Mladic was also indicted. Later indictments were issued for violating the customs or laws of war, breaches of the Geneva Convention (international law addressing humanitarian concerns) in Croatia, and genocide in Bosnia-Herzegovina.

Milosevic attempted to gain another term as president of the much-reduced Yugoslav Federation in September 2000 but lost. He contested the election result, but a mass demonstration in Belgrade on October 5, 2000, eroded Milosevic's remaining authority. The newly elected president took office the next day. The Serbian government arrested Milosevic in April 2001 on charges of corruption and handed him over to the ICTY, an act Milosevic and his supporters claimed was illegal.

Trial of Milosevic

The trial of Milosevic began in February 2002. Because of Milosevic's position as a head of state, his war crimes trial received a great deal of

Slobodan Milosevic's war crimes trial received a great deal of world attention. AP IMAGES.

world attention. Milosevic accused the tribunal of attacking him in an evil and hostile manner. He refused to recognize the jurisdiction of the tribunal, a claim that gained support among many Serbs in his homeland. They viewed the indictment as a violation of national sovereignty. During the trial, however, Milosevic sat and listened to testimony from Bosnians and Croats that supported the indictments.

The prosecution case took two years to review the wars in Croatia, Bosnia, and Kosovo. During the presentation of the prosecution's case, Milosevic became increasingly ill, suffering from high blood pressure and serious bout of influenza that worsened his heart condition. The trial was delayed periodically due to his declining health. Finally, in 2004 it was time for Milosevic to present his defense. His defense attorneys, however, attempted to resign because Milosevic was uncooperative with them.

After numerous delays Milosevic's trial ended abruptly on March 11, 2006, when he was found dead in his jail cell. The Hague tribunal at the time was reviewing his request to further delay the trial in order for him to travel to Russia for medical treatment to relieve high blood pressure and heart difficulties. Some on the tribunal were not convinced that Russian officials could prevent Milosevic from escaping once he arrived there.

Following his death questions arose as to whether Milosevic was poisoned as he often suggested he would be. However, medical examination of his body found no irregularities in his bloodstream. It appeared that Milosevic died solely from complications resulting from his deteriorating heart condition.

The ICTY handed down its final indictment in 2005. The ICTY had indicted 161 people since it began in 1993. It planned to conclude all trials in 2008 and all appeals of its rulings by 2010.

For More Information

BOOKS

Bell-Fialkoff, Andrew. *Ethnic Cleansing*. New York: Palgrave Macmillan, 1999.

Cohen, Lenard J. *Serpent in the Bosom: The Rise and Fall of Slobodan Milosevic*. Boulder, CO: Westview Press, 2002.

Judah, Tim. *Kosovo: War and Revenge*. New Haven, CT: Yale University Press, 2000.

Lieberman, Benjamin. *Terrible Fate: Ethnic Cleansing in the Making of Modern Europe*. New York: Ivan R. Dee, 2006.

Naimark, Norman M. *Ethnic Cleansing in Twentieth-Century Europe*. Cambridge, MA.: Harvard University Press, 2002.

Sell, Louis. *Slobodan Milosevic and the Destruction of Yugoslavia*. Durham, NC: Duke University Press, 2002.

Weine, Stevan M. *When History Is a Nightmare: Lives and Memories of Ethnic Cleansing in Bosnia-Herzegovina*. Piscataway, NJ: Rutgers University Press, 1999.

Woodward, Susan L. *Balkan Tragedy: Chaos and Dissolution after the Cold War*. Washington, DC: Brookings Institution, 1995.

WEB SITES

"A Brief History of Ethnic Cleansing." http://www.foreignaffairs.org/ 19930601faessay5199/andrew-bell-fialkoff/a-brief-history-of-ethnic-cleansing.html (accessed on November 22, 2006).

"The Dayton Peace Accords on Bosnia." *University of Minnesota Human Rights Library*. http://www1.umn.edu/humanrts/icty/dayton/daytonaccord.html (accessed on November 22, 2006).

"Milosevic Trial Public Archive." http://hague.bard.edu/ (accessed on November 22, 2006).

16

The Arab-Israeli Conflict

The land located along the eastern shore of the Mediterranean Sea is at the center of a long-standing conflict between Arabs and Jews. Both groups of people claim territorial rights over this relatively small piece of land measuring approximately 10,000 square miles, about the size of the state of Maryland. These claims are rooted in history and seek to establish who can rightfully say that this territory is their homeland (a group's native land).

The land in question has gone by various names: Palestine, Israel, and Judea, depending on which group held control. The struggle for the land has often degenerated into violence and bloodshed that has passed down through many generations. The origins of the Arab-Israeli conflict are extremely complex and difficult to understand given the differing claims and counter-claims made by Arabs and Israelis, as each has interests in controlling this region of the world. This conflict is based in religion and politics as well as the strong human desire to have a secure homeland. Because Palestinian Arabs and Israelis strongly feel that they each deserve a nation on the same land to the exclusion of the other, each group often demonstrates its hatred and mistrust for the other. These attitudes are expressions of prejudice so deeply held that Palestinians and Israelis have often participated in horrific acts of violence against each other.

While the Arab-Israeli conflict is a struggle over a small piece of land with few natural resources, it has ignited a clash in the larger Middle East and the countries where Islam (the major religious faith of Muslims in the world) is the predominant religion. Indeed, the Arab-Israeli conflict has at times caused the world's superpowers to choose sides against each other. Therefore, the struggle between Palestinian Arabs and Jews has threatened to spill over into a much larger global conflict. This long-standing conflict began with the establishment of Israel as an independent state in 1948.

WORDS TO KNOW

Diaspora: The dispersal of Jews to other countries after being forced to live outside their traditional homeland.

Holocaust: Literally meaning a burnt sacrifice, the program pursued by the Nazis to eradicate Jews from the world leading to the murder of six million European Jews, Gypsies, Catholics, and homosexuals.

nationalism: One nation promotes its interests over the interests of other nations.

refugee: A person seeking safety in a foreign country to escape persecution.

Zionism: Movement that arose with the aim of reestablishing a Jewish state in Palestine.

The land of historic Israel and Palestine has been repeatedly invaded and conquered over the past 2,500 hundred years. According to history Hebrew tribes entered this land in the thirteenth century BCE. The abbreviation BCE refers to the time before the Christian era on calendars, or before the time of the birth of Christ around two thousand years ago. From the eleventh century to the sixth century BCE, these tribes were known as the Israelites, and they ruled the land. At the end of this period, the Israelites (or Jews) were conquered and at times carried away as slaves by the Assyrians, Babylonians, Persians, and Greeks. In 168 BCE, the Jews overcame the control of the Greeks and established an independent Jewish state called Judea. By 63 BCE, the Romans were the unwelcome occupiers of Judea. In the year 135, most all of the Jews were expelled from Judea by the Romans as the result of a violent uprising led by a Jewish revolutionary named Bar Kochba.

The following are two historical timelines that give an overview of historic Israel's or Palestine's development to its current political arrangement. From these timelines, several key features provide a solid understanding of the Arab-Israeli conflict. It is important to remember that the Israeli side believes the chronology should begin early in the history of historic Israel, while the Arab side believes the proper starting point for the chronology should begin in the late nineteenth century.

The chronology Israelis think is most accurate and fair would include the following events:

- 1800 BCE: Abraham migrates to Canaan (ancient name for land of Palestine)

- 70 CE: Romans destroy Jerusalem and much of the Jewish homeland; beginning of the Diaspora

- 135: Bar Kochba revolt suppressed by the Romans; Jews expelled from Palestine
- 632: Islamic armies conquer large areas of land, including Palestine
- 691: Dome of the Rock mosque built on the site of the Jewish Temple destroyed by the Romans
- 1516–1918: Ottoman Empire rules over Palestine
- 1860–1904: Life of Theodor Herzl, founder of the Zionist movement
- 1882: First group of Jews migrate to Palestine
- 1947–48: Warfare between Jewish and Palestinian communities begins
- 1948: Israel declares itself to be an independent state
- 1956: Outbreak of war between Israel and neighboring Arab countries
- 1964: Founding of the Palestine Liberation Organization
- 1967: Outbreak of the Six-Day War between Israel and neighboring Arab countries
- 1973: Outbreak of the Yom Kippur War between Israel and neighboring Arab countries
- 1978: Camp David Accord signed, involving U.S. president Jimmy Carter, Egyptian president Anwar Sadat, and Israeli prime minister Menachem Begin
- 1982: Israeli invasion of Lebanon
- 1987: Outbreak of intifada
- 1988: Declaration of the independent state of Palestine
- 1989: Yasser Arafat elected president of Palestine
- 2000: Outbreak of intifada
- 2004: Death of Yasser Arafat
- 2006: Hamas wins surprising election in Palestine

The chronology Arabs think is most accurate and fair would include the following events:

- 1882 Beginning of modern Jewish immigration to Palestine
- 1897: First Zionist Congress
- 1917: Balfour Declaration issued

- 1918: All of Palestine occupied by Allied forces
- 1936: Arab revolt against British rule and Zionism
- 1939–45: World War II and the extermination of six million Jews (Holocaust) in Europe
- 1947: Palestine problem submitted to the United Nations
- 1948: Israel declares itself as an independent nation; war breaks out in Palestine
- 1950: West Bank united with Jordan; Gaza Strip administered by Egypt
- 1956: Outbreak of war between Israel and neighboring Arab countries
- 1964: Founding of the Palestine Liberation Organization
- 1967: Outbreak of war between Israel and neighboring Arab countries
- 1973: Outbreak of war between Israel and neighboring Arab countries
- 1978: Camp David Accord signed, involving U.S. president Jimmy Carter, Egyptian president Anwar Sadat, and Israeli prime minister Menachem Begin
- 1982: Israeli invasion of Lebanon
- 1987: Outbreak of intifada
- 1988: Declaration of the independent state of Palestine
- 1989: Yasser Arafat elected president of Palestine
- 2000: Outbreak of intifada
- 2005: Death of Yasser Arafat
- 2006: Hamas wins surprising election in Palestine

It can be readily seen that the division between the Palestinian and Israeli perspectives is centered on the beginning of the chronology. While Israelis think a much longer view of history gives the right answers to the questions regarding the status of Israel, Palestinians believe that a more just approach is to keep the discussion in the modern period. These differing points of view have proven to play a key role in the attempts to create peace between Israelis and Palestinians by discovering who has rights to the land. Therefore, coming to a conclusion about whether the Arabs or Israelis have a stronger set of claims to Palestine depends in part on one's view of history. This means trying to answer the question about who are the legitimate residents of Palestine based on who lived there first.

The development of Zionism

Although the Jews were systematically removed from Judea by the Romans, many Jews clung to the dream of returning to their homeland to reestablish the nation of Israel. This idea gathered strength in the late nineteenth and early twentieth centuries. Led by the thoughts of Leon Pinsker (1821–1891), a Russian Jew, and Theodor Herzl (1860–1904), a Jewish journalist residing in Austria, many Jews urged creating a Jewish state in Palestine. This movement became known as Zionism. Zionism is defined as the reuniting of Jewish people in Palestine. The idea of Zionism, named after a hill in biblical Jerusalem named Zion, grew through the nineteenth century. Zionism was prominent in Eastern Europe where persecution against Jews was the strongest. Zionist ideals were powerful enough to cause many European Jews to migrate to Palestine.

Jewish journalist Theodor Herzl. COURTESY OF THE LIBRARY OF CONGRESS.

The growing number of Jews arriving in Palestine caused increasing strife and tension between the immigrants (people who leave their country of origin to reside permanently in another) and the Palestinian Arabs, who were the long-standing residents of the area. Generally, Arabs were not opposed to Jewish emigration to Palestine so long as it was not rooted in political motives. They did not want Jews to build up political power to rule over Arabs or establish a separate country. The greatest numbers of Arabs living in Palestine were Muslims (followers of Islam) who conquered the region in the seventh century. Because the Jews living in Palestine adhered to Judaism, the stage was set for the Arab-Israeli conflict to take on its religious characteristics. These religions have many common roots. Islam and Judaism (as well as Christianity) regard such important religious figures as Abraham, Moses, and the Hebrew prophets as key to their respective faiths. But the conflict between Jews and Arabs has intensified in part because both Judaism and Islam claim a God-given right to the land of Palestine.

Fall of the Ottoman Empire

From the sixteenth to the early twentieth century, Palestine was ruled by the Ottoman Empire. This empire was Turkish in origin and existed from 1299 to 1922. At the height of the empire's strength it ruled the Middle East, parts of North Africa, and even a portion of southeastern Europe. The Ottomans aligned themselves with Germany during World War I (1914–18). After Germany and its allies were defeated, control of Palestine was in the hands of Great Britain.

British promises to the Arabs and Jews

As reward for siding with Britain and its allies during the war, promises were made to both Zionists and Arabs that they would have their own homelands. Sir Henry McMahon (1862–1949), the British high commissioner in Egypt, exchanged letters with a ruler on the Arabian Peninsula promising that a new Arab nation would be formed from the lands of the former Ottoman Empire. Simultaneously, a similar promise was made to the Jews in the form of the Balfour Declaration (1917). This declaration reads as follows:

> His Majesty's Government view with favour the establishment in Palestine of a national home for the Jewish people, and will use his best endeavours to facilitate the achievement of this object, it being a clearly understood that nothing shall be done which may prejudice the civil and religious rights of non-Jewish communities in Palestine, or the rights and political status enjoyed by Jews in any other country.

With the approval of the League of Nations (a world political body dedicated to resolving disputes between nations that was later replaced by the United Nations), the British enacted the principles of the Balfour Declaration and partitioned (divided) Palestine into two separate regions. For this reason, many Arabs believe they have been treated in a prejudicial way by strong western countries. For them, this was cause to think that many westerners see Arabs as an inferior group of people. The larger portion of land became known as the Emirate of Transjordan (now the modern nation of Jordan). The remaining territory, bordered by Lebanon and Syria in the north and Egypt in the south, was still called Palestine. The Arab-Israeli conflict has mostly taken place in this limited territory.

Prior to World War II, Great Britain maintained a policy designed to limit the number of European Jews migrating to Palestine. However, this policy was only partially effective. After World War II ended, the world became aware of the Holocaust. Many people began to believe that it was necessary to create an independent Jewish state. The Holocaust, literally meaning a burnt sacrifice, was the program pursued by the German Nazis to primarily eradicate Jews from Europe. The Holocaust led to the murdering of six million European Jews in addition to millions of other peoples, such as Gypsies, homosexuals, and Catholics. In 1947, the United Nations passed Resolution 187, dividing Palestine into two new states, one for Jews and one for Arabs. In 1948, the Jewish state of Israel came into existence. This move angered not only the Palestinian Arabs but Arabs in other countries surrounding Israel.

Israel at war with the Arab world

From 1948 to 1949, Israel fought a war against its Arab neighbors as a direct result of declaring its independence in 1948. This war is sometimes called the Israeli War of Independence. While the Israelis were greatly outnumbered, they were successful in defeating the combined armies of Egypt, Jordan, Syria, Lebanon, and Iraq. The fighting ended in 1949 with the signing of the Rhodes Armistice (a ceasefire agreement), an agreement to at least temporarily stop fighting but did not give Arab recognition of Israel's right to exist. The conclusion of the war officially affirmed the borders of the Jewish state and added more territory to Israel. It also created a significant refugee (people seeking safety in a foreign country to escape prejudice or persecution) problem. About seven hundred thousand Palestinians were displaced from their homes. Many Palestinians fled or were expelled from Israel after the Rhodes Armistice was signed. Similarly, about nine hundred thousand Jews fled or were expelled from the Arab countries that fought against Israel. Of this number, about six hundred thousand migrated to Israel while the remainder moved to Europe or the United States.

The continuing Arab-Israeli conflict

While the Rhodes Armistice ended open warfare between Israel and its neighbors, most Arabs did not accept the principles of the armistice that included areas that should be free of military forces, called demilitarized zones. Rather, the conflict reemerged as a guerilla war where Palestinians led raids against Israel, often attacking and killing innocent Israeli citizens. The guerilla war continued into the twenty-first century. This led to a series of reprisals in the form of Israeli attacks against Palestinian military targets. These acts of revenge maintained a cycle of sustained violence between Israelis and Palestinians. However, following 1948,

Egypt, led by President Gamal Abdel Nasser, took complete governmental control of the Suez Canal. © BETTMANN/ CORBIS.

several conventional wars also contributed to the continuation of the Arab-Israeli conflict.

The 1956 War The first in the series of these wars was fought in 1956 from October 29 to November 6. For a variety of reasons, the Israelis believed Egypt was preparing to make war against Israel. Egypt, led by President Gamal Abdel Nasser (1918–1970), nationalized (took complete governmental control of) the Suez Canal. The Egyptians blocked Israeli ships that were passing through the canal. The canal was vital for world trade because it connected the Indian Ocean with the Mediterranean Sea. Prior to its nationalization, the canal was jointly controlled by Great Britain and Egypt.

In response to Egypt's military buildup and nationalization of the Suez Canal, Israel launched an attack into the Sinai Desert (Egyptian territory) while Great Britain and France took control of the canal by force. Finally, a ceasefire was arranged by the United Nations with the backing of both existing world superpowers: the United States and the United Soviet Socialist Republics (USSR). But Israel's military success left the country in control of the Sinai Desert and the Gulf of Aqaba. This gulf provided direct access to the Indian Ocean for Israel. Israel agreed to retreat from this captured territory only after the United Nations guaranteed Israel's continued access to these vital waterways.

The 1967 War In 1967, Israel again went to war, this time against Syria, Egypt, and Jordan. This war is sometimes referred to as the Six-Day War because it was fought between June 5 and June 10. The war was in part fought in the Sinai Desert. Egypt's President Nasser again closed the Gulf of Aqaba to Israel after compelling United Nations troops to leave Egyptian territory. This move allowed Nasser to mobilize his troops in the

Yasser Arafat. AP IMAGES.

Sinai Desert in preparation for war against Israel. Israel again defeated the Egyptian military. It also captured the Old City of Jerusalem (sometimes referred to as East Jerusalem) from Jordan and the Golan Heights from Syria. While Israel eventually retreated from the Sinai Desert due to pressure from the United Nations, it retained control of all of Jerusalem.

The 1973–74 War The next war between Israelis and Arabs was fought from 1973 to 1974. The war began on October 6, 1973, the date of a very important Jewish religious holiday called Yom Kippur. Egypt and Syria launched surprise attacks against Israel on two fronts that day. Often this war is referred to as the Yom Kippur War. At first this war did not go well for Israel. Other Arab countries, including Libya, joined in the struggle along with Israel's established enemies, Syria, Jordan, and Egypt. As things grew difficult for the Israelis, the United States stepped in and supplied Israel with large quantities of sophisticated weapons. This aid greatly increased Israel's military capabilities and gave it the power to push its enemies back inside their own borders.

The 1982 War In 1978, the Palestine Liberation Organization or PLO (see box) based in southern Lebanon (Israel's immediate neighbor to the north) attacked Israel. Israel responded by sending its troops into

Palestine Liberation Organization (PLO) and Hamas

The PLO was created in 1964 as a political organization to support the creation of an independent Palestinian state. After the Arab-Israeli war of 1967, Yasser Arafat emerged as the president of the PLO. The PLO was not really a singular organization but was made up of various political parties that had differing perspectives on how to view and respond to Israel. While the PLO officially renounced terrorism and recognized Israel's right to exist in 1988, it was not clear that every group under the umbrella of the PLO believed that terrorism should be abandoned.

The most prominent PLO group was the political party known as Fatah. Until January 2006, Fatah was the dominant party in the Palestinian parliament. But another party known as Hamas came to power and held the majority of seats in the Parliament. Hamas still retained the view that justice and peace could only be established in the Middle East when the state of Israel was destroyed. Many believe that the political victory won by Hamas undermined the possibility of peace between Israelis and Palestinians. Others thought that Hamas's win at the polls would force it to moderate its political views and renounce terrorism as well as recognize that Israel has a right to exist.

Lebanon to create a buffer zone of about 5 miles to prevent further attacks from PLO guerillas. While the United Nations sent a peacekeeping force into this region, it did not stop the fighting.

In an effort to eliminate the PLO bases in southern Lebanon, Israel attacked with the full weight of its military might in 1982. Ultimately, the PLO guerillas were forced to leave Lebanon and were dispersed into several Arab countries. A plan was brought forward by the United States to end hostilities. Israel withdrew all its forces from Lebanon in 1985. Further conflict between Israelis and Palestinians was in the form of two distinct intifadas (uprisings), one lasting from 1987 to 1993 and another in 2000 (see box).

In all wars fought between Israelis and Arabs, there has been a series of agreements and armistices, with little effect on the Arab-Israeli conflict. Most of the wars and their treaties achieved little to resolve the political roadblock between Arabs and Israelis. They did nothing to decrease violence between the two populations, either.

The worldwide importance of the Arab-Israeli conflict

The Arab-Israeli conflict has never been not seen by most of the world as having an impact only in the lives of Arabs and Israelis. A majority of the world's leaders have historically seen the Arab-Israeli conflict as one that has implications for the security of the world. Many have feared that this conflict could spill over the borders of the Middle East as well as cause confrontations between countries that have historically supported one side or the other. This was clearly the case when tensions rose between the world's two superpowers at the time. The United States supported Israel and the USSR supported the Arab cause in the 1973 war between Israel and its Arab neighbors. The Israelis received military aid from the United States and the Arabs received military aid from the Soviet Union.

Intifada

Intifada is the Arabic word meaning "uprising." The intifadas have usually been in response to a perceived Israeli act of injustice that harmed the Palestinian cause. In the modern conflict of Israel and Palestine, this term usually referred to two specific events called the first (1987–93) and second intifadas (2000–05).

The first intifada took place as a revolt against the Israeli occupation of the West Bank and Gaza. This uprising was also driven by Palestinian citizens who were facing the humiliation of having to show identity documents and special permits as they traveled into Israel to provide much-needed labor. Palestinian workers went on a general strike and got into violent confrontations with Israeli police and soldiers.

The second intifada was economic in nature. Israel sought to secure its borders against terrorist acts by blocking Palestinians from working in Israel. This intifada was made worse when an Israeli leader named Ariel Sharon (1928–) took a group of followers to the Temple Mount in Jerusalem. It was rumored that Sharon actually went inside the Dome of the Rock mosque that sits on the Temple Mount, perhaps in defiance of Islamic beliefs. This mosque is one of the holiest sites for Muslims around the world; regular people are forbidden to enter it. Angry Palestinians responded by creating a more violent and bloody uprising.

Much of the world's oil reserves are found within the borders of Arab countries such as Saudi Arabia, Iraq, Kuwait, and a traditional Muslim country like Iran. Iranians are not ethnically Arab but support the Arab cause against Israel because most Iranians are Muslim. These countries and others showed sympathy for the plight of Palestinian Arabs. Their oil wealth gave them great economic leverage in advancing the Palestinian cause. Since many western countries depended on Middle East oil to meet their energy needs, they were compelled to give attention to the difficulties faced by Palestinian Arabs.

On the other hand, Israel had its strong supporters too. For example, the United States, Great Britain, and France were firmly resolved to support Israel's right to exist within secure borders. These countries have at times given Israel key military hardware, such as artillery shells and combat aircraft, to block attempts by Arab countries to destroy Israel. In return Israel has been a faithful ally helping countries such as the United States retain its influence in the Middle East.

Because the world has a keen interest in resolving the deeply felt tensions between Israelis and Arabs, many attempts have been made to arrive at a fair and long-lasting peace in this region of the world. Arab nationalism (promoting the creation of new nations) and political

Zionism laid claim to the same land placing two nationalistic movements in direct conflict. Nationalism is often behind the attempt of one nation to promote its interests over the interests of other nations. When nationalist attitudes become too strong, the ideals of one nation become more highly valued than the ideals of other nations. This means there is a greater opportunity for prejudice, hatred, and mistrust to arise. Because of these nationalist attitudes, there have been many attempts in recent history to create a just and lasting peace between Israelis and Palestinians, such as the 1998 Camp David Accords and the 2003 Geneva Accord. However, nothing resolved the conflict. Both sides tried to make their claims to the land the strongest not only against each other but by appealing to the court of public opinion around the world. For example, a list of the kinds of claims that each side made have the following characteristics. On the Jewish side:

> The continuous presence of Jews in Israel for four thousand years.

> The persecution of the Jews of the Diaspora (see box), and the Holocaust as the climax of this persecution.

> The fulfillment of God's promise in the return of the land to the chosen people.

> The phenomenal contribution of the Jews to the development of the land and the welfare of the world.

> Arab failure to make peace with the Jews when they were willing to negotiate for peace.

> The importance of the present and future security of Israel for the Jewish and Western worlds.

But Palestinian Arabs have their claims as well and oppose the Jewish side by saying:

> For two thousand years, since Roman times, Palestinians have been a majority in historic Palestine, which is now Israel.

> The establishment of Israel has been at the expense of the Palestinians who have been displaced through wars and other forceful means.

> Palestinians are now ready to compromise and accept a share of the land, but Israel refuses to negotiate for peace.

> Palestinians belong to Palestine. They do not wish to be sent away to other Arab countries.

> Palestinian nationhood is as valid as Zionist nationhood, if not more so when viewed in terms of a common history, language, and culture.

> The two million Palestinians that live in the occupied territories are not treated as equal citizens since they are not free to choose their own system of government.

In the background of these claims as to who are the rightful residents of Palestine is the belief that people from the other side are bad and repulsive, while those on "our" side are good. Many people in the world, including many Israelis and Palestinians, had hoped that moderate voices would come to the forefront recognizing of the rights of both the Palestinians and Israelis. Palestinians and Israelis have held the common human vision of wanting to live in their own land in peace and security with the hope that justice will prevail.

The basic Israeli perspective

Israel insists that peace is impossible until Palestinians first recognize Israel's right to exist. This means that Israel maintains a strong and modern military to defend itself against what it thinks is the ultimate Palestinian goal, namely to destroy the state of Israel. Until those who govern the Palestinians as well as other Arab and Islamic countries publicly declare that Israel has a basic right to exist as a secure nation, there can be no permanent peace between Palestinians and Israelis, according to the Israeli government.

The basic Palestinian-Arab perspective

Most Arabs think Israel cannot make a legitimate historical claim to have a separate Jewish state since doing so displaces Palestinians from their homeland. Though in the long past Jews did have control of the area, this did not mean that Jews who have lived in other parts of the world for nearly two thousand years now have a right to return to Palestine and create a new Jewish homeland. Further, some Israelis believed that they had the right to expand their territory by building settlements in the West Bank. This area immediately on the west side of the Jordan River has been the homeland for a large number of Palestinians at least since World War I. Palestinian Arabs also believed that the United Nations had generated many resolutions (Resolution 194, Resolution 242, and Resolution 446) designed to protect Palestinian rights that Israel had ignored.

Possibilities for peace

Geneva Accord and the Road Map for Peace The Geneva Accord of November 2003 was developed and written by representatives of Palestine

Terrorism often took the form of suicide bombing especially against Israeli citizens. AP IMAGES.

and Israel in order to bring an end to hostilities between Israelis and Palestinians. The accord became the official document recognizing the right of Palestinians and Israelis to have independent statehood. As provided in the *American Task Force on Palestine* website (http://www.americantaskforce.org/geneva.htm), the Geneva Accord stated that it aspired to the view that " . . . both peoples need to enter an era of peace, security, and stability.' Out of the Geneva Accord arose the hope that Israelis and Palestinians would cooperate and commit themselves to coexist side by side as good neighbors, that they would aspire to the well-being of Palestinian and Israeli citizens. The Geneva Accord also had a goal of not only reconciling Palestinians and Israelis but of promoting normal, peaceful relations between Israel and other Arab states.

The Road Map to Peace initiative was brought forward in a speech by U.S. Republican president George W. Bush (1946–; served 2001–) on June 24, 2002. With the support of many countries in Western Europe, Russia, and the United Nations, the initiative called for a two-state solution to the Arab-Israeli conflict. The Road Map to Peace called for the Palestinian leadership to move decisively toward ending terrorism. Terrorism often took the form of suicide bombing especially against Israeli citizens. Israel was also challenged to take strong steps to support the emergence of a stable and secure Palestinian state by ending its occupation of historic Palestinian territory.

Developments in the early twenty-first century

In April 2002, Israel began construction of a security barrier to keep suicide bombers from making their way into Israel from the West Bank. The Israelis believed the security fence was necessary for the protection of its citizens. However, human rights groups, Palestinians, and much of the world complained that the barrier cut across territory that had been declared to be Palestinian by international law. This was another case of mounting tensions between Israelis and Palestinians.

Diaspora

The Diaspora is a term usually applied to Jews who have been forced to live outside their traditional homeland. In historic Israel, Jews were often expelled or taken into captivity by empires that conquered them. The Babylonian, Persian, Greek, and Roman empires are examples of nations that participated at different times in the Jewish Diaspora. This term evokes strong emotions, as it is often employed by Zionists to support the view that Jews have a right to return to their traditional homeland to recreate an independent Jewish state.

In the early twenty-first century, many Palestinians viewed themselves as victims of a Diaspora at the hands of Jews who have displaced them from their traditional homeland. Because of this turn of events, many Palestinians were forced to live in other Arab countries such as Saudi Arabia, Egypt, Jordan, Syria, and Lebanon. Because Palestinians and Israelis believed they were the genuine victims of displacement and exile, both sides were committed to actions that led to violence and retaliation.

In January 2006, a radical Palestinian group known as Hamas (see box) won the majority of seats in Palestine's parliamentary elections. Hamas gained this political victory over the PLO (see box). The PLO had been the controlling political party in Palestine since 1967. When PLO president Yasser Arafat (1929–2004) renounced terrorism and recognized Israel's right to exist, many world leaders held high hopes for eventual peace between Israelis and Palestinians. However, a part of Hamas's charter called for the destruction of Israel. In the view of many, this meant the prospects for peace between Palestinians and Israelis were greatly reduced unless Hamas recognized Israel's right to exist. Several European countries that give financial assistance to the Palestinians threatened to discontinue this aid unless Hamas renounced terrorism and recognized Israel's right to exist.

Violence in the region escalated through much of 2006. Israel continued its occupation of Palestinian Arab territories and conducted raids into Arab neighborhoods to arrest or kill Hamas leaders. In addition, Israel launched a massive bombing and artillery attack on neighboring Lebanon that lasted weeks. The attack was in reaction to the Lebanese government harboring Hezbollah, an anti-Israeli Arab group. Peace for the region seemed as remote as ever.

For More Information

BOOKS

Cattan, Henry. *The Palestine Question.* New York: Croom Helm, 1988.

Cohen, Michael J. *The Origins of the Arab-Israeli Conflict.* Berkeley: University of California Press, 1987.

Gelvin, James L. *The Israel-Palestine Conflict: One Hundred Years of War.* New York: Cambridge University Press, 2005.

Khouri, Fred J. *The Arab-Israeli Dilemma.* 3rd ed. New York: Syracuse University Press, 1985.

Lesch, Ann M, and Dan Tschirgi. *Origins and Development of the Arab-Israeli Conflict.* Westport, CT: Greenwood Press, 1998.

Wasserstein, Bernard. *Israelis and Palestinians: Why Do They Fight? Can They Stop?* New Haven, CT: Yale University Press, 2003.

WEB SITES

"The Geneva Accord." *American Task Force on Palestine.* http://www.americantaskforce.org/geneva.htm (accessed on November 29, 2006).

"Palestine Liberation Organization (PLO)." *FAS.* http://www.fas.org/irp/world/para/plo.htm (accessed on November 29, 2006).

17

Racial Segregation in the American South: Jim Crow Laws

Racism is the belief that the physical characteristics of a person or group determines their capabilities and that one group is naturally superior to other groups. Racism has been a major factor of society in the United States throughout its history. Racial prejudice has even been central to the development of American laws, basically legalizing white dominance over others.

The historical plight of black Americans presents a classic example of what happens when a group becomes defined as weaker and less intelligent and overall, less valued. As time passes, those prejudices become long-lasting behavior patterns carrying over from one generation to the next. They became highly resistant to challenge by social movements and even new laws banning discrimination (treating some differently than others or favoring one social group over another based on prejudices) against the minority. Discrimination means one group enjoys an undeserved advantage over another group with the same capabilities. For example, some groups may freely attend certain prestigious schools or obtain better paying jobs while others are not. In the twenty-first century, blacks are still recovering from centuries of prejudice against them. Injustices in the present have strong roots in the past.

A long history of racism

Racism was prominent during the colonial period in the seventeenth and eighteenth centuries when the North American colonies were a part of the worldwide British Empire. Britons had traditionally associated dark skin color with negative behavioral traits such as evil and filth. Colonists brought this prejudice with them to North America when they crossed the ocean to settle in the seventeenth century.

By the late seventeenth century, race became the basis of slavery (people being held captive and treated as property in order to perform

WORDS TO KNOW

boycott: A protest by not buying certain products or using certain services until demands are met.

freedom rider: A civil rights activist who rides on interstate buses to test their compliance with court orders to end segregation on buses and bus facilities.

segregation: Using laws to separate whites and blacks.

sit-in: When black activists walk into an establishment such as a restaurant for whites-only and refuse to leave until they are served or the business closes.

slavery: People being held captive and treated as property in order to perform free labor.

free labor). Blacks did not come to the United States by choice but were brought to North America through an international slave trade. Forced into a life of slavery, they were captured by European slave traders and shipped to the New World in trade for sugar, rum, and various goods that were then shipped back to Europe. The colonists had severe labor shortages and an immediate and pressing need to clear the forests of the Eastern Seaboard from Georgia north through New England and plant crops. The Africans provided a large and free labor pool. They also provided a social group that to which the predominately white western European colonists could feel superior. Whites could gain social status by becoming planters and slave owners. The prejudice shaped colonial laws that banned intermarriage and considered slaves not as humans, but as property with no rights. Any child of mixed blood (one white parent, one black) was considered black and forced to live as a slave, among slaves with few exceptions.

Throughout the 1700s, Britons and their colonists were convinced that slavery was an essential element to national prosperity and world power. To justify slave trade, black Africans were dehumanized, often referred to as black cattle. The prejudiced attitudes held by the colonists focused on what they considered the uncivilized and un-Christian nature of the black Africans. They held a widespread belief reinforced by popular writings and religious sermons that Africans were naturally inferior to white Europeans.

Only part-human

Through the American Revolutionary War (1775–83), Americans won their freedom from British rule and a new nation of the United States of America, as officially named in 1777, began taking shape. However,

334

freedom was not extended to the black slaves. Even Thomas Jefferson (1743–1826), who authored the Declaration of Independence in 1776 and included the famous phrase that "all men are created equal," came from a wealthy Virginia planter's family and was himself a slave owner. In fact, in the late twentieth century it was discovered that Jefferson probably had six children with a slave woman, Sally Hemings. He freed all six of the children, but never Hemings herself. By the 1780s, slavery was being phased out of the Northern states. But Southern states stubbornly hung on to slavery as a cornerstone of its agricultural economy. The plantations relied heavily on the free labor and they could not economically survive without it. Slavery was such an emotional topic that it was not discussed during the Constitutional Convention held in the summer of 1787 in Philadelphia. There the nation's Founding Fathers shaped a new national government and system of justice. Many of them were slave owners who privately thought, or hoped, that slavery would just slowly fade away for the sake of the country.

When the topic of black slaves did enter into the discussion in the convention, it was related to how the national census (a regular count of people in a country) should be taken. A key question was whether blacks should be counted. The census was to be crucial for determining how many members of the U.S. House of Representatives could be sent from each state, therefore it would determine how much political influence each state would hold. If slaves were to be counted, then the Southern states would have greater political power in relation to the Northern states. If not counted, the Southern states would have less. The debate raged for days before convention participants reached a compromise. Black slaves were to be counted as three-fifths of a person. Blacks were still not full humans in the eyes of the law.

Southern delegates to the 1787 Convention also won a compromise that the new U.S. government could not abolish the importation of slaves for at least twenty years after adoption of the new Constitution. During the next two decades, public pressure continued to increase to prohibit slave trade on U.S. shores. As soon as it could do so, Congress responded, in 1808 with legislation banning U.S. participation in international slave trade.

Growth of slavery

The first census ever taken in the United States occurred in 1790. It showed that 757,000 blacks lived in the United States, of whom 700,000

The emergence of the cotton gin meant that more slaves were needed to pick the crops because the work once done by hand was now done much faster by machine. © BETTMANN/CORBIS.

were slaves. Over 22 percent of American families owned at least one slave. The hopes that slavery would fade out of American life were dashed only a few years later. In 1793, American inventor Eli Whitney (1765–1825) developed a much-improved cotton gin, a machine that separates cotton fibers from seed. The cotton gin made cotton a highly marketable crop in the South; its emergence meant that more slaves were needed to pick the crops because the work once done by hand was now done much faster by machine. New cotton fields spread across the Deep South and slavery boomed. Despite a ban on the importation of new African slaves, the black population in the United States grew to approximately 4.5 million by 1860. Some 90 percent of blacks in America were slaves. However the number of slave owning families had dropped to 10 percent. Large cotton plantations had overpowered smaller farms.

Prior to the American Civil War (1861–65), black slaves were at the bottom of a caste system (a very strict division of a society). At the top were rich plantation owners. In the middle were merchants, small farmers, and laborers. Slaves lived in housing provided by their owners. The owners also provided food and clothing. The quality of these basic necessities varied widely depending on the owner. The field laborer worked normally from sunrise to sunset. Ten or more slaves lived in a single room shack. The beds consisted of straw and old rags and the floors were dirt. Black families tried to maintain connections with one another, but that often became impossible as the slaves were sold like property on a regular basis. Slaves had no right to marry, vote, own firearms, own property, learn to read or write, possess books, testify in court against whites, or speak abusively toward whites.

The rise of Jim Crow

Slavery ended in 1865 with the South's defeat in the Civil War. However, the life of black Americans improved little. Three amendments were added to the U.S. Constitution guaranteeing rights to freed slaves. Slavery, though outlawed, was merely replaced with racial discrimination and injustice that was upheld legally by Black Codes (laws restricting rights of blacks). The Black Codes denied freed slaves the right to vote, to possess any form of weapon, and to leave a job and move elsewhere. They were considered servants now instead of slaves. Disobeying a Black Code could lead to imprisonment. Efforts by the federal government to rebuild the South's economy and society in the 1870s, called Reconstruction, abolished the Black Codes though open racial prejudice and discrimination persisted.

When Reconstruction ended in 1877, Southerners began passing new laws enforcing racial segregation (separation of black people from whites) known as Jim Crow laws. It was the Jim Crow laws through which the beliefs about the inferior nature of blacks were perpetuated throughout much of the twentieth century. The term Jim Crow comes from a racist fictional character popular in America in the early 1800s. The character, played by a white person with blackened face, expressed racial prejudice against black Americans depicting an uneducated, poor rural black person.

Racial prejudices led to these discriminatory measures passed by state and local governments that sought to keep blacks at a lower social and economic position. Jim Crow laws strictly enforced public racial segregation in almost every aspect of Southern life. The segregation laws did not exist in the North, but racial discrimination by Northerners was widespread nonetheless. For example, blacks could not buy houses in the same neighborhoods as whites. Economic and educational opportunities for black Americans were greatly restricted.

Separate but equal

To contest the growing number of Jim Crow laws, a black shoemaker named Homer Plessy (1862–1925) boarded a train in New Orleans, Louisiana, and defiantly found a seat in a railroad car reserved for whites. Refusing to get off when commanded by the conductor, Plessy was arrested for violating segregationist laws. The case went to the U.S. Supreme Court, where his defense lawyer argued that the law violated the Thirteenth Amendment to the Constitution, which granted freedom to slaves, and the Fourteenth Amendment, which maintains that a state cannot deny privileges to people without applying fair lawful procedures known as due process of law.

The Court in *Plessy v. Ferguson* (1896) ruled against Plessy and upheld laws enforcing segregation in railway car accommodations on the condition that the facilities were of equal quality. This decision became known as the "separate but equal" principle—the cornerstone of Jim Crow laws. However, the facilities were usually far from equal; those for blacks were always much inferior. For example, restrooms for blacks were filthy and often little more than outhouses. Also, black entrances to public facilities were usually, if not always, in the rear or the alley. With the introduction of motorized buses in the 1920s, seats for blacks were located in the hot and crowded back rows and the stink of exhaust fumes prevailed.

In reaction to Jim Crow laws, various scientists refuted the notion of inferiority of the black race, or even the very existence of true races. In futility, they claimed that genetics was too complex, that one group gradually blends into another with no sharp break. Their perspectives were generally ignored by the public and politicians and racial prejudice continued.

The inhumanity of Jim Crow

By 1915, all Southern states had some form of Jim Crow laws. Blacks could not eat in the same restaurants, drink out of the same water fountains, watch movies in the same theaters, play in the same parks, or go to the same schools as whites. Blacks had to sit in the back of buses and streetcars and give up their seats to whites when instructed to do so. Blacks could not nurse whites in hospitals. Signs reading "Colored Only" or "White Only" could be seen everywhere.

Blacks could not eat in the same restaurants, drink out of the same water fountains, watch movies in the same theaters, or go to the same schools as whites. © BETTMANN/CORBIS.

In addition to laws, there were certain unwritten social expectations. For example, a black man was not to shake hands with a white man and he could not make eye-contact with a white woman or else he would be accused of highly inappropriate sexual advances. When speaking, blacks were expected to address whites as "Mr.," "Sir," or "Ma'am."

Jim Crow laws also blocked most blacks from voting in public elections. Local authorities charged fees, called poll taxes which most blacks could not afford, and required blacks to pass literacy (reading and writing) tests not required of whites. Deprived of a formal education, most blacks could not read and write well and failed these tests. In addition to voting barriers in general elections, blacks were excluded from Southern politics in other ways. Southern states introduced the "white primary." The Democratic Party, the only real political party of power in the South, claimed their primaries to select candidates for various officers were private events. They banned participation by blacks.

Prejudice in the Modern World: Almanac

By 1910, this practice was used in every Southern state. As a result of voting restrictions and exclusion from primaries, blacks had little political influence in the South.

In addition to legal and social restrictions, terrorism by white suprema-cists was also used to discourage blacks from voting. These combined measures were very effective. In Louisiana, more than 130,000 blacks were registered to vote in 1896. By 1905, that number dropped to just over 1,300. If blacks violated Jim Crow rules, they could expect swift and perhaps brutal punishment, such as whippings or even death.

According to a report published by the National Association for the Advancement of Colored People (NAACP) in 1919 titled *Thirty Years of Lynching in the United States: 1889–1918,* 2,522 black Americans were lynched—hanged, burned alive, or hacked to death—between 1889 and 1918. Lynching was the most violent form of discrimination. Offenses the victims were accused of were usually minor, such as stealing a cow, attempting to register to vote, or speaking out for equality. Often there were allegations of sexually assaulting a white woman or talking back to a white person. Rather than receiving a fair trial, blacks were lynched by white mobs. Of course, many victims were innocent. Lynching was a major means used during this period to control blacks. However, blacks were not the only victims of lynching; whites sympathetic to blacks were as well. Ida B. Wells-Barnett (1862–1932) became a leading African American advocate to outlaw lynching. Though she traveled the world speaking out against it, lynching would continue into the 1960s.

As prejudice, discrimination, and violence against blacks increased, a call to action by black leaders spread. An outspoken critic of the segrega-tionist policies and racial prejudice was sociologist and activist W. E. B. Du Bois (1868–1963) at Atlanta University. In 1905, Du Bois and other black leaders met in Niagara Falls, Canada, to map out a strategy to fight prejudice in America. It became known as the Niagara Movement. Their focus was broad including voting rights for blacks, right to good educa-tion, better job opportunities, equal treatment as whites before the law in courts, and an end to Jim Crow laws. They had limited effectiveness due to lack of funds, but did establish a foundation for other groups to come along.

Meanwhile, Southern hostility toward blacks boiled over on several occasions. Major race riots broke out in 1906 in Brownsville, Texas, and Atlanta, Georgia, and in 1908 in Springfield, Illinois. Alarmed, black leaders gathered again and in 1909 established the NAACP to fight

Rather than receiving a fair trial, blacks were lynched by white mobs. COURTESY OF THE LIBRARY OF CONGRESS.

lynching and other racist activities. The organization would be highly influential throughout the twentieth and into the twenty-first centuries. The primary focus of the NAACP was legal action against racism, educational programs for black adults and children, and encouraging voter participation.

World War I (1914–18) created new jobs in various war industries, such as shipbuilding, and other factories in the North. Hundreds of thousands of blacks left the rural South in what became known to as the Great Migration. Black Americans arrived in the industrial North looking for good-paying war industry jobs. The Great Migration would last into the second half of the twentieth century.

The National Urban League, founded in 1910 by George E. Haynes (1875–1960), the first African American to earn a doctorate degree from Columbia University, social activist Frances Kellor (1873–1952), and others, helped blacks adjust to city life. However, many never found the economic betterment they were seeking. They were unskilled and uneducated and relegated to jobs as laborers and servants, much as they had been in the South. The growing numbers of poor blacks crowded into

Members of the KKK dressed in white robes for secrecy and to create fear. A burning cross was it symbol of terror. © GREG SMITH/CORBIS.

cheap, deteriorating housing areas in the inner cities of the North called ghettos. These communities became known for their poverty and high crime rates.

The growing black population in the North also led to conflicts with whites that included rioting in several cities between 1917 and 1919. In the summer of 1918, racial conflicts in Chester and Philadelphia, Pennsylvania, led to ten deaths and sixty injured. That was only a prelude to 1919, when twenty-five race riots erupted across the United States, leaving about one hundred people dead. During these years, membership in the Ku Klux Klan (KKK), a white supremacist hate group, also grew rapidly and continued following the war. The KKK was founded only a few years earlier in 1915 in the Southern state of Georgia. It continued to grow in the 1920s to a membership of four million. Klansmen dressed in white robes for secrecy and to create fear. A burning cross was its symbol of terror. In the 1930s the KKK greatly declined in popularity only to come back in the 1960s in some Southern states in reaction to the fight for civil rights protections for blacks.

Last hired and first fired

Difficult conditions for blacks in America would only get tougher in the 1930s. When the value of stocks (partial ownership in a company) dropped sharply in October 1929, the United States—and later much of the world—entered a severe economic crisis known as the Great Depression (1929–41). Many people lost their jobs as production plummeted. Times became tougher yet for American blacks and prejudice increased dramatically through the 1930s. As related by authors Robin D. G. Kelley and Earl Lewis in the 2000 book *To Make Our World Anew: A History of African Americans,* the saying "Last Hired and First Fired" applied to black Americans, who were the first to be let go at factories and other businesses. Racial discrimination increased even more during tough times.

Black Americans began to see some hope in the New Deal programs of Democratic president Franklin D. Roosevelt (1882–1945; served 1933–45). The New Deal was a set of federal programs established in the 1930s to bring economic relief to those most affected by the Depression. Though not specially designed for blacks, this population benefited from the programs, though in the Jim Crow South discrimination affected the distribution of benefits.

Roosevelt organized a group of black advisors that became known as the Black Cabinet. Among them was William H. Hastie (1904–1976), who would become the first black federal court judge. However, many blacks were frustrated that the president was not more dedicated toward ending Jim Crow policies. The president did not want to loose political support of Southern politicians for his economic programs. The person in the White House most admired by blacks was President Roosevelt's wife, first lady Eleanor Roosevelt (1884–1962). Eleanor was outspoken about the underprivileged, particularly the conditions in the American

Musicians Duke Ellington, left, and Louis Armstrong.
AP IMAGES.

South. Being less politically restricted than her husband, she publicly favored dismantling Jim Crow laws.

As jobs became available with the arrival of World War II (1939–45), more than two million blacks moved from the rural South to the North, again to find jobs in war industries to leave behind Jim Crow. Much to their dismay, they still faced pronounced prejudice and discrimination because many Northerners shared Southerners' attitudes about the abilities of blacks. Blacks were usually hired for jobs such as janitors at factories rather than on the actual assembly lines where war materials were made. Black leaders called for a march on Washington in 1942. Desperately not wanting to see a controversial political protest in Washington while trying to keep a unified war effort underway, Roosevelt issued an executive order forbidding racial discrimination in government agencies and the war industries. Still, more than a million blacks serving in the U.S. military served in largely segregated units. Segregation in the military would not end until 1948 when U.S. president Harry S. Truman (1884–1972; served 1945–1953) signed another executive order requiring equal treatment for all races.

Black Contributions During Jim Crow

Despite the oppressive laws and policies of the Jim Crow era, during the 1920s an exceptionally gifted group of black authors produced literature that all Americans could appreciate. They wrote of their experiences in the rural South as well as Northern cities. Most of the authors were located in Harlem; therefore, the period from 1919 to the mid-1930s became known as the Harlem Renaissance. The group included Langston Hughes (1902–1967) and James Weldon Johnson (1871–1938). Black musicians also gained considerable fame. In 1914, bandleader W. C. Handy (1873–1958) composed the "St. Louis Blues," one of the first Blues songs to become a popular hit. The Blues was a form of music first made popular by black American musicians in the early 1910s. The music derived from spiritual songs and often portrayed a depressed outlook. Handy became known as the father of Blues. Jazz was also born during this period from black folk ballads. Louis Armstrong (1901–1971) and Duke Ellington (1899–1974) became the nation's leading jazz musicians. Other noted black leaders of the time included labor leader A. Philip Randolph (1889–1979), who founded the first black union, the Brotherhood of Sleeping Car Porters. Also capturing the headlines were such black athletes as track runner Jesse Owens (1913–1980) and heavyweight boxers Jack Johnson (1878–1946) and Joe Louis (1914–1981). The Harlem Renaissance helped build a foundation for the later civil rights movement by demonstrating the cultural contributions that black Americans were capable of making. It also provided inspiration for future black artists in America.

Later in the Jim Crow era, other firsts came for black Americans. Blacks became accepted in sports after Jackie Robinson (1919–1972) shattered the color barrier when he joined and starred with the Brooklyn Dodgers major league baseball team in 1947. Robinson became a larger than life hero and a symbol for blacks throughout America into the twenty-first century. U.S. diplomat Ralph J. Bunche (1904–1971) became the first black to receive the Nobel Peace Prize in 1950. The Nobel Peace Prize is a prestigious annual award given in Oslo, Norway, to a person who has made notable achievements in promoting peace and goodwill in the world. Gwendolyn Brooks (1912–2000) was the first black to win the Pulitzer Prize in 1950 for a collection of poems published in the 1949 book *Annie Allen*. In 1955, Marian Anderson (1897–1993) became the first black singer to play a leading role in New York City's Metropolitan Opera. In 1963, actor Sidney Poitier (1927–) became the first black to win an Academy Award as best actor for his role in the film adaptation of *Lilies of the Field*.

Legal victories

During the war years, the NAACP increased its legal efforts in the fight against Jim Crow racial discrimination. It won several Supreme Court rulings, including a 1944 ruling in *Smith vs. Allwright* that the Southern white primary was illegal. Other anti-discrimination activities also took place during the war. In 1943 the Congress of Racial Equality (CORE), founded the previous year in Chicago to combat racial segregation through non-violent means, supported a sit-in (the act of entering an establishment such as a restaurant and peacefully refusing to leave in protest of their prejudicial policies) in a racially segregated Chicago restaurant.

Following the war, the NAACP gained new members as black servicemen returning home were again shocked by the blatant cruelty of the Jim Crow prejudice and discrimination that was still going on in the United States. A new group of young lawyers saw more legal successes between 1948 and 1951, including decisions against discrimination in higher educational institutions and in housing. In 1948 the Supreme Court ruled in *Shelley v. Kraemer* that restrictions could not be placed on real estate to forbid its sale to people on account of race. In *Sweatt v. Painter* the Court ruled that blacks could not be denied entrance to a state university law school on account of race.

The biggest legal victory for the NAACP against Jim Crow laws came in the 1954 U.S. Supreme Court decision of *Brown v. Board of Education.* A lawsuit challenged a local school board decision in Topeka, Kansas that denied black student Linda Brown, a third-grader, from attending the all-white public school, which was the school nearest her home. Several other similar instances had occurred in other states, and they were all combined into a single Supreme Court case. The resulting Court decision over-turned the 1896 *Plessy* decision. The "separate but equal" principle was no longer valid. The *Brown* decision stated that racially segregated public schools were illegal. The ruling did not provide a specific time by which schools had to desegregate, a fact that kept some schools segregated for another decade. Much to the frustration of black Americans, the ruling only applied to schools and not other public places such as theaters, restaurants, and places of employment.

The *Brown* decision posed dramatic implications. Black Americans were inspired to seek an end to other Jim Crow segregationist laws and to end all discriminatory practices as soon as possible. However, in the Jim Crow South, whites resisted the Court ruling. School employees who helped black children enroll at white schools were fired. A Virginia school system closed all of its public schools to avoid integration and sent their white children to private schools.

Growth of the Civil Rights Movement

Blacks, frustrated by the slow pace of change following the *Brown* decision, decided they had to fight for their rights. Protests against Jim Crow laws became widespread and used strategies such as sit-ins.

Protestors would walk into hotels, restaurants, and libraries where blacks were not allowed and sit down, quietly refusing to leave when asked. In one famous incident, four black college students sat at a Greensboro, North Carolina, lunch counter. Refused service, they sat there for hours until the restaurant closed. Sit-ins spread across the South. As businesses increasingly feared losing income, "White Only" signs began coming down.

Protests spread to other areas of discrimination in the South. In August 1955, Rosa Parks (1913–2005), a seamstress and secretary for the local chapter of the NAACP in Montgomery, Alabama, was arrested for not giving up her seat to a white man on a Montgomery city bus. Local Jim Crow laws and traditions required blacks to sit toward the back of buses and give up their seats if the white section was full and whites wanted seats further back. Parks, with her bag of groceries, was tired of giving in. Her arrest triggered a boycott (to stop buying a certain product until demands are met) of the Montgomery buses by blacks, who comprised almost 70 percent of the bus riders. For 382 days, the boycott persisted, significantly reducing the revenue of the city bus department. Blacks rode in carpools, took taxis, or walked. In some instances, police arrested carpool drivers and charged them with picking up hitchhikers, which was illegal in Alabama. Bombs were thrown at the homes of black leaders. The boycott ended when the city bus department changed its policy shortly after Parks, defended by NAACP lawyers, won a Supreme Court decision that ruled bus segregation was illegal. It was another major victory against Jim Crow laws segregating public transportation. The boycott was the first organized mass protest by blacks and catapulted their leader, Martin Luther King Jr. (1929–1968), a young Montgomery Baptist minister, into the national spotlight.

Protests against Jim Crow laws paved the way for a broad social movement known as the Civil Rights Movement. Activists included whites as well as blacks, and all sought equal rights for black Americans. It was also known as the Black Freedom Movement. Following the Montgomery boycott, King and other leaders formed the Southern Christian Leadership Conference (SCLC) in 1957 to coordinate work of the various civil rights groups around the South. Preaching nonviolent resistance to Jim Crow laws and other discriminatory policies, King pressed forward, challenging long held segregationist traditions.

Resistance to school desegregation in the Jim Crow South continued. Three years after the *Brown* decision, there were still no blacks attending schools with whites anywhere in the South. In 1960, when a six-year-old girl enrolled in a white school in New Orleans, parents withdrew their white children in her class. She was the only child in her classroom for over a year. In defiance of a federal court order, Arkansas governor Orval E. Faubus (1910–1994) sent the state's National Guard to block the entrance of black students into a Little Rock high school. U.S. president Dwight D. Eisenhower (1890–1969; served 1953–61) responded by mobilizing federal troops to enforce the court order to integrate the schools. In response, school officials closed the high school for two years rather than admit blacks.

New organizations

Continued frustration over persistent prejudice and discrimination brought cries for more aggressive steps than those promoted by the NAACP and SCLC. In 1960, black and white college students organized the Student Nonviolent Coordinating Committee (SNCC). The SNCC sponsored protest marches, boycotts, sit-ins, and other confrontational action against Jim Crow laws and policies. These actions served to increase national public awareness about the social barriers black Americans faced.

The Supreme Court in December 1960 ruled that bus and railroad companies traveling across state lines could not impose racial segregation on the vehicles or in waiting rooms, water fountains, and restrooms. To test the compliance with the new ruling, another activist group the Congress of Racial Equality (CORE) organized Freedom Rides in the spring of 1961. Both black and white activists rode two buses from Washington, D.C., to New Orleans. They encountered considerable hostility from whites along the way. Some were beaten and one bus was bombed and burned. The Freedom Riders received considerable attention in the news. Through the summer more than three hundred Freedom Riders were arrested in the South. Many were convicted of disturbing the peace and sent to jail for weeks.

In 1962 and 1963, the spotlight fell on segregation at Southern universities. James Meredith, a student at nearby Jackson State College, applied for law school at the University of Mississippi and was rejected. He went to court challenging his rejection. The Supreme Court ruled that the school must admit him. When the state governor took steps to block Meredith's entrance, President John F. Kennedy (1917–1963; served 1961–63) sent federal marshals to enforce the court ruling. However, the marshals came under attack and a riot broke out on campus, killing 2

A Freedom Rider bus goes up in flames after a fire bomb was tossed through a window in 1961 in Alabama. AP IMAGES.

bystanders and injuring about 375 students, federal marshals, and others participating in the riots. Despite the problems concerning his acceptance as a student, Meredith graduated from the university in 1964.

In 1963, Alabama governor George Wallace (1919–1998) attempted to block the entrance of blacks at the University of Alabama. This time, Kennedy sent National Guard troops to help the students. In a speech at the door to the university building, Wallace denounced federal efforts to support the civil rights of blacks. Kennedy angrily responded on a nationally televised address calling segregation morally wrong.

The fight over Jim Crow escalates

In the spring of 1963 the SCLC organized marches and sit-ins in Birmingham, Alabama protesting lingering Jim Crow policies. On May 2 thousands of schoolchildren took part in one march. The Birmingham police arrested some six hundred children. The following day police used high-powered fire hoses knocking down marchers including children. Police also unleashed dogs on the marchers. News of the events brought more protesters and news coverage to Birmingham. The KKK bombed homes and churches of black people.

Alabama governor George Wallace attempted to block the entrance of blacks at the University of Alabama. AP IMAGES.

Violence spread elsewhere in June 1963 as civil rights activist Medgar Evers (1925–1963) was murdered in Jackson, Mississippi. Evers had organized various protests, including sit-ins, and was helping blacks to register to vote. KKK member Byron de la Beckwith (1920–2001) was arrested and charged with murder. Two juries found him not guilty. In 1994—thirty-one years after Evers's murder—Beckwith was convicted and sentenced to life in prison.

Discrimination spurred by Jim Crow laws was gradually being overcome in some areas but violence was escalating in others. Discrimination persisted in many other areas untouched by protests and legal challenges. Pushing for stronger federal action, King and other black leaders, including labor leader A. Philip Randolph (1889–1979), Roy Wilkins

Black Power

During the turbulent 1960s, black groups formed, eager to take more militant action than what Martin Luther King Jr. had preached. Disappointment mounted over the lack of change in American society's prejudice since the Jim Crow era. Activists advocated forming all-black communities and using violence in reaction to discriminatory practices. Among the groups were the Black Muslims and the Black Panthers. The Black Muslims had formed in 1934 under the leadership of Elijah Muhammad (1897–1975), who advocated creation of a black nation within the United States. By the 1960s, Malcolm X (1925–1965) assumed the leadership role of the Black Muslims and pressed for blacks to fight back as well as separation of the races. He was assassinated in 1965 by members of the Nation of Islam, a religious organization that promoted improved social and economic conditions for black Americans, with whom Malcolm X had political feuds.

Malcolm X. AP IMAGES.

Inspired by the ideas of Malcolm X, Huey P. Newton (1942–1989) and Bobby Seale (1936–) founded the Black Panthers in 1966 shortly after Malcolm X's death. The organization initially promoted violent revolution against government authorities. After numerous clashes with police leading to the deaths of some Black Panthers and imprisonment of others, the Black Panthers became less violent. They began providing job training classes for blacks and other peaceful programs.

Also in 1966, members of the Student Nonviolent Coordinating Committee (SNCC) including Stokely Carmichael (1941–1998) and H. Rap Brown (1943–) formed the Black Power Movement to more militantly combat racial violence. They sought to increase the political power of blacks. One way was to take political and economic control of their communities away from whites and promote a black culture. The movement stressed that "black is beautiful" to increase self-respect and pride in the black communities. In addition, the terms "Negroes" and "colored people"—relic terms from the Jim Crow era—were replaced by such terms as black Americans, African Americans, and Afro-Americans. Trouble followed Brown in later years. After serving five years in prison for robbery in the 1970s he was convicted in 2002 for the killing of a black sheriff's deputy in a grocery store he owned in Atlanta, Georgia, and was sentenced to life in prison.

(1901–1981) of the NAACP, James Farmer (1920–1999) of CORE, and Whitney M. Young Jr. (1921–1971) of the Urban League, organized a massive protest march on Washington, D.C. On August 28, 1963, over two hundred thousand blacks and whites descended on the nation's capital. The highlight of the March on Washington was a series of speeches given from the steps of the Lincoln Memorial. Most notable was King's appeal for racial equality in America, in which he stated that he had a dream that one day all Americans would enjoy equality and justice. King's words came to symbolize the goals of the Civil Rights Movement. Perhaps in response to the March, a month later in September 1963 a bomb went off at a black church in Birmingham on a Sunday morning killing four young girls.

Following the March, President John F. Kennedy proposed civil rights legislation to end the Jim Crow era discrimination. However it attracted strong opposition in Congress.

Following Kennedy's assassination in November 1963, President Lyndon B. Johnson (1908–1973; served 1963–69) pressed forward with the legislation leading to passage of the landmark Civil Rights Act in July 1964. The act prohibited discrimination in all public places and called for equal opportunity in education and employment. It also authorized the federal government to withhold funds from school districts that refused to admit blacks. Enforcement was difficult because of the lack of cooperation of local authorities in many areas as racial prejudices persisted. The act was a major statement against Jim Crow laws. King won the Nobel Peace Prize that year for his effective non-violent strategies.

Right to vote

Despite the major gains made in civil rights, many officials in the Jim Crow South still resisted enforcing federal laws and court rulings, including the right to vote. Voter registration drives (efforts to register people eligible to vote but not yet registered with local authorities) to register blacks began in 1963 in Mississippi, Alabama, and Georgia. The voter registration drives escalated in the summer of 1964, nicknamed Freedom Summer due to the belief that the ability to vote would lead to greater social justice and freedom from prejudiced governmental policies and laws. SNCC held Freedom Schools, teaching blacks to read and write so they could pass literacy tests required to vote. In June, three

Protests against local authorities in Alabama escalated, leading to three deaths and hundreds of beating victims. AP IMAGES.

voter registration activists two of whom were white were kidnapped and murdered in Mississippi. They were missing for forty-four days until their bodies were found buried in a dam. The deaths spread much fear among blacks in the South that they might face violent deaths if they dared to register to vote. However, the crime proved a rallying point for the civil rights movement and greatly increased public awareness elsewhere in the nation about the persecution minorities faced in the South. Eighteen suspects were arrested, but only seven were convicted.

In January 1965, King journeyed to Selma, Alabama, to help erase voting rights barriers. The resulting protests against local authorities escalated, leading to three deaths and hundreds of beating victims. On March 7, police on horseback clubbed protestors, dramatizing Southern resistance to equal rights. Eight days later on March 15, President Johnson introduced a voting rights bill to Congress. To bring national attention to the bill, King began a massive four-day march on March 20. Thirty thousand protesters walked from Selma to the state capitol building in Montgomery. They were protected by federal troops mobilized by President Johnson. Another fifty thousand supporters joined the marchers in Montgomery. In another historic speech to the crowd and national media, King demanded that blacks be given the right to vote without unjust restrictions posed by Jim Crow laws and policies.

In reaction to the harsh scenes portrayed on the national news programs of peaceful protesters being beaten by Southern law authorities, the American public pressed for further legal safeguards against racial discrimination. Later that year on August 6, Congress passed the Voting Rights Act of 1965. The act banned the poll tax as a voting requirement and placed close federal oversight over Southern voting practices such as voter registration. Any changes in state voting laws had to be approved by the U.S. Department of Justice, and federal officials supervised voter registration where problems had existed in the past. One million black Americans who had never been allowed to cast their ballot before, voted between 1965 and 1968.

Affirmative action

In 1965, President Johnson continued to ease discrimination. Declaring it was not enough to end legally enforced discrimination, he pressed to end Jim Crow discriminatory social customs through affirmative action programs. These programs, some directed by the federal government, were to open up opportunities in education and employment long denied to minorities. Affirmative action programs required that employers and schools favor minority and female applicants in an effort to create a more socially diverse workforce or student body.

In setting examples of his new policy, Johnson appointed Robert C. Weaver (1907–1997) as secretary of housing and urban development in 1966. Weaver was the first black cabinet member in the United States. The following year, Johnson appointed Thurgood Marshall (1908–1993), a former NAACP lawyer, as the first black member of the U.S. Supreme Court.

Legacy of Jim Crow

Despite the major political gains, the lasting effects of Jim Crow remained strong. Many black Americans resided in inner-city slums and faced abusive policing. They enjoyed little change from the earlier decades in terms of prejudice and discrimination. The resulting frustration exploded into violence in the mid-1960s. A series of riots occurred in various cities beginning in Harlem in 1964. In 1965, the South Los Angeles community of Watts rioted killing thirty-four, injuring nine hundred and

Martin Luther King Jr. at a Tennessee hotel shortly before his assassination. AP IMAGES.

causing $40 million in damage. Four thousand rioters were arrested. Major riots also occurred in Detroit and Washington, D.C. President Johnson established a commission to study the riots and determine the causes. In a report issued in March 1968, the commission focused on racial prejudice promoted by the Jim Crow era that led to persistent segregation, poor housing, high unemployment, few educational opportunities, and hunger. The report stated that the United States was becoming two societies, one black and one white. The commission recommended major federal programs to address the needs of black America to recover from Jim Crow discrimination.

Only a short time after the report was released, King was assassinated on April 4 in Memphis, Tennessee. He was there to support a strike by city workers. Riots erupted in response to the assassination in almost one hundred communities. In response, Johnson pushed through the Civil Rights Act of 1968, which included the Fair Housing Act. The housing act prohibited racial discrimination in the rental and sale of most housing in the United States.

Recovery from Jim Crow

Laws banning discrimination aided by affirmative action programs ended the Jim Crow era in the late 1960s. The actions of courageous activists and government leaders contributed to a significant increase in black student enrollments in previously all-white schools. The 1970s saw the high school enrollments of black youth increase from 1.8 million in 1970 to 2.2 million in 1979; students and college enrollment rose from 600,000 to one million from 1970 to 1979. In addition, the number of black-owned businesses grew from 185,000 to 235,000 during the same time period. During this period, a black studies movement developed, increasing awareness and appreciation of black heritage to further the psychological and social healing from Jim Crow prejudices.

With blacks' right to vote protected, the number of blacks elected as government officials rose sharply by the late 1970s. Before long, blacks were elected as mayors of cities including Tom Bradley (1917–1998) of Los Angeles who became one of the first black American mayors of a major city in 1973. Despite these gains, the fight against racial prejudice and discrimination in America continued into the twenty-first century.

For More Information

BOOKS

Chafe, William H. *Remembering Jim Crow: African Americans Tell About Life in the Segregated South.* New York: W. W. Norton, 2001.

Collier, Christopher. *Reconstruction and the Rise of Jim Crow, 1864–1896.* New York: Benchmark Books, 2000.

Darby, Jean. *Martin Luther King.* Minneapolis: Lerner Publications, 1990.

Horton, James O., and Lois E. Horton. *Slavery and the Making of America.* New York: Oxford University Press, 2005.

Kelley, Robin D. G., and Earl Lewis. *To Make Our World Anew: A History of African Americans.* New York: Oxford University Press, 2000.

National Association for the Advancement of Colored People. *Thirty Years of Lynching in the United States: 1889–1918.* New York: Negro Universities Press, 1969.

Packard, Jerrold. *American Nightmare: The History of Jim Crow.* New York: St. Martin's Press, 2002.

Wormser, Richard. *The Rise and Fall of Jim Crow.* New York: St. Martin's Press, 2003.

WEB SITES

National Civil Rights Museum. http://www.civilrightsmuseum.org/ (accessed on November 29, 2006).

"The Rise and Fall of Jim Crow." *pbs.org* http://www.pbs.org/wnet/jimcrow/ (accessed on November 29, 2006).

18

Native Americans

Native Americans are the indigenous peoples of the United States. Indigenous peoples are the first or earliest inhabitants of a region. As with indigenous populations in many other parts of the world, indigenous peoples differ in skin color and ethnic customs from the dominant society that assumed control of their lands sometime in the past five hundred years. The term Native American is commonly used to refer to American Indians living within the United States. However, it also includes Hawaiians and some Alaskan Natives not considered American Indians. Therefore, American Indians refers to most Native Americans in the main continental United States plus some native groups in Alaska.

The complex legal standing of Native Americans in the early twenty-first century resulted from governmental laws and policies that built up over centuries. By the twenty-first century over five hundred Native American tribes were officially recognized by the federal government. Although many similarities existed among them, each tribe had its own unique cultural and legal history. Their overall relationship to the U.S. government for over two centuries followed a pattern shifting between periods of support for tribal self-government and economic self-sufficiency to periods of forced Indian inclusion into the dominant white society, known as assimilation.

This relationship began taking shape during the seventeenth century. European colonists, who settled along the Eastern Seaboard, negotiated treaties with the local indigenous groups. These colonists brought with them a long-established international policy that treated individual native groups as politically independent nations. During early colonial settlement natives were dying in large numbers from violent conflicts and diseases their immune systems had no resistance to, which were introduced by the colonists from the Old World (the Eastern Hemisphere). Where native groups were able to persist at their settlements, in the

WORDS TO KNOW

assimilation: Forced inclusion into the dominant society.

indigenous: The first or earliest inhabitants of a region.

sovereignty: A nation's ability to govern its own internal affairs.

termination: A tribe no longer having the U.S. government representing its best interests and providing special social services.

trust: Holding and managing something of value for the benefit of another person or organization.

treaties the colonists recognized the Indian right of possession to lands they were occupying and using. In return the colonists received promises of peace and security.

As a result of these treaties, the tribal groups were internationally recognized as nations well before the United States gained its independence as a nation from Great Britain. This process of formal recognition established the basis for future U.S.–Indian relations from the very beginning of U.S. existence into the early twenty-first century as American Indian communities made a strong economic and political recovery from centuries of prejudice and oppression.

The arrival of European settlement

Contact between Western Europeans and Native American societies in North America began in the seventeenth century as the first European colonists settled along the East Coast. The early colonists found numerous Native American settlements across the landscape. Consistent with the European doctrine of discovery used by early explorers in claiming New World lands, the colonists claimed exclusive right for the area they settled to negotiate with peoples who still occupied those lands.

At first the small numbers of colonists were outnumbered and vulnerable to hostile attack by the more numerous Indians. Though outnumbered, the colonists carried forward the ethnocentrism (believing one ethnic group's way of life is superior to all others) that dominated Europe for centuries. They intended to carry civilization as known in Europe to the rest of the world's populations while helping themselves to the wealth of natural resources available in native-held lands. At first however, the colonists eagerly signed treaties of peace and friendship with

A drawing of Indians trading furs with colonists. COURTESY OF THE NATIONAL ARCHIVES OF CANADA.

Indian groups to ensure their own safety. However, the balance of strength changed as the number of colonists steadily grew and the Indian population along the coast rapidly declined. By the mid-1700s the coastal native population had been dramatically reduced by war, isolated skirmishes, disease, and starvation. Many surviving Indian peoples moved west of the Appalachian Mountains away from the colonial settlements.

In the 1783 Treaty of Paris ending the American Revolution (1775–83), the newly independent United States gained a claim to lands between the Appalachians and the Mississippi River from Britain. The United States now had the right to negotiate with tribes residing in this western region for the actual possession of their lands for new American settlement. However, racial prejudices of American citizens toward Indian peoples were strong. Not only were Indians considered uncivilized, they had also sided with the British during the Revolution. Now they were considered a defeated enemy. As a result, settlers poured across the Appalachians to settle the fertile Mississippi and Ohio River valleys regardless if the appropriate treaties acquiring possession of the land were completed or not.

Establishing U.S.–Indian relations

Adding to the growing conflicts on the American frontier, the Articles of Confederation governing the young nation through its first years largely left Indian relations to the individual states. The new and very weak central government could only take actions that did not get in the way of the states' activities. Greater decisiveness to address the chaos came soon when the Second Continental Congress adopted the Northwest Ordinance in 1787. The Ordinance formally established the Northwest Territory from lands west of the Appalachian Mountains. Having no funds to finance military conflicts with Indians, the Ordinance attempted to secure peaceful and orderly relations with Indians. While asserting its claim to the newly gained lands from Britain, the Ordinance recognized existing Indian right of possession to those lands. The Ordinance prohibited private individuals and local governments from negotiating treaties or buying these lands directly from Indians. Only the federal government could now negotiate treaties with tribes in that region and guide overall relations with Indians.

The policies defining U.S.–tribal relations by the Northwest Ordinance were carried forward into the new U.S. Constitution, adopted in 1789. An example of Congress's broad powers over Indian relations was Article I, section 8, clause 3 of the Constitution. This clause gave the federal government sole authority to regulate all trade not only with foreign nations and between individual states, but also with Indian tribes. The Constitution also recognized the importance of treaties with Indians. According to Article VI Indian treaties ratified (approved) by the U.S. Senate have the same legal force as federal laws and have priority over state laws.

One of the first actions of the new U.S. Congress in 1790 was passage of the Indian Trade and Intercourse Act. The act formed the basis for

U.S.–Indian relations for the next two centuries. It gave Congress broad powers over Indian peoples including control of all interaction between Indians and U.S. citizens. Like the Ordinance, it prohibited states or private citizens from purchasing land from Indians. In addition, any merchant selling to Indians without first receiving government permission could face criminal penalties.

The 1790 act started a new era of treaties. Their primary purpose was removing Indians out of the way of the constantly expanding U.S. settlement. In 1800 the native population still possessed three-fourths of what would later be the United States. Between 1790 and 1871 the U.S. Senate ratified over 370 treaties with Indian nations. The treaties not only served to acquire lands, but to gain Indian allegiance to the newly formed nation instead of Britain which had maintained friendly relations with many of the tribes prior to American independence.

The treaty process clearly reflected the prejudices of the government negotiators and the society they represented. The treaties largely took place in English and normally in an atmosphere of extreme duress for the tribes. U.S. officials chose which tribal members to negotiate with. Usually those selected had no real tribal authority to sell (cede) tribal lands. The United States always purchased the lands for prices well below fair market value, only a few cents an acre for good farmland. The treaties also promised annual payments to the tribes and delivery of agricultural equipment and other basic necessities, such as blankets to protect against winter cold. These payments and goods frequently never appeared.

The treaty process gave the newly established democratic nation a false sense of fairness in the face of bitter prejudice shown by U.S. settlers toward the Indians and the blatant conquest of Indian lands. The treaty process made this transfer of land appear more peaceful and voluntary. Regardless of whether the U.S. government had negotiated treaties for removal of Indians from their land, the new settlers moved in anyway, clearing the natural woods and plowing agricultural fields. Game and natural foods the Indians had relied upon for centuries vanished. In some cases the settlers moved into areas reserved in treaties for Indian use only. The pioneers of predominantly white European ancestry only wanted the dark-skinned Indians out of the way, either peacefully or not.

Hostile conflicts

U.S.–Indian relations through the nineteenth century involved numerous skirmishes and battles. The Indians peoples suffered a heavy loss in life. Much bitterness developed, particularly owing to the brutal hand-to-hand combat that these battles frequently involved. The U.S. Army possessed more advanced military technology and a larger supply of arms and ammunition making the outcome of U.S. conquest inevitable. Fighting the outnumbered and outmatched Indians produced new American heroes including future U.S. presidents William Henry Harrison (1773–1841; served 1841) and Andrew Jackson (1767–1845; served 1829–37).

The Indian peoples repeatedly stiffened their resistance to the continued loss of their homelands to American settlers. On different occasions new Indian leaders promoted a return to traditional beliefs and ways of life, called revitalization. They rejected American goods including alcohol and other undesirable American habits.

The civilization program

The U.S. government constantly sought ways of avoiding conflicts with Indians and protecting lives of its citizens. In the early nineteenth century the government introduced a program to civilize indigenous peoples. Displaying prejudices toward ethnic lifestyles of natives, the U.S. leaders wanted to turn Indians from hunters into farmers in order to civilize them. The government provided agricultural implements and spinning wheels to encourage the farming lifestyle. The Office of Indian Affairs (later Bureau of Indian Affairs) in 1824 was created to administer government Indian policies. However, surprisingly to the ethnocentric Americans, Indians consistently showed a stronger determination to maintain their traditional economies. Indians did not find this new European way of civilized life acceptable. Many Indians sought wage labor in the newly established frontier towns. However, there exclusion from residing in these communities based on racial prejudice made it difficult.

States mounted legal challenges to U.S. recognition of tribal sovereignty and the exclusive control over Indian relations held by Congress. Sovereignty represents a nation's ability to govern its own internal affairs. States wanted to gain control over Indian relations. As a result, U.S. Indian policy became further defined by three landmark Supreme Court decisions between 1823 and 1832, known as the Marshall Trilogy after legendary Supreme Court chief justice John Marshall (1756–1835). The Court's opinions expressed in *Johnson v. McIntosh* (1823), *Cherokee Nation v. Georgia* (1831), and *Worcester v. Georgia* (1832) reaffirmed

A painting of The Trail of Tears, the forcible removal of the Cherokee Indians to the West. THE GRANGER COLLECTION, LTD.

the tribal right to occupy and govern its own lands that were free from state jurisdiction (the geographic area over which law enforcement or courts have legal authority) on their own lands, referred to as Indian Country, and defined a U.S. moral trust responsibility to the tribes. Marshall called tribes domestic dependent nations. The trust obligations meant the United States was responsible for Indian health and welfare and their economic well-being.

The Marshall Trilogy established the legal status of the Indian tribes in the United States. Unfortunately for Indian peoples at the time, these legal principles were not well received by the U.S. population. Even President Jackson ignored the Court's rulings and pressed on with harsh Indian policies.

Before long, the U.S. government abandoned efforts to civilize Indian peoples. Instead, it adopted policies to isolate Indian peoples including even forced removal. The 1830 Indian Removal Act led to mass relocations of those surviving Indian peoples still remaining east of the Mississippi River. Under this policy, the United States forcefully removed members of the Five Civilized Tribes (Choctaw, Seminole,

Cherokee, Creek, and Chickasaw) from the Southeastern United States to the newly created Oklahoma Indian Territory. Thousands of deaths directly resulted from initial long-term detention followed by the 1,800-mile, six-month march known as the Trail of Tears.

Reservation period

Through much of the nineteenth century American settlement continued its relentless march westward under the highly prejudiced notion of Manifest Destiny. Under this idea, U.S. citizens believed they had a God-given right to spread its influence across the North American continent to the shores of the Pacific Ocean. This expansion involved removal of Indian peoples they considered uncivilized and not making good use of the land by farming.

Following the acquisition of the Southwest from Mexico and the opening of the Oregon Trail to the Pacific Northwest in the 1840s, Indian removal policies of the 1830s continued into the 1870s. Through more treaties, tribes exchanged land, water, and mineral rights for promises of peace, security, healthcare, and education. The western treaties created a vast reserve system in which surviving Indian peoples could exclusively exercise their inherent (acquired at birth) rights within certain defined territories, called reservations. The reservations were usually located in remote areas judged unsuitable for white settlement. In 1871 Congress officially closed the treaty period with more than 650 treaties signed and 370 ratified into law.

Signing these treaties was one matter for the U.S. government, honoring them was another. Many believed that the dwindling native populations in the late nineteenth century would eventually cease to exist altogether. Consequently, some U.S. leaders considered the treaties only a temporary measure. Instead, these reservations formed the basis for Indian communities and governments into the twenty-first century.

With Congressional action in 1871 Indian removal was considered essentially complete. However, with discoveries of new goldfields in the 1860s, the remote reservation lands increasingly looked attractive to prospectors and settlers. Some of the last treaties forced tribes to greatly reduce the size of reservations promised in earlier treaties.

Throughout the nineteenth century Indians were banished from towns and relegated to remote reservations. A system for policing Indians developed largely outside the normal U.S. court jurisdiction. Indian agents working for the Office of Indian Affairs had ready access to the U.S. military and exercised broad authority. They routinely detained individual Indians for a wide range of alleged actions. Finally advocates for Indians took a case to federal courts. In 1879 a federal court ruled that Indians off-reservation were persons as defined in the Fourteenth Amendment of the U.S. Constitution. They had the same constitutional due process (legal protections through established formal procedures) and equal protection rights (all persons treated fairly before the law) as U.S. citizens. The ruling meant the U.S. Army could no longer exercise broad authority to detain Indians while off the reservation without full civilian constitutional protections.

Assimilation policies

By the 1880s, many believed the only chance of survival for Indians was through integration into society. A major period of forced cultural assimilation began with the General Allotment Act of 1887. To a large degree this act marked a return to the highly prejudiced desire of civilizing Indian peoples. Believing the indigenous tradition of communally owning land was a major cultural barrier to Indians adopting Western ways, Congress passed the Allotment Act, also known as the Dawes Act. The act authorized the Bureau of Indian Affairs (BIA) to divide communal reservation lands into smaller, privately owned parcels. The agency allotted 160-acre parcels to families and 80-acre parcels to single adults over eighteen years of age. Indians receiving allotments also received U.S. citizenship supposedly to speed their assimilation. U.S. policymakers reasoned that if they owned their own property, Indians would most likely become farmers and adopt the U.S. social values.

Given the dramatic decrease of the Indian population before 1887, a large amount of reservation land was left over after each tribal member or family had received their allotment. The BIA declared those unallotted lands as surplus and sold them to non-Indians. Often these were the more agriculturally productive lands on reservations. In addition to the loss of these so-called surplus lands, much allotted land went into forfeiture (was lost) when many Indians could not afford to pay taxes on their often remote, unproductive desert properties. This land, too, went to non-Indians eventually. Even when land was productive, markets were usually still too distant to deliver produce in this era before refrigerated railway cars. As a result, the allotment policy was an economic disaster for Indian peoples. The size of Indian Country in the United States decreased from 138 million acres in 1887 to just 48 million acres by 1934.

As part of its assimilation policies, Congress later passed the Indian Citizenship Act of 1924. The act granted all Indians citizenship. The act also made Indians citizens of the states in which they resided.

More legal challenges

The legal status of Indian tribes once again became a topic of the U.S. Supreme Court in the early twentieth century. Some of these decisions focused on the results of the early prejudices associated with the early treaty negotiations. In *Lone Wolf v. Hitchcock* (1903) the Court ruled that Congress has the plenary (absolute) power to take away tribal rights. However, the federal trust responsibility identified by Supreme Court chief justice Marshall eighty years earlier required careful exercise of this absolute power, using it only when Congress believed it was beneficial to Indian peoples.

In *United States v. Winans* (1905), the Supreme Court established the Reserved Rights Doctrine. The doctrine meant that tribes retain inherent rights until explicitly taken away by Congress. For example, a tribe retains its hunting and fishing rights even if its reservation is taken away by Congress unless legislation specifically states that the rights are no longer valid.

In *Winters v. United States* (1908), the Supreme Court ruled that the creation of reservations through treaties also carried with them implied (unwritten) water rights (right of a user to a particular water source) necessary to support residential and economic use of the reservation. The decision, known as the Winters Doctrine, remained central to water rights negotiations into the twenty-first century involving tribes, private landowners, and public agencies, particularly in Western states.

To resolve legal disputes over how treaties are to be interpreted, the Court created the doctrine known as "canons of construction" in its 1908 *Winters* ruling. This doctrine stated that courts should always interpret unclear treaty language from the tribal perspective.

Renewed hope at survival

It is estimated the peak Native American population was perhaps as high as ten million people prior to the arrival of European explorers and settlers in the Western Hemisphere in the sixteenth century. The population plummeted to less than 300,000 by the 1920s, at its lowest point.

By the late 1920s American Indians had been stripped of almost all their traditional lands. Surviving Indians were isolated on remote reservations or in rural communities, trapped in oppressive poverty with few opportunities for an education and poor access to health services. Highly prejudiced government programs prohibited them to practice ancient Indian traditions. A 1928 study by the Brookings Institution, *The Problem of Indian Administration,* documented in detail the dire situation of Native Americans in the United States.

In the midst of this desperate situation, hope came in 1933 when newly elected president Franklin D. Roosevelt (1882–1945; served 1933–45) named Harold Ickes (1874–1952) as secretary of the interior. Ickes was a champion of civil liberties and not prejudiced against traditional native cultures. Ickes appointed John Collier (1884–1968), a leading critic of earlier federal Indian policies, to serve as U.S. commissioner of Indian affairs. Collier recommended an end to assimilation policies and Congress responded.

Under the guidance of Ickes and Collier, the 1930s became a turning point in American Indian history. The decade was marked by the Great Depression, a major decline in the nation's economy. Numerous federal programs of the Roosevelt administration designed to help those Americans suffering the most from hunger and unemployment were collectively known as the New Deal. Those programs aimed more directly toward Native Americans became known as the Indian New Deal. Using the 1928 report as a guide, Collier reformed the governmental policies guiding American Indian affairs. The U.S. Office of Indian Affairs (later renamed the Bureau of Indian Affairs or BIA) now promoted the continued political and cultural existence of tribes. American Indians would not be forced to blend into the dominant American white culture. Importantly, social services available to Indians were improved.

Collier wanted to provide tribes a way to pursue economic development while maintaining their individual tribal cultures. To achieve this goal he guided through Congress the Indian Reorganization Act (IRA) of 1934. Still based on Western society racial prejudices, the act gave tribes an option of adopting written constitutions establishing democratic forms of government and forming federally chartered corporations. In creating an IRA government, a tribe could receive federal funds to purchase land, start businesses, and receive social services.

Some 252 tribes held elections to decide whether to create an IRA government. Of these 174 tribes voted to accept IRA conditions. However, ultimately only 92 tribes actually adopted IRA constitutions.

John Collier with Blackfoot Indians. Collier served as commissioner of Indian affairs. © BETTMANN/CORBIS.

Other tribes chose to organize new governments under their own tribal rules. Despite its limited acceptance by tribes, the IRA stopped the ongoing loss of American Indian lands and provided a major source of funds for tribes to pursue economic recovery. The IRA took a big step toward increasing tribal economic and political independence. On the other hand, the IRA-established tribal governments often clashed with the tribe's traditional leaders causing strife within tribal communities. Nonetheless, some tribes with a sufficient land base and marketable natural resources, such as timber, developed a strong economy and prospered during this period.

Collier orchestrated other reforms. To improve education and health services, Congress passed the Johnson-O'Malley Act in 1934. The act authorized the federal government to pay public school districts for expenses related to educating Indian children in their classrooms.

In 1935 Congress created the Indian Arts and Crafts Board to encourage American Indians to produce traditional as well as contemporary arts and crafts. The Board adopted standards for Indian crafts to guarantee their value. Indians could also now trademark their designs. The Board established galleries where Indians could market their crafts. The locations were in Washington, D.C.; Montana; South Dakota; Oklahoma; and at the World's Fair in San Francisco, California, in 1939 and 1940. In New Mexico the New Deal's Works Progress Administration (WPA) hired artists and musicians to teach Indian crafts and traditions that had been almost lost. A small group of Indian artisans whose influence would grow later in the twentieth century emerged from these governmental programs.

Assimilation through termination

Thousands of Indians served in the U.S. military abroad during World War II (1939–45) while others worked in defense plants. Much like African Americans at the time, their exposure to mainstream society during the war made life on poverty-ridden reservations less acceptable as they returned from active duty or the assembly line following the war. A population shift from reservations to cities began.

Meanwhile, the U.S. Indian policies took another turn away from promotion of Indian traditions. As the population trend toward cities increased, special interests longing for valuable Indian-owned assets persuaded Congress to shift policy back to assimilation, this time known as termination. Termination of a tribe meant ending its special trust relationship with the U.S. government and converting tribal reservation lands to private lands. Access to federal health and education services was also curtailed.

The assimilation policies in the 1950s were designed to increase integration of Indian peoples into mainstream U.S. society. The government created the Adult Vocational Training Program and the Employment Assistance Program to promote urban relocation. From 1952 to 1972 the government sent over one hundred thousand Indians from reservations to urban job placement centers. The percentage of Indians living in cities expanded from only 10 percent in 1930 to almost 30 percent in 1960.

Approximately one hundred tribes were selected for termination through acts passed by Congress. As in the allotment period, much Indian land was sold to non-Indians or became public lands including

National Forests. The economic base for those Indian communities was devastated. Also as part of termination, Congress passed Public Law 280 in 1953. The act expanded state jurisdiction onto tribal lands in selected states. Tribal sovereignty was decreased even further.

A return to tribal support

Congressional support for the termination policies did not last long. Once again U.S. Indian policy took another dramatic shift. The 1970s saw renewed support for tribal government independence. What was referred to as the tribal self-determination era began in which the tribes could govern their own internal affairs.

Changes in support of tribes began again in the 1960s. Title VII of the 1964 Civil Rights Act exempted Indians from job discrimination in certain circumstances. For example, the BIA could favor Indian applicants in filling jobs within the agency. The 1974 Supreme Court ruling in *Morton v. Mancari* affirmed that the federal government can treat American Indians differently from other U.S. citizens, despite anti-discrimination laws, when applying for jobs in the BIA. The Court ruled that when a government agency acts to protect Indian interests and promote tribal sovereignty, then tribes are considered political groups, not racial or ethnic groups.

Other legal distinctions for Indians were also identified. To ensure consistent civil rights protections within the individual tribes Congress passed the Indian Civil Rights Act (ICRA) of 1968. The act extended most of the U.S. Constitution's Bill of Rights (first ten amendments to the U.S. Constitution recognizing certain rights and protections) to Indian peoples. These individual rights and protections included free speech protections, free exercise of religion, and due process (designated to protect the legal rights of individuals) and equal protection of tribal government laws. The act did not extend to Indians the prohibition on government support of a religion. Tribal governments were free to promote their own tribal religions.

The biggest boost in support of tribal sovereignty and self-sufficiency came in 1975 when Congress passed the Indian Self-Determination and Education Assistance Act. The act gave the BIA and other agencies authority to transfer responsibility for administering certain tribal programs to the tribes. The programs must be those federal programs benefiting Indian peoples, such as programs providing health and education services to tribal communities.

As the Indian population shift from reservations to cities progressed, problems of racial discrimination and poverty became prevalent for urban Indians. Underemployment led to homelessness, rampant substance abuse, and unusually high injury, disease, death, and infant mortality rates. To provide support for the expanding Indian urban population, Indian centers, clubs, and churches appeared in many cities. In 1976 Congress passed the Indian Health Care Improvement Act to address the urban Indian plight by bringing increased healthcare services to Indians.

Resurgence gains momentum

With the resurgence of some tribal economies in the 1980s and resulting improved living conditions on reservations, Indians began moving back to their rural tribal communities from the cities. The educations and skills they acquired in mainstream society further propelled Indian Country resurgence. As the wealth of some tribes increased, questions and issues related to tribal membership and rights, claims to Indian ancestry or tribal affiliation, and intellectual property issues (who has the right to represent Indian interests to the mainstream society) became key areas of concern.

Determining who was Indian had increasingly important financial and legal consequences. Individuals could gain tribal membership through birth or marriage and may have substantial non-Indian ancestry. However, a person of total Indian ancestry who never establishes a relationship with a tribe cannot claim legal Indian status. Because of tribal sovereignty, each tribe was responsible for determining the basis for its membership. Generally, an Indian could be anyone having some degree of Indian ancestry, considered a member of an Indian community, and promoting himself as Indian.

Congress continued passing acts protecting tribal rights and interests, including the American Indian Religious Freedom Act (1978), the Indian Mineral Development Act (1982), the Native American Graves Protection and Repatriation Act (1990), and the Indian Self-Governance Act (1994). The 1994 act amended the earlier 1975 Self-Determination Act making more federal government services to tribes subject to tribal administration.

A key player on the national scene

By the late twentieth century, a special branch of law in the U.S. legal system had even become recognized, referred to as Indian law. In the early twenty-first century 554 tribes were formally recognized as sovereign nations located within the boundaries of the United States. These tribal governments oversaw about 56 million acres, or just over 2 percent of lands within the United States. In 2000 approximately two million Native Americans lived on 314 reservations and in cities. More than 250 native languages were still spoken in Indian Country. The percentage of Indians living in cities grew to 56 percent by 1990. The majority of American Indians now lived in urban areas. Despite the population shift, the reservations in Indian Country remained the focus of native pride and political identity separate from American white culture.

Issues of tribal sovereignty persisted into the new century related to natural resource management and economic development. By the beginning of the twenty-first century tribal lands held much of the last remaining deposits of natural resources in North America. Ongoing issues involved water rights, forest management, restoration of fish runs, mineral development (including gold, copper, zinc, oil and gas, uranium, and coal), cleanup of heavy-metal poisoning left from earlier mining activity, and management of major waterways including the Columbia, Snake, Colorado, and Missouri rivers. Legal conflicts frequently pitted private interests and state governments against tribal governments with the federal government weighing in on various sides depending on the circumstances behind the particular dispute.

Tribal governments and their peoples continued to enjoy a unique legal status. Under the sovereignty concept, tribes could form and reorganize their own governments, determine tribal membership, regulate individual property, manage natural resources, provide health services, develop businesses, regulate commerce on tribal lands, collect taxes, maintain law enforcement, and establish tribal court systems. Members of federally recognized tribes were both U.S. and tribal citizens, simultaneously receiving benefits and protections from federal, state, and tribal governments.

Indian gaming

A new era of tribal economics arrived in 1988 when Congress passed the Indian Gaming Regulatory Act. By the end of the twentieth century, one-third of the 554 federally recognized tribes operated some form of gaming establishment. Annual revenue was estimated at $6 billion. Due to tribal sovereignty, casino revenues were tax free. However, agreements with individual states required by the act often provided some funding to states to pay for increased community needs due to their popular businesses.

By the end of the twentieth century, one-third of the 554 federally recognized tribes operated some form of gaming establishment.
AP IMAGES.

These needs included improved roads and sewers and expanded police capabilities in the communities.

The financial success of the individual gaming businesses varied greatly. The most notable success in gaming was the Foxwoods Casino and Resort, operated by the Mashantucket Pequots of Connecticut, a tribe of only five hundred members. Comprised of three million square feet plus a high-rise hotel and twenty-four restaurants, in 1998 it was the largest tribal facility in the country. By the late 1990s the tribe was making over $1 billion a year through its casino and other businesses. It had become the largest employer in New England and largest land-owner in Connecticut with the land purchases the tribe made.

Similar stories unfolded elsewhere in the country though normally at a lesser scale. The Coeur d'Alene Tribe of northern Idaho with its new-found gaming income built a $5 million wellness center and a 8,000-bed hospital. For the Ojibwa of Minnesota, who built two lavish casino and hotel complexes in the early 1990s including the Grand Casino Mille

Lacs, unemployment fell from 46 percent to less than 10 percent. Housing for tribal members improved and the tribes acquired new lands. The Oneida of Wisconsin became the largest employer in the Green Bay area due to gaming and other business ventures.

Other economic gains

Gaming revenues first went into education, housing, health and elder care, and law enforcement. But as wealth accumulated, investments in a wide range of developments grew. In addition, donations were made to local non-Indian community needs.

Indian gaming successes gave rise to a new generation of Native American entrepreneurs. Economic issues involving casino development usually grabbed the public's attention, but tribes were also investing in a diversity of other long-term business ventures. Economic investments involved billions of dollars. Many of these new business leaders saw gaming as a means to establish long-term more diverse tribal economies involving non-gaming developments. Tribal acquisitions ranged from golf courses to industrial parks. Unemployment rates in many areas plummeted.

Their goal was a lasting increase in quality of life. Tribes also built new cultural centers to help reconstruct tribal identities lost over the centuries of oppression from dominant societies. They focused on lost languages, songs, dances, and other traditions.

A prejudiced reaction

The substantial economic gains some tribes were able to achieve brought a backlash from the federal and state governments and the general public. Issues of economic development and tribal sovereignty became increasingly intermixed. With incomes growing for some tribes, opposition rose to the tax-free and largely regulation-free status of tribes. Many complained that tribal businesses operating free of state taxes and regulations had an unfair competitive edge against non-Indian businesses.

The concept of tribal sovereignty came increasingly under attack. Tribal leaders responded that this challenge only represented what tribes had faced for centuries: whenever Indians gained something of value, the dominant white society wanted it. Opposition grew against placing more land in trust for tribes as tribes purchased more lands. When lands are placed into federal trust they become exempt from local taxation and zoning requirements since they are not privately owned.

Members of the American Indian Movement at a rally with the founder of the AIM, Dennis Banks, holding his daughter.
MS. ILKA HARTMANN.

Tribes began spending millions of dollars in donations to political parties and hiring lawyers, lobbyists, and public relations firms. Some tribes have even opened lobbying offices in Washington.

During the summer of 1999, Indian peoples filed a class-action lawsuit against the BIA alleging over two centuries of misuse of Indian assets held in trust by the U.S. government. They were asking for tens of billions of dollars in payment. The lawsuit captured national headlines in the following years as major changes were made in the way the government administered tribal programs.

Prejudice and poverty remained

Despite dramatic economic gains by some tribes in the late twentieth century, by 2000 Indian reservations overall still had a poverty rate of 31 percent, six times the national average at the time. Health and education needs were high. Almost 60 percent of Native Americans lived in substandard housing while large numbers were homeless.

American Indian Movement

The civil rights movement of the 1950s and 1960s, which made progress toward ending certain forms of racial discrimination of African Americans, inspired Indian activism and radicalism including growth of what became known as the Red Power movement. Among various organizations was the American Indian Movement (AIM) in the summer of 1968 by Dennis Banks (1937–) and others on the Pine Ridge Indian Reservation, an Indian community long known for its poverty and isolation.

AIM was formed to protect traditional ways of the Indian communities and inspire a cultural rejuvenation. Specific issues included from alleged heavy-handed police actions against tribal members and government takeover of Sioux lands in the Black Hills of South Dakota for gold mining. AIM was more confrontational than most social activist organizations of the time. They confronted government agencies and organizations that sought to marginalize American Indians. AIM caught national attention in November 1972 when AIM members seized the Washington, D.C., headquarters of the BIA in protest of the agency's policies. Twenty-four were arrested. The following year a gun battle erupted between Banks and approximately two hundred AIM members and FBI on the Pine Ridge Reservation at Wounded Knee, South Dakota. The standoff lasted seventy-one days. Three tribal members were killed. In 1975 more violence erupted between AIM members and FBI leading to the deaths of two tribal members and two FBI agents in separate incidents. AIM member Leonard Peltier (1944–) was convicted in 1977 for the murder of the agents and became a symbol of American Indian radicalism as he served a life sentence in prison.

AIM remained active in the early twenty-first century advocating American Indian interests. Their involvement included the protest of schools and sports teams using indigenous caricatures as mascots and protests of the Lewis and Clark Bicentennial celebrating U.S. exploration of the American West in the early nineteenth century. Another early leader of AIM, Russell Means (1939–), ran for governor of New Mexico in 2001.

American Indians in the United States suffered higher rates of tuberculosis, liver disease, cancer, pneumonia, diabetes, suicide, and homicide than the general U.S. population. In many tribes amputations, blindness, and dialysis were a way of life as diabetes is rampant.

The Indian Health Services (IHS), a U.S. federal agency, provided health care for about three-fourths of the two million Native Americans in the United States. Health care was provided at both reservation health centers and in urban clinics. Recognizing the hopelessness and despair still prevalent in much of Indian Country, in March 2000 the U.S. Commission on Civil Rights recommended formation of a federal task force to seek solutions. In April 2000 President Bill Clinton (1946–; served 1993–2001) visited the Navajo Nation to stress how the American economic boom of the 1990s had bypassed some Native American communities. Almost 40 percent of Navajo households were still without electricity, 70 percent were without telephones, and the unemployment rate was 50 percent.

Despite foreign incursions of epic proportions into their native lands over the past five centuries, Native Americans refused to just disappear. Though isolated on poverty-stricken reservations and in inner cities for much of two centuries, the Native population had rebounded in population size as well as economically and politically.

For More Information

BOOKS

Dowd, Gregory. *A Spirited Resistance: The North American Indian Struggle for Unity, 1745–1815.* Baltimore: Johns Hopkins Press, 1992.

Matthiessen, Peter. *In the Spirit of Crazy Horse.* New York: Penguin Books, 1992.

Washburn, Wilcomb E., ed. *Handbook of North American Indians: History of Indian-White Relations.* Vol. 4. Washington, DC: Smithsonian Institution, 1988.

Wilkinson, Charles F. *American Indians, Time, and the Law: Native Societies in a Modern Constitutional Democracy.* New Haven, CT: Yale University Press, 1987.

WEB SITES

American Indian Movement. http://www.aimovement.org/ (accessed on November 29, 2006).

National Congress of American Indians. http://www.ncai.org/ (accessed on November 29, 2006).

19

The Holocaust

Holocaust (a program of genocide pursued by Nazi Germany during World War II to rid Europe of Jews and others leading to the murder of eleven million people including six million Jews) refers to the systematic killing of almost six million Jewish men, women, and children by the German government under approval of German dictator, or ruler, Adolf Hitler (1889–1945). Hitler directed this massive and centrally organized plan of murder during World War II (1939–45). World War II was a global conflict between the Axis powers of Germany, Japan, and Italy, and the Allied powers led by Britain, the United States, and the Soviet Union. Hitler intended to racially purify Germany by ridding nation of its Jewish population in addition to Roma (Gypsies), ethnic Slavs of eastern Europe, and others considered undesirable. Race refers to a segment of the world's population that is socially identified by certain physical characteristics, usually skin color but also hair texture, eye shape, or some other physical trait.

For Germany, a primary goal of the war was the extermination of all Jews in Europe. The Holocaust lasted from 1933 to 1945, with the most intense activity occurring in the war years between 1942 and 1944. The killing was carried out using the most advanced technology available to kill as many people as possible. As stated by author Martin Gilbert in his 1986 book *The Holocaust: A History of the Jews of Europe during the Second World War,* the German leaders referred to the mass murder of Jews as "the final solution of the Jewish question."

The term holocaust is derived from the Greek word *holokauston* that refers to a sacrifice, burned in whole, to God. The word was used since the late nineteenth century to describe major disasters. However, since World War II the term has been solely associated with Nazi (a political party in Germany more formally known as the National Socialist German Workers' Party led by Adolf Hitler from 1920 to 1945) Germany's genocide of Jews since the dead bodies were burned in

WORDS TO KNOW

anti-Semitism: Prejudice against members of the Jewish faith.

concentration camp: A location set aside to hold detainees, such as prisoners of war, refugees, or political prisoners, usually in crowded conditions.

crime against humanity: A criminal offense in international law that refers to murderous actions on such a large scale that it affects the global population as a whole.

genocide: A deliberate destruction of a political or cultural human group.

Holocaust: A program of genocide pursued by Nazi Germany during World War II to rid Europe of

Jews and others, leading to the murder of eleven million people including six million Jews.

Nazi: A political party in Germany more formally known as the National Socialist German Says Workers' Party led by Adolf Hitler from 1920 to 1945.

prejudice: A negative attitude, emotion, or behavior towards individuals based on a prejudgment about those individuals with no prior knowledge or experience.

scapegoat: A person or people blamed or punished for the things done by others.

whole in crematoriums and open fires. Genocide is a planned, systematic attempt to eliminate an entire targeted group of people by murdering all members of that group.

Long-standing prejudice (a negative attitude towards others based on a prejudgment about those individuals with no prior knowledge or experience) against the Jews allowed Hitler and the Nazis to pursue the Holocaust. Prejudice against Jews extended back for centuries in ancient Europe. This prejudice, both religious and racial forms, became known as anti-Semitism (prejudice against members of the Jewish faith). The term "Semites" comes from a biblical term referring to ancient peoples of the Near East, including early Israelites, who spoke languages related to Hebrew. Even though Semites included Arabs and other peoples besides Jews, in modern times anti-Semitism refers specifically to prejudicial attitudes against anyone of the Jewish faith. Jews who had converted to other religions and no longer practiced Judaism were still victims of anti-Semitic prejudice.

A basic goal of the Nazi Party was promotion of a pure German race they considered superior to all others, the Aryans. Aryan race refers to people living mostly in northern Europe. They are characterized as tall, blond, and blue-eyed. Though no such thing as an Aryan race actually exists, Hitler promoted it as the master race with the Germans at the top.

The Holocaust represents to the world the utter depths to which humans can descend in their treatment of others based simply on prejudice as is typical in genocides. Germans referred to Jews as subhumans. Jews were scapegoats, blamed for many of the problems plaguing Germany in the 1930s. Scapegoats are people blamed for the actions of others. Scapegoating is a major factor in most forms of prejudice. The prejudice against Jews became central to German society and governmental actions.

The rise of anti-Semitism

For the past two thousand years since the rise of the Jewish faith, anti-Semitism could be found wherever Jews lived outside the Palestinian homeland located at the eastern end of the Mediterranean Sea. Anti-Semitism in the early Greek and Roman civilizations focused more on religious prejudice. Judaism was based on the worship of a single God. The other societies had different religions in which they worshiped many gods. Jews were seen as different and disloyal.

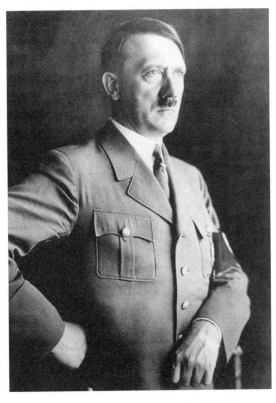

Nazi leader Adolf Hitler.
© BETTMANN/CORBIS.

Strife between Jews and Christians, followers of Jesus Christ, began not long after the crucifixion of Jesus in about the year 29. With the approval of Jewish leaders, the Roman Emperor killed Jesus, a Jew. By the year 70, Christians, who believed Jesus was the Son of God, were blaming Jews for allowing his death. Jews denied that Jesus was the Son of God, that he was neither a prophet nor divine. Jews believed that God could not be separated into different parts, but is a unified whole. They were called Christ-killers and considered evil.

Jewish-Christian strife continued through the next few centuries as Jews continued to reject the increasingly popular Christian faith. Jewish communities were attacked on occasion. In the predominantly Christian Roman Empire (27 BCE–476 CE), which included territories from Great Britain and Germany to North Africa, laws enforced prejudices against Jews by restricting their freedoms, such as living in certain areas or pursuing certain occupations. During the eleventh century, Christian crusaders targeted Jews and murdered thousands of them in the name of God.

Centuries of persecution

During the Middle Ages (from the fifth to the sixteenth centuries), Jews were denied citizenship and rights enjoyed by others in most of Europe. They could not become members of craftsmen guilds. In 1096, open violence against Jews broke out in Europe and the Holy Roman Empire. Jews were required to wear yellow badges identifying them as Jews. Jews in some towns were placed in ghettos, separate from the rest of society. (Ghettos were small, run-down sections of cities where Jews were forced to live, usually behind stone walls or barbed-wire fences policed by armed guards.) This practice of segregation (using laws or social customs to separate certain social groups based on some characteristic, such as race, gender, or religious affiliation) continued for centuries in Europe. In the fourteenth century, Jews were blamed for the plague, a very contagious, usually fatal epidemic disease, which killed millions of people in Europe. The Jews were blamed for poisoning the water wells thus causing the disease.

As commerce (business) expanded in the late Middle Ages, some Jewish businessmen prospered in trade, banking, and financing. These financial successes increased resentment—along with greater prejudice and discrimination—against Jews. They were expelled from England and a growing number of regions in Europe from the late thirteenth century to sixteenth century. Even in Spain, where Jews were numerous and a key part of society, they were expelled in the 1490s. These series of expulsions from Western Europe led to centers of Jewish life shifting to Turkey, Poland, and Russia. Jewish persecutions in Western Europe continued through the eighteenth century. The French Revolution in 1789 finally lessened discrimination against Jews as equality for all was emphasized.

From religious to racial prejudice

With the rise of nationalism in Europe in the nineteenth century, conflicts between countries were largely fueled by racial or ethnic differences rather than religious ones. Nationalism refers to a belief that a particular nation is superior to other nations. Jews began to be persecuted as a race with distinct physical differences, such as facial characteristics or body form, rather than as a religious group. The term "anti-Semitism" was first used around 1873. The new nations sought racial or ethnic purity within their boundaries. Jews were now considered inferior to the Aryan race through propaganda of the Nazi Party as promoted in speeches and books. Anti-Jewish riots called pogroms broke out in western Russia in the 1880s when many Jewish homes were destroyed and their occupants left impoverished, and Jews were restricted in their activities, such as living in rural areas, participating in local elections, or working in certain occupations, such as law practices. These pogroms led to emigration to other countries such as the United States.

World War I (1914–18), fought in Europe, led to many population displacements (being forced to leave traditional homelands). This triggered an increase in anti-Semitism as displaced peoples needed a scapegoat on which to blame their misery. In trying to ease tensions, Britain, which gained control of much of the Middle East from Germany following the war, declared a part of the Palestine area as the Jewish National Home in 1917. It also identified an area for Palestinian Arabs. The action only served to inflame hatreds between the two groups, who both claimed the same sacred grounds.

The Nazis gain followers

The National Socialist Germany Workers' Party, called Nazis for short, came to power in Germany in January 1933 with their leader Adolf Hitler. The strongly nationalistic Nazis offered hope for the German public still suffering under difficult economic conditions that began at the end of World War I. Many experiencing poverty and hunger were angry over their nation's plight. The Nazis promised jobs and food. The Nazi Party was founded on racist ideas that purifying the German population would be a cure for Germany's ills. Hitler had written of the removal of Jews from Germany as early as 1919, right after Germany's defeat in World War I. Others discussed the elimination of what they considered worthless people. The Jews, again made scapegoats, were blamed for Germany's loss in World War I.

Hitler's 1925 epic book *Mein Kampf (My Struggle)* portrayed the Jews as an evil race that was seeking domination of the world. He praised the virtues of the Aryan race and claimed it was the government's duty to protect the purity of the race. It was the duty of the Germans to rid their beloved country of the evil Jews, according to Hitler. As Hitler began his rise to power, the book became a best-seller in Germany. Jews were portrayed as a race, not a religious group. Even those who had converted to other religions were still considered Jews by German authorities and the public.

German girls show their support for the Nazi party, waving Nazi flags by a roadside. © BETTMANN/CORBIS.

Hitler promotes a New Germany

Upon assuming leadership, the Nazis immediately began strengthening political control over the country. Jews were considered the chief enemies of the state. In reaction to the growing anti-Semitism in Germany, many countries boycotted (refused to buy goods or services from a business or country until their demands are met) German goods. On April 1, 1933, the German government responded with a boycott of Jewish-owned businesses. On that day, German soldiers were positioned in front of every Jewish business forbidding anyone from going into the stores and businesses. The boycott further escalated anti-Semitism in the country. Only one week later, Germany passed the first anti-Jewish law, the Law for the Restoration of the Civil Service. Under the law Jews were fired from government positions. In addition, by May the government also restricted the number of Jewish students admitted to German schools.

On May 10 of that year, anti-Semitic violence escalated as thousands of German students, along with many professors, stormed university libraries and bookstores in cities across Germany. In great bonfires they burned books written by Jews and other authors considered non-Aryan. Any books that were critical of Nazi policies were thrown into the fires. One-third of the books in Germany were destroyed. The first concentration camps within Germany were established in 1933, primarily for political prisoners and those considered undesirable because of their ethnic background or disabilities. A concentration camp is a location set aside to hold detainees, such as prisoners of war, refugees, or political prisoners, usually in crowded conditions. These early camps did not include the gas chambers that came into existence several years later.

In September 1935, the Nazi Party at its annual rally in Nuremberg adopted a set of laws that became known as the Nuremberg Laws. One was the Law for the Protection of German Blood and German Honor. The second was titled the Law of the Reich (German government) Citizen. These laws provided a legal definition of a Jew and an Aryan. They were used to categorize people in German-controlled territories over the next several years. Marriage and sexual relations between Jews and others were prohibited. Jews no longer held political and civil rights. They could not vote or hold political office and had no legal protections. Jews also had to register the property they owned with government authorities. They were now simply subjects of the German state. The categorization of Jews was not based on religious beliefs, but on the number of Jewish grandparents a person had. Any Jewish blood at all meant a person was a Jew.

Alarmed by the formalization of these policies, Jews began seeking refuge (safety) in other countries. However, most countries, including the United States, were not sympathetic to the growing Jewish plight in Germany due to prevalent anti-Semitic attitudes in their own societies as well as not fully understanding the genocide that was developing in Germany. As with other immigrant groups such as Asians, the government set strict limitations on the number of Jews that were allowed to immigrate into their countries. The small Jewish community in Palestine in the Middle East was most willing to accept Jewish immigrants. Many Jews had little option but to persevere through the growing anti-Semitism in Germany.

Violence begins with escalating anti-Semitism

Carefully orchestrated by the German government, violence against Jews erupted on the evening of November 9, 1938, across Germany and German-controlled Austria. Over the next two days, rioters burned or damaged over one thousand Jewish synagogues (places of worship) and damaged almost eight thousand Jewish-owned businesses. Approximately thirty thousand Jewish men between the ages of sixteen and sixty were arrested and sent to concentration camps. This was the first of hundreds of mass arrests of Jews. Around one hundred Jews died from sporadic beatings and shootings. Another two thousand died in the concentration camps over the next three months before their release. Fireman stood by during the riots, primarily making sure fires did not spread to non-Jewish property. The riots became known as *Kristallnacht,* or the "Night of Broken Glass." Those arrested were released once their families paid a fine.

Three days later, German leaders met to assess the cost of the damage from the rioting. They fined the Jewish community for the damage costs and made them responsible for cleaning up and repairing the damage. Victims were prohibited from collecting insurance payments for their losses. After *Kristallnacht* the German Jewish population saw there was no hope for them under Nazi rule leading to likely hundreds of suicides. Those Jews who could leave did with some 115,000 emigrating to other European countries or elsewhere including the United States, Palestine, and Asia.

Laws already existed that banned Jews from obtaining college degrees, owning businesses, or practicing law or medicine for non-Jewish clients. New laws were passed following *Kristallnacht,* restricting Jews from public places such as theaters and public schools and banning the use of radios and telephones. They also had to sit in separate compartments on trains. Confiscation of property, known as Aryanization of the German economy and begun in 1937, continued. By April 1939, almost all Jewish businesses had closed. The closures were especially devastating to Jews because they were, by and large, merchants. They commonly did not work for other companies or people, but worked in family-owned or Jewish businesses. Without this ability, their incomes were virtually nonexistent. By September 1941, all Jews in Germany were forced to wear a yellow star patch on their clothes in public.

Germans were eager to send the Jews elsewhere, even including the prospect of establishing a large reservation (a tract of public land set aside for a special purpose, such as placement of an undesired social group away

During **Kristallnacht,** *or the "Night of Broken Glass," rioters burned or damaged over one thousand Jewish synagogues and damaged almost eight thousand Jewish-owned businesses.* © BETTMANN/CORBIS.

from mainstream society) in Poland. Other options more distant included the possibilities of creating a state of Israel (new sovereign nation with a biblical name) in the Middle East or shipping the Jews to the large island of Madagascar off the coast of Africa. Poland, however, refused to accept more Jews after November 1939 due to the severe anti-Semitic attitudes there and the British navy blocked the Madagascar option.

The Germans under Hitler made life so unbearable for German Jews that hundreds of thousands decided to leave the country of their own accord. Between 1933 and 1941, the number of Jews in Germany declined from 500,000 to 164,000. Those who left carried with them only suitcases, leaving all else behind. Those who stayed did not think conditions could get any worse. It was difficult for the Jews to anticipate what was coming in the form of the Holocaust and they had few places to go where they were welcomed. Some Jewish parents, fearing the worst, sent their children away on trains, later referred to as orphan trains when the Holocaust claimed the lives of the parents who stayed behind.

Other targeted groups

Others besides Jews who were considered politically undesirable or racially inferior were also targets of Nazi prejudicial policies. These included political opponents, members of the Social Democrat Party, union members, those who refused to serve in Hitler's army, homosexuals, the physically or mentally disabled, and Gypsies.

Around twenty thousand Jehovah's Witnesses (an international religion) were imprisoned because they refused to serve in the military or hold Hitler in great esteem. (Jehovah's Witnesses are members of a religious group who oppose war and preach the imminent end of the world.) Approximately twelve hundred of them died in the camps.

Nazi police raided gay bars beginning in 1933, arresting male homosexuals. Homosexuals would not be contributing to the reproduction of the master race, so they were deemed useless. Nazis also believed homosexuality could be contagious, like a disease. Females were not targeted since they were not considered a threat to future generations of the German race. Many homosexuals were convicted under anti-gay laws and sent to prison. Some were castrated (had their private parts removed). Others were placed in mental hospitals. About fifteen thousand died in concentration camps, where they were forced to wear special yellow armbands and pink triangles to signify their homosexuality.

The mentally and physically disabled were viewed as contrary to Nazi ideas of a master Aryan race. In addition, they posed a burden on society. German leaders believed that eliminating those considered physically or mentally unfit would result in an improved Aryan race. This was the first group to be exterminated (systematically killed) under the 1939 T-4 Euthanasia Program. At first mentally and physically handicapped children were executed by individual lethal injections. Then as the number of victims grew including large numbers of handicapped adults, the Germans began using carbon monoxide gas pumped into rooms referred to as gas chambers. By 1939, six large concentration camps existed where the handicapped were bused. German officials told their families that they were being taken to a place where they would receive improved treatment by the state. Following their execution and cremation, an urn of ashes and a false death certificate were sent to the families. Of course, the ashes were not of the specific individual since the victims were cremated en masse. The practice of extermination using gas chambers and mass crematories began with the T-4 Program. The Germans rounded up the mentally retarded, physically disabled, and others with mental health problems and murdered them in mass numbers. The T-4 Program killed over 200,000 people between 1939 and 1941. Another four hundred thousand were sterilized, or surgically made unable to have children, against their will.

Like the Jews, another group that faced brutal treatment was the Gypsies. (Gypsies, also known as Roma, are people of several different tribes that are believed to have originated in India.) By the end of World War II, around 220,000 Gypsies—almost half of the entire Gypsy population—would be exterminated.

The assault on Polish Jews

As Germany expanded its control in 1938 and early 1939 over Austria, Moravia, and Bohemia (later the Czech Republic), more and more Jews came under German control. On September 1, 1939, the military invasion of Poland, where many Jews lived, brought the Final Solution to the Jewish Question, or what Nazis wanted to do with the Jewish people, to the critical point. (The Final Solution, devised by high-ranking Nazi officials, involved the murder of every Jew in Europe, regardless of age, gender, or social status.) Poland contained most of Europe's Jews, almost five million people. Jews in Poland were less integrated into the general Polish society than in Western Europe and were more readily identifiable merely by their appearance. Many lived in rural communities, spoke Yiddish, and dressed traditionally with beards, hats, and long coats. The same was true of Jews in Russia who had distinctive language, customs, and dress.

Cruelty by Germans toward Polish Jews occurred immediately upon the German invasion. Dehumanizing tactics such as pulling out by hand or setting fire to Jewish men's beards were common. Approximately five thousand Jews were killed in Poland in the first two months of German rule before the later death camps were established.

With a desire to increase the size of Germany, the Germans sought Polish land by first destroying Polish society so that the German army could take control without opposition. The Nazi army rounded up about thirty thousand Polish intellectuals and political figures. Approximately seven thousand of them were eventually killed. Polish political leaders and priests were also captured and killed. Poland was then divided between Germany and the Soviet Union. About two million Jews lived in the part controlled by Germany. German leaders debated ways to rid the region of Jews. Thoughts of shipping the Jews to the southeast coast of Africa proved impractical because there were too many.

On September 21, 1939, the Germans began concentrating Jews into large ghettos located in the oldest and most run-down sections of town where sanitation was very poor. The Nazis selected willing Jews to serve on Jewish councils. They were responsible for governing the ghetto and carrying out Nazi orders. The largest ghetto was located in Poland's capital city of Warsaw and called the Warsaw Ghetto. It contained around 380,000 people, comprising 30 percent of the Warsaw's population. The ghettos were like large crowded prisons, as barbed wire fences surrounded them. Schools and religious practice were banned. From 1940 to 1942, extreme overcrowding led to infectious diseases such as typhoid, malnutrition, and poverty during the bitter cold winters. Approximately sixteen thousand died of typhus in the Warsaw Ghetto in 1941. Death from starvation was also common. Many Jews figured this would be their plight for the remainder of the war.

A decision for genocide

By early 1941, Hitler and German leaders had decided how to eliminate the Jewish population. They chose genocide. Germany began a program of systematically killing Jews in June 1941 when it invaded its former ally, the Soviet Union. Entering the Soviet territory along with the German army were three thousand men who volunteered to serve in special killing units, called Einsatzgrappen. In a July speech, Hitler encouraged the death squads. Following the main army by two or three days, they were responsible for killing all Jews, Gypsies, and Soviet officers in areas captured by the German army. Their general process was to enter a captured town, round up targeted individuals, take them to the edge of town, and shoot them. The bodies were buried in mass graves at the location where they were executed. In some cases, mobile death vans drove around eastern Europe and Russia, with gunmen killing as they went. It was not uncommon for entire rural villages to be executed. During the summer of 1941, around seventy thousand Jews were killed outside Vilna, Lithuania. On June 30, approximately fourteen thousand Romanian Jews were murdered. In two days in late September, almost thirty-four thousand Jews were killed outside Kiev, Ukraine. Another nine thousand were killed in late October in Kaunas, Lithuania. Over twenty-five thousand were killed outside Riga, Latvia, by early December.

Altogether, almost two million Jews, Gypsies, and Soviets were murdered. When the Soviets mounted a counterattack, Nazi special units different from the killing units, whose members were volunteers, dug up as many bodies as possible in the mass graves to burn them and destroy the evidence.

During the summer of 1941, the Germans began experimenting with poison gas for mass killings to keep the costs down and to not involve a large number of German troops who were needed at the battle fronts. They used Zyklon-B at the Auschwitz concentration camp in southern Poland, killing 250 hospital patients and 600 Russian prisoners. The experiment was successful and construction of death camps began. Ironically, Zyklon B had been developed by a German Jew during World War I.

Experimenting in Mass Killing

When Germany occupied Belarus during its invasion of Russia in 1942, the Germans began experimenting with captured mental patients on how to most efficiently kill multiple people at once. They would stand victims in a line to see how many could be killed by firing a single bullet. They also experimented with dynamite but this proved ineffective by not killing all the victims immediately. Neither approach proved very effective. In October 1941, Germans began experimenting with carbon monoxide gas, using truck exhaust fumes piped into the back of a truck filled with people. By using bigger trucks they were able to kill larger groups in shorter periods of time. This method led to the creation of gas chambers for use during the war.

Creation of extermination centers

By the fall of 1941, Hitler and Heinrich Himmler (1900–1945) finalized plans for killing Jews in mass numbers. The Jews were now firmly under German control especially since their avenues for flight to other countries were limited. The Germans also sought to rid Europe of Slavs (Polish, Russian, and Ukrainian peoples) as well as Latvians, Estonians, and Lithuanians. The first to die were the political leaders and most educated of these populations who constituted much of the leadership.

Rather than sending out death squads to kill people, the victims would now be transported by train to the seven newly built extermination centers—Auschwitz, Belzec, Chelmno, Majdanek, Sobibor, Treblinka, and Maly Trostenets. All were located in Poland and all were finished by summer of 1942.

The extermination centers were designed to make mass killing most efficient using permanently built gas chambers and adjoining crematoriums to burn the bodies. Gas chambers were disguised as showers. It would take only a small number of camp staff to kill tens of thousands of people a month. Carbon monoxide was first used as the poisoning gas. Later Zyklon-B was used.

SS troops leading Jews in the forcible deportation from the Warsaw Ghetto. NATIONAL ARCHIVES/USHMM PHOTO ARCHIVES.

Extermination begins

Himmler gave the order on July 19, 1942, to begin deporting Jews from the Polish ghettos. Three days later, deportation from the Warsaw Ghetto began. To make the transport of thousands from the ghettos to the death camps go smoothly, the Germans called the process "resettlement" rather than "deportation." They promised more food, warmer clothing, and work. Over the following fifty-two days, around three hundred thousand people were transported by rail to the Treblinka extermination camp from Warsaw.

The Germans kept detailed records of the killings in thousands of reports. Detailed lists of the victims were compiled and their seized personal property was catalogued and tagged. Germans removed gold teeth from the bodies and sorted the clothing, including shoes and coats. Valuables went into special bank accounts or were sold. The overall value gathered throughout the entire Holocaust was $128 million. Women's hair was cleaned and woven into gloves and socks for German submarine crews to stay warm.

Much manpower was dedicated to the extermination program. At the forefront was the special German military force, the SS (abbreviation of the German word *Schutzstaffel*), led by Himmler. The SS served as guards and killers. The regular German army ran the camps, formed the ghettos, transported prisoners, and supervised slave labor. Those Germans involved in the Holocaust were not only soldiers, but also civilian clerks and officials as well in addition to physicians, a number of ministries, and local police. Citizens of countries occupied by German forces also helped round up and kill Jews.

The process of extermination

The deportations were massive in scale. The Germans used thousands of railway freight cars traveling over hundreds of thousands of track. Up to 130 inmates rode in a single windowless cattle car with no room to sit or lie down for trips that lasted several days. The Germans provided no food, water, or heat. Deportees froze to death in the winter and suffocated in the summer months. In an effort to keep the prisoners disorganized and in shock, German guards orchestrated what appeared to prisoners as a chaotic situation upon arrival of each train at a death camp. The Germans then quickly marched the inmates in large lines, tearing apart families while deciding who would die immediately and who would work in labor camps. The gas chambers were disguised as shower rooms and the victims were handed towels and soap (children received candy), before going in. Therefore, people walked quietly and obediently to their deaths. Once in, the doors were locked behind them and gas piped in. Death occurred within five to forty-five minutes. The bodies were then taken next door to the crematorium to be burned.

Thousands of other concentration and labor camps were built through the German-occupied territories of Europe. Life in these camps was brutal, with torture and beatings routinely carried out. An industry was established at every camp to make use of the slave labor. Private industry, including the companies Siemens, Porsche, and Bayer, would buy inmates for the day. Adult males might cost $3.60, while a child cost 90 cents. The labor camps often had no barracks; workers would simply sleep on the bare ground. They had little to eat and no warm clothing. Fighting was common among the prisoners for items such as a stale loaf of bread, a blanket, or a pair of shoes. When they became too weak or sick to work, they were shot or beaten to death. The death camps themselves were built by slave labor. Inmates were literally worked to death.

Those not killed immediately were shaved of all hair, sent to real showers, sprayed with a disinfectant, and given uniforms of rough cloth and wooden shoes. Each prisoner was assigned an identification number, which was tattooed on the inside of the forearm. Besides Jews wearing yellow patches, prisoners wore color-coded triangular patches. Political prisoners wore red triangles, asocial people (those who did not blend in to German society) black, homosexuals pink, Jehovah's Witnesses purple, and habitual criminals green. They never received a change of clothes and became infested with fleas and contagious lice. Every action of the Germans was designed to break the spirit of the inmates. In barracks, four to five people slept on a single bench level with a mattress of filthy straw on a wooden plank. Buckets served as toilets. Daily roll call occurred at 4:00 A.M., and even those who had died in the night were dragged out to be accounted for. Food usually consisted of watery, saltless soup made with rotten vegetables and spoiled meat, and a few ounces of bread. Hunger was persistent. At some camps, gruesome medical experiments were performed on live victims, such as seeing the effects of freezing to death, testing various drugs, and performing amputations without medication. Some prisoners threw themselves into the electrified fences to give themselves a mercifully quick death. Those few who manage to survive did so through bribery and stealing for extra food and clothing.

Killing by the numbers in Poland

At Auschwitz, between 1.1 and 1.6 million people were killed. The extermination camp of Auschwitz became the most notorious of the camps for the large numbers of people killed there. Around eight thousand innocent people were killed there each day. It was divided into three camps: a prison camp, an extermination camp, and a slave-labor camp. Upon arrival, Jewish prisoners would be sorted into the camps. Pregnant women, handicapped, sick, elderly, and young children were sent straight to the extermination camp for killing. Those who were able-bodied were sent to the labor camp for work at factories built next to the camp to aid the German war cause. Given insufficient food, shelter, medical care, and clothing, the laborers often worked themselves to death. Those unable to work further were sent to the gas chambers. The prison camp was also used for non-Jewish prisoners. Over 200,000 Gypsies were killed at Auschwitz.

The number of deaths also mounted at other Polish camps. Treblinka operated for seventeen months. A staff of 120 killed between

Polish children standing behind a barbed wire fence in the extermination camp Auschwitz. USHMM.

750,000 and 900,000. Belzec operated for ten months and claimed the lives of 434,000 Jews. About 250,000 were killed at Sobibor. When the killings ended at both Treblinka and Sobibor, all traces of the camps were removed and farms were built on the sites.

Extermination elsewhere

Twenty-one countries were directly affected by the mass killings. Central and eastern Europe were most affected. Besides Poland in eastern Europe, Germany invaded Hungary (in March 1944). Until then, the Hungarian government had refused to transport its Jews to German camps. However, with the change in government, 440,000 Jews were rounded up for deportation. After being initially confined in ghettos, beginning in mid-May they were transported to Auschwitz. The entire process took less than two months and 147 train trips. In addition to those transported on trains, about 20,000 Budapest Jews were shot on the banks of the Danube River and another 70,000 were sent on a death march to Austria. Along the way thousands died of starvation, exposure to weather, or a bullet to the brain.

Some countries, in support of Germany, did the killings themselves. Among these were Romania and Croatia whose leaders agreed with Nazi policies. Romanians killed up to 380,000 Jews. At one Romanian

Between 1.1 and 1.6 million people were killed at Auschwitz. © BETTMANN/CORBIS.

concentration camp at Bogdanovka, 54,000 Jews were exterminated between December 21 and 31, 1941. The Croatian government killed up to 390,000 Jews.

Other countries tried sending their Jews to safety as quickly as possible when they fell under German control. Denmark did not have a history of anti-Semitism. As a result, it sent almost 7,500 Jews to Sweden in fishing boats in October 1943. Bulgaria also refused to deport the 50,000 Jews living there to German camps as they stayed relatively safely in Bulgaria.

The occupation of France was divided between Germany and Germany's war ally, Italy. The Italians did not pursue mass killing of the four thousand Jews in their region until they themselves were overtaken by Germany. However the French leaders in the German-controlled area, known as Vichy France, assisted in killings.

The final count

It is estimated that between five and seven million Jews were killed, or 64 percent of the Jews in Europe. This amounted to 35 percent of the world's Jewish population. The Germans killed three million Jews in Poland alone (over 90 percent of the Jewish population in that country) and over one million in the Soviet Union. Over 70 percent of the Jewish population was killed in Yugoslavia, Greece, the Netherlands, Hungary, Lithuania, Bohemia, Slovakia, and Latvia. Over 50 percent of the Jewish population in Belgium, Romania, Luxembourg, Norway, and Estonia was killed. Over 25 percent of the Jewish population in France and Italy was killed. Overall some nine to eleven million people were killed including non-Jewish peoples. This included millions of Soviet prisoners and Slavic civilians.

Among the Jews that died, some researchers figured that over 800,000 died in ghettos, close to two million were shot in open areas primarily in 1941 before the death camps were built, and almost three million were killed in the camps.

Unprepared to fight back

Efforts to rescue Jews from the Holocaust were widespread. However, people involved in helping Jews faced death if caught. Some people risked all to aid Jewish families. They generally helped by providing hiding places and food for weeks or longer. Among Germans who sought to save Jews from death was Oskar Schindler (1908–1974), a German business-man who used Jewish slave labor in Poland. He went to great lengths using his exceptional persuasive skills to protect his Jewish workers from persecution.

The Jewish population found it almost impossible to defend itself against the massive German war machine. Overall, the Jews were unprepared and did not anticipate the German plan of extermination. Also, the rapid expansion of Germany into Eastern Europe caught everyone by surprise.

Various factors discouraged meaningful resistance. Jews had no access to arms. They were often surrounded in their own neighborhoods by anti-Semitic people. The Germans continuously disguised what was going on, and they threatened reprisals against people's friends and relatives if they resisted. Deceptions included having prisoners send postcards to friends and relatives upon their arrival at camps.

To stop a rebellion that had started in the Warsaw Ghetto, Nazi troops burned the ghetto to the ground, killing all remaining Jews. © HULTON-DEUTSCH COLLECTION/CORBIS.

Jews had known a long history of persecution, yet had always recovered. They never had their own nation or an army, and Judaism discouraged fighting their persecutors. They believed whatever travesty was occurring was God's will and they were martyrs for God. In addition, any form of resistance was essentially suicide against the more numerous, well-armed Nazis and the Jewish faith prohibited suicide.

Fear of imminent death did lead to some acts of organized resistance in ghettos and camps including over one hundred armed uprisings. None of the ghetto uprisings was successful. The largest organized Jewish resistance, the Warsaw Ghetto Uprising, occurred in April 1943, nine months after the Germans began transporting ghetto inhabitants to Treblinka (see box).

Several uprisings occurred in the Treblinka extermination camp in August 1943, at Sobibor in October 1943, and at Auschwitz in January

Warsaw Ghetto Uprising

On September 5, 1942, the German military began rounding up to deport the last 115,000 Jews left of the original 500,000 that had been crowded into the Warsaw Ghetto. They shipped out approximately 10,000 people each day. When there were only 42,000 Jews remaining, a rebellion erupted. Jews formed the Jewish Combat Organization (ZOB) and busied themselves digging a network of bunkers and secret passageways in preparation for making a last stand of resistance against the Nazis.

On January 18, 1943, German troops entered the ghetto to round up more Jews for transport and met gunfire. Fifty German soldiers were killed or wounded as they retreated. This initial success by the rebels led to increased support of the ZOB as it grew to include around one thousand members. They even received more weapons from the Polish resistance fighters operating nearby. Meanwhile, the Germans regrouped.

On April 19, two thousand German soldiers with tanks entered the ghetto. After eleven hours of intense fighting they once again retreated. The Germans cut off gas, electricity, and water and began shelling the ghetto with heavy artillery. The fighting continued until May 16 when the ghetto was burned completely to the ground by the Germans, killing all remaining Jews.

1944. Few prisoners found freedom from all the escape attempts in the ghettos and camps. Most of those who did manage to escape were usually captured, killed by anti-Semitic public, or died of exposure in the unforgiving cold of the countryside.

A main point of controversy between Western leaders and surviving Jews was the lack of action by Allied forces, even after intelligence information began filtering to British and American authorities about what was occurring as early as 1941. By the end of 1942, knowledge of the use of gas chambers and the Holocaust in general had become clear. The Allies believed that the problem could not be resolved until the war was over. No action was taken such as bombing the camps or railroad tracks used to deliver the victims. Even the German public, aware of mass killing of Jews but perhaps not about gas chambers, did nothing. In effect, they gave consent if not active support. Even the Catholic Church leadership, which had signed an agreement with the German Nazis in 1933 agreeing to stay out of politics in return for freedom of worship for German Catholics, never publicly criticized the mass killings. One reason given was fear of Nazi retaliation against German Catholics. The Catholic Church, which had a long history of anti-Semitism, had supported Hitler's rise to power.

Conclusion of the Holocaust

The extent to which Germans tried to conceal the still ongoing Holocaust toward the end of the war revealed the continued dedication they had to the mass killing of Jews. Even in the last months of the war when the Germans knew their cause was lost, they continued the mass killings and worked hard to destroy the evidence. Special German units dug up mass graves and burned the remains.

By mid-1944, Allied forces were closing in on Germany. In July, advancing Soviet troops discovered the first major camp, Majdanek. Germans frantically evacuated the various camps as Allied forces approached each one. They forced remaining prisoners to march long distances in the winter conditions toward central Germany. Those who could not keep up with the pace were shot. For example, as Soviet troops were approaching Auschwitz in January 1945, the Germans marched 60,000 remaining prisoners 35 miles before boarding them on trains to other concentration camps. Approximately 15,000 died on the way.

American and British forces approaching from the west in spring of 1945 unexpectedly came upon concentration camps. There they discovered gruesome reminders of what had gone on at these camps. At Dachau, the Allied troops found twenty-eight railway cars stuffed with corpses. At Bergen-Belsen, the surviving 60,000 prisoners were in such bad condition that some 28,000 died shortly after being rescued.

Displaced persons

At war's end, the Allied forces found between seven and nine million displaced people living outside their home countries. Displaced persons camps were established according to nationalities for Jews and others. Over six million returned to their home countries. However, over one million refugees refused to return. Some refugees had assisted Nazis during the war and feared retaliation if they returned to their communities. Others did not want to return to territories that were now under Soviet occupation and Communist governments (system of government in which the state controls the economy and a single party holds power). For many Jews, there was no home to return to. The communities were destroyed and families eliminated. Few nations were willing to accept them. In addition, physical recovery from near-starvation was lengthy. Over 250,000 remained in displacement camps for years suffering severe psychological effects from the death camps, the horrific conditions, and extensive loss of friends and family.

American soldiers walk by rows and rows of corpses at a Nazi concentration camp. The Army found more than 3,000 bodies, and a handful of survivors. AP IMAGES.

Increasingly, people looked to the establishment of a Jewish homeland in the British-controlled Middle East region of Palestine. Creation of Israel in 1948 provided a solution to the Jewish refugee problem. The displaced persons camps were finally closed by 1952.

The aftermath of genocide

Not surprisingly, the immediate aftermath of the Holocaust was also a very difficult period for survivors. With millions of families broken apart and whole communities destroyed, the search for friends and loved ones was difficult. For the survivors, the Holocaust was not an experience that could be forgotten. Memories of inmates being humiliated, tortured, and killed remained unspeakable. By the twenty-first century, searchable computer databases contained the names of three million Jewish victims.

A number of courtroom trials were held over the next several decades related to atrocities associated with the Holocaust. One of the more famous was the Nuremburg trials, held immediately after the war in 1945 and 1946. Nuremburg had been the site of Nazi Party rallies through the 1930s. An International Military Tribunal, a military court, was established in August 1945 by Allied forces in U.S.-controlled section of Germany in Nuremburg. It tried twenty-two high-ranking Nazi officials on charges of various war crimes. One newly established type of war crime was called crimes against humanity. These crimes included various inhumane acts against civilians, such as mass murder, extermination, and enslavement. Over five thousand Germans were convicted of war crimes by 1949. The defendants included physicians, judges, commanders of killing squads and concentration camps, German military leaders, and business leaders who made profits from slave labor. The trials brought the Holocaust to the attention of the world.

As a result of the Holocaust, human rights international law grew. The United Nations adopted the Convention on the Prevention and Punishment of the Crime of Genocide in 1948. The Holocaust trials, which continued through the remainder of the twentieth century, also set a precedent for future war crimes trials conducted by international tribunals, such as cases involving atrocities in Bosnia and Rwanda.

Settling claims

The return of property taken by German authorities from Jewish people during the war was a major issue that continued to be debated into the twenty-first century. For example, in the late 1990s, the world learned that Swiss bankers had received gold and other valuables from the German Nazis and kept it. International criticism of Switzerland led to a backlash of anti-Semitic sentiment in the country.

The fall of the eastern European Communist governments in 1990 opened new avenues for tracing seized property. Legal struggles over pieces of seized artwork that had been sold and resold developed in several countries. In addition to the recovery of seized property, the German government established a special fund to compensate with payments those who had been subjected to slave labor during the war. However, the funding proved difficult to raise among German companies and the government.

Tributes to Holocaust victims

Following the war, Germany was divided into two parts, one occupied by the Allied forces and the other occupied by the Soviet Union. This partition into West and East Germany lasted the next several decades. Following the reunification of the two sections of Germany in the 1990s, the German parliament voted in 1999 to build a Holocaust memorial in the capital of Berlin.

Pope John Paul II (1920–2005), the first and only pope from Poland, witnessed the Holocaust as a youth. He improved relations between followers of Judaism and Catholicism and became the first pope to visit a Jewish synagogue in 1986. While visiting Israel in 2000, Pope John Paul asserted that anti-Semitism was anti-Christian.

By late 2005, about 120,000 Holocaust survivors still lived in the United States. The Los Angeles area included around 10,000, one of the largest survivor groups in the world. They formed The 1939 Club, a reference to the year Hitler invaded Poland and the mass killings began. The club meets regularly and develops its own educational programs to combat anti-Semitism and donates money to other organizations that also pursue similar goals.

Holocaust Denial

By the twenty-first century, a major issue arose when some public figures claimed the Holocaust never happened or was not nearly as severe as commonly portrayed. These included Iranian president Mahmoud Ahmadinejad (1956–), who made threatening statements about the continued existence of Israel in 2006. This attitude, known as Holocaust denial, had originally surfaced in the 1960s in France. At the time, oral history projects were busy recording the memories of Holocaust survivors for future generations. Holocaust denial was labeled as another form of anti-Semitism. Several countries made the public expression of Holocaust denial a crime, including France, Poland, Austria, Switzerland, Germany, Belgium, and Romania.

To keep alive memories of the Holocaust, in November 2005 the UN General Assembly designated January 27 as the International Day of Commemoration in Memory of the Victims of the Holocaust. This date commemorated the day in 1945 that the remaining inmates of Auschwitz were liberated by Allied troops.

Interest in the Holocaust continued into the twenty-first century. Besides continuing as a major influence on art and literature, two major movies were released in the 1990s that kept the issue at the public forefront: *Schindler's List* (1993), which offered a fictionalized account of Oskar Schindler's life, and *Life Is Beautiful* (1997), a foreign language romance that won three Oscar Awards. The number of memorials and museums continued to grow. Built in 1993, the United States Holocaust Museum on the Mall of Washington, D.C., serves not only as a memorial to the Holocaust victims, but as a center for public interpretive displays and resources for the study of the Holocaust. The public still wondered how so many seemingly reasonable and educated people could obey such immoral orders in the mid-twentieth century.

For More Information

BOOKS

Altman, Linda J. *Hitler's Rise to Power and the Holocaust.* Berkeley Heights, NJ: Enslow, 2003.

Des Pres, Terrence. *The Survivor: An Anatomy of Life in the Death Camps.* New York: Oxford University Press, 1980.

Frank, Anne. *The Diary of a Young Girl.* New York: Doubleday, 1995.

Friedlander, Henry. *The Origins of Nazi Genocide: From Euthanasia to the Final Solution.* Chapel Hill: University of North Carolina Press, 1995.

Gilbert, Martin. *The Holocaust: A History of the Jews of Europe during the Second World War.* New York: Holt, Rinehart, and Winston, 1986.

Levi, Primo. *Survival in Auschwitz: The Nazi Assault on Humanity.* New York: Collier Books, 1993.

Sereny, Gitta. *Into That Darkness: An Examination of Conscience.* New York: Vintage Books, 1983.

WEB SITES

Holocaust Survivors. http://www.holocaustsurvivors.org/ (accessed on November 29, 2006).

United States Holocaust Memorial Museum. http://www.ushmm.org (accessed on November 29, 2006).

20

Religious Politics: Northern Ireland and England

The United Kingdom of Great Britain and Northern Ireland is located in Western Europe. Separated from the mainland continent by the North Sea and English Channel, Great Britain includes England, Scotland, and Wales. West of Great Britain and separated by the Irish Sea, Northern Ireland is located at the northern end of an island mass that includes the modern independent nation of Ireland. England, its capital is London, is the administrative and economic center of the United Kingdom.

By the late sixteenth century, England had become the world's leading military and commercial power. With its superior naval fleet, England took control of countries and regions worldwide. Collectively these holdings, called colonies, were known as the British Empire.

England's worldwide dominance came to an end in the first half of the twentieth century following World War I (1914–18) and World War II (1939–45). Many English colonies, predominately these in Africa and Asia, were granted independence between 1945 and 1951. Ireland became a nation independent of England in 1949. Northern Ireland remained a part of the United Kingdom.

Prejudice (a negative attitude towards others based on a prejudgment about those individuals with no prior knowledge or experience) between Irish Catholics and Irish Protestants in Northern Ireland led to centuries of war with England. The suppression of Irish Catholics in Northern Ireland resulted in open rebellion to English rule. Political and religious discrimination (treating some differently than others or favoring one social group over another based on prejudices) divided the country into the twentieth century. The long-running conflict reached its most violent phase between 1968 and 1994. By the time an agreement was reached between the two sides, thousands had died and many more had their lives permanently altered by prolonged disruption of day-to-day life under the constant threat of violence.

WORDS TO KNOW

ceasefire: Stopping active hostilities.

guerrilla warfare: Irregular fighting by independent bands.

internment: To confine or imprison a person without a trial.

Parliament: The national legislative body in various nations including Great Britain.

stereotyping: An oversimplified prejudgment of others using physical or behavioral characteristics, usually exaggerated, that supposedly apply to every member of that group.

History of English rule over Ireland

The English government took control of Ireland in the twelfth century, and a long struggle developed between the Irish and their English rulers. The English based their army in Dublin, Ireland's capital city. An Anglo-Irish Parliament was established by the English conquerors, who held most of the seats of power in the Parliament (government). They allowed only a few native-born Irishmen to participate in the governing body, and those representatives had no real power. "Anglo" is a term used interchangeably with the term "English." Wars broke out between the army and the Irish population who were opposed to English rule. By the fourteenth century, Scottish invaders landed in Ireland and allied with local Irish tribal chiefs to weaken English rule. Eventually, English power was limited to an area around Dublin called the Pale. By the mid-fifteenth century, English noblemen living in the Pale of Ireland participated in the Wars of the Roses (1455–85) with hopes of increasing their control. The name of the wars came from the depiction of roses on badges representing the two warring English royal factions. Unsuccessful in their attempts, the wars only further weakened England's power in Ireland. Nevertheless, in 1495, the English Parliament subjected all of Ireland to their direct command with an act called Poyning's Law, named after the English-appointed governor of Ireland who sought to secure Ireland under English rule.

The social fabric of Ireland further unraveled when the English tried to force their own religion on the Irish. In 1534, King Henry VIII (1491–1547) formed the Anglican Church, or the Church of England. Citing political and religious differences, King Henry broke ties with the Roman Catholic Church, whose seat of power was in Rome. Henry named himself

Orangemen

Orangemen belong to a Protestant men's organization called the Orange Order. Founded in 1795 in Loughgall, Ireland, it is largely based in the province of Ulster and western Scotland, but it is a worldwide organization. Separate chapters are located in England, Australia, Canada, New Zealand, the United States, and West Africa. Its supporters see the Orange Order as a means to celebrate Protestant culture and identity.

Throughout its history, the Orange Order has been associated with politics in Northern Ireland. From the beginning, there was a formal association with the Ulster Unionist Party. The Party was established in 1905 to resist Home Rule, Irish self-government independent from the British Parliament in London. Catholic membership in the party was discouraged. Unionist members were most always Orangemen as well, and Catholics were barred from membership in the Orange Order. The influence of the Orangemen in the government of Northern Ireland was deep and wide-ranging. The Unionist Party was the controlling government from 1921 until 1972. Until 1969, all of the prime ministers of Northern Ireland and all but three cabinet ministers were Orangemen. Eighty-seven of the ninety-five Members of Parliament and every Unionist senator but one was an Orangeman until 1969.

The political connection between the two remained until March of 2005 when most Orangemen transferred their allegiance to the Democratic Unionist Party.

The Orange Order holds annual marches or parades along traditional routes on roadways in their chapter's home town. The first Orange parade was held in 1796 in County Armagh, Ireland. Marches have led to rioting, violence, and death in the twentieth century. In Northern Ireland, problems became more intense when traditional routes for Orangemen parades, with their anti-Catholic theme, took them into housing areas now occupied by Catholics. In 1935, thousands of Catholics were forced to leave their homes in Ulster after rioting sparked by a parade left several dead. Many of the bands hired by the Orangemen for their parades openly advertised their association with paramilitary groups (units formed on a military pattern to wield military force against Catholics). The traditional songs at the Orange parades contain lyrics that are insulting and threatening to Catholics and have led to some serious disturbances. Both sides take their community's rights very seriously. Protestants declare their right to freedom of speech and Catholics respond with their right to freedom from fear.

head of the new church he created in England. This protest against Roman Catholicism marked the beginning of Protestantism in England. Despite the fact that most of Ireland's inhabitants were Catholic, England's King Henry VIII created a Protestant "Church of Ireland" in 1541. Catholic monasteries were abolished and Roman Catholicism was prohibited in England and Ireland. This blatant discrimination against their religion intensified Irish hatred of the English rule.

When the English suppressed an Irish rebellion in 1649, they seized much of the land in the northeastern province of Ulster. English and Scottish

Protestants settled this land as part of the large-scale colonization of Ireland. As the Protestants moved into Ireland, many Catholics were driven off their lands. Irish farmers found themselves in a tenant farm system. Under the tenant system, Irish farmers worked the land for English landlords who often lived elsewhere. Landlords took the profits while providing the farmers who rented and lived on their land with bare basic necessities.

Continuous open rebellion in Ireland led to the reversal of Poyning's Law in 1782. That meant Ireland's Parliament was no longer under direct control of the English Parliament. It was a real step forward for Irish independence but Catholics were still denied the right to hold office. In 1791, an underground movement called the United Irishmen was founded to oppose English rule and fight for separation of Ireland from England. Called separatists, they believed that the only way to get England out of Ireland was by force. England was in competition with rival European powers at that time, and political control of the Irish island was a military necessity for protection from the French navy. Irish separatists looked to England's enemies for assistance and support. To resist and exercise political power over the Catholics, a Protestant organization called the Orangemen (see box) formed in 1795.

By the beginning of the nineteenth century, there was a movement in England to resolve the separatist issue in Ireland. In 1800 the British Parliament passed the Act of Union that merged the kingdoms of Ireland and England into the United Kingdom of Great Britain and Ireland. Put into effect on January 1, 1801, they were united under a central parliament and monarchy (royalty line of kings and queens) based in London. Irish politicians were allowed to serve in the English Parliament. In 1829, Parliament passed the Catholic Emancipation Act, overturning all laws directed specifically against Catholics. Further legislation followed further uniting Ireland with the rest of Great Britain. The Parliament passed the Disestablishment Act in 1869 that formally dissolved the Anglican Church in Ireland. British Parliament then passed a series of acts between 1870 and 1903 referred to as the Irish Land Acts to aid tenant farmers. Despite these efforts, Irish independence remained a controversial issue. In Ireland, Catholics supported the rise of the Home Rule movement in the late nineteenth century for self-government. Protestants, who were in the minority on the island, opposed it; they feared Catholic domination. Protestants supported continued English rule. The Home Rule movement was the beginning of a political rivalry between the two groups that continued through the twentieth century.

Irish independence

At the dawning of the twentieth century, politics in Ireland divided communities between the Unionists and the Nationalists. Unionists were mainly Protestant descendants of Scottish and English settlements, and they wanted to remain under direct rule from London. The Orangemen closely associated with the Unionist Party. Nationalists were largely Catholic descendants of the original Irish population and they desired independence from England. In 1905, Sinn Fein (see box) was organized as a political party to secure Irish independence. Sinn Fein's roots go back to 1791 when the Catholic underground movement (secretive organized effort) formed the United Irishmen.

On April 24, 1916, while England was engaged in World War I, a revolt against English rule broke out in Ireland. The fighting began in the streets of Dublin and spread to other parts of the island before the leaders were caught and executed. Known as the Easter Rising, or Easter Rebellion, it seemed a total failure until the English executed its leaders. The general Irish populace reacted with disgust and anger believing the leaders were unjustly killed. The Easter Rising is credited with paving the way for the eventual establishment of the Irish Free State. In 1916, the Irish Republican Army (IRA) formed to fight for Irish independence. A guerrilla war (irregular fighting by independent bands) began between the IRA rebels and British government forces.

When the First World War ended, the idea of Home Rule gained momentum. It was proposed that Ireland be divided into two separate Home Rule areas, northern and southern. Unionists were in the minority on the island but held a majority in the four northern counties of Antrim, Armagh, Down, and Londonderry, in the province of Ulster. The addition of the two Ulster counties of Fermanagh and Tyrone left northern Ireland with a workable economic plan for Home Rule. It seemed like a good compromise to everyone except the hundreds of thousands of Nationalists from Fermanagh and Tyrone, who found themselves included in the northern area with the predominant Unionists. The other three of the nine counties of Ulster were left in control of the south because of their prevailing Nationalist populations. The outcome of the Home Rule proposal in 1920 was that twenty-six counties, in the south of Ireland, would be ruled from Dublin. Six northern counties— Antrim, Armagh, Down, Londonderry, Fermanagh, and Tyrone—would be ruled from Belfast in northern Ireland. Provision was made for both parliaments to eventually join into one parliament for all of Ireland.

Sinn Fein

Sinn Fein is the oldest political organization in Ireland. Its roots can be traced to the Catholic underground movement of the United Irishmen in 1791. Created to oppose English rule in Ireland, the early leaders believed that only an independent Ireland could guarantee equality and prosperity for the people. The organization evolved over the centuries until it emerged in the twentieth century as Sinn Fein. Sinn Fein is a political party that seeks the unity and independence of Ireland. The theories of the separatist political movement were first published in 1905 under the title "The Sinn Fein Policy."

Sinn Fein takes its name from an Irish Gaelic expression, which translates into English as "We Ourselves," or "Ourselves Alone." The modern Sinn Fein party prefers "We Ourselves." During the 1918 general election in Ireland, Sinn Fein won a landslide victory. It set up a separatist parliament, Dail Eireann (Irish assembly), and proclaimed Ireland a Republic with its own Irish army called the Irish Republican Army (IRA). Following several years of guerrilla warfare, the party split over support of the Government of Ireland Act of 1920. The act divided Ireland with an international land border.

Reorganized in the 1960s, Sinn Fein launched a political campaign to gain support on issues other than separation. The party split once again and the Provisional Sinn Fein emerged as the party known in the late twentieth century. Provisional means temporary or serving for the time being. From the 1970s onward, Sinn Fein took the role of leading advocate for English withdrawal from Ireland. It campaigned on the streets throughout Ireland for a reunited thirty-two-county island. The IRA also experienced a split in 1969 over political differences among the members. One branch took a more political and less violent approach. The other branch that split off called itself the Provisional IRA and continued the same armed strategies of the earlier IRA. It is the group recognized as the IRA today. Sinn Fein combined with the IRA and came to symbolize militant Irish nationalism to the rest of the world. The IRA conducted armed campaigns of violence within England and Northern Ireland until 1994. By the time a peace settlement was reached in 1998, more than three thousand people had been killed, most of them civilians. It was the longest unbroken period of armed resistance in the long and troubled history shared between Irish Catholics and England.

The Government of Ireland Act of 1920 resulted in the creation of the six-county Northern Ireland and provided for Home Rule. An international land border, the only one within the United Kingdom, was established to separate Northern Ireland from the south of Ireland. The act provided for parliaments in Dublin and in Belfast. Northern Ireland chose to remain part of the United Kingdom, and the remaining twenty-six counties of the south and west formed the Irish Free State under the Anglo-Irish Treaty of 1921. These actions failed to end the unrest. Although the Irish had finally gained some independence from England, the long-standing resentment over English domination remained.

In 1926, the Fianna Fail party was founded in Ireland with the goal of severing all ties with England. Eamon de Valera (1882–1975), former president of the Irish Republic and member of Sinn Fein, founded the political party. Through the next several years an economic war existed between Ireland and Britain. As an Irish leading official, de Valera stopped paying annual land payments owed to Britain. Britain responded with restrictions on Ireland's exports to Britain. In 1937, the Irish Free State declared independence as Eire. Eire used its independent status to remain neutral throughout World War II. England suffered heavy losses during the war, both in combat and in sweeping German air attacks on its cities, and was in no position to resist the independence move by Eire. In 1949, Eire was renamed the Republic of Ireland. The Republic of Ireland declared final independence from Britain on April 18, 1949. It then renewed its efforts in the movement to unite Protestant Northern Ireland with the Catholic Republic of Ireland.

Eamon de Valera, former president of the Irish Republic and member of Sinn Fein. COURTESY OF THE LIBRARY OF CONGRESS.

Two distinct ethnic groups

Riot reports of the early twentieth century recorded the ongoing violence between Catholics and Protestants. The reports focused mainly on troubles within Belfast and Londonderry, where most of the bloody conflicts took place. Until the 1960s, most Catholics and Protestants throughout Northern Ireland dealt with problems locally. It had been forty years since the creation of Northern Ireland and, while there was neither unity nor stability, both sides had more or less accepted the reality of the six-county province. However, Catholics and Protestants still saw themselves as belonging to distinct groups, and the underlying conflict was rooted in their differences and cultural identity. Northern Ireland Protestants were the majority group and strongly favored by London.

There was a high level of stereotyping (an oversimplified prejudgment of others using physical or behavioral characteristics, usually exaggerated, that supposedly apply to every member of that group) between the Protestants and Catholics. Catholics considered the Protestants to be

Signs of Northern Ireland Ethnic Division

Northern Ireland ethnic division can be seen in the absence of any universally accepted national symbols as a national anthem or national flag. Northern Ireland lacks an official national anthem. When one is required for an event, "God Save the Queen" is most often played and the English Union Flag is displayed. At the Commonwealth Games "A Londonderry Air," the old anthem of Northern Ireland, is played while the Ulster Banner, or Red Hand Flag, is flown. The Commonwealth Games are similar to the world-wide Olympics but with even more sports included that are common mainly to the Commonwealth countries, such as lawn bowling and rugby. The Ulster Banner is based on the flag of Ulster and occasionally still flies, even though it lost its official status when the Parliament of Northern Ireland was abolished in 1972. In an attempt to promote unity the Flag of St. Patrick has been raised by some organizations. It too has failed to receive universal approval because it represented Ireland during English rule and it is still used by some English army regiments.

Nationalist and Unionist communities fly different flags. Nationalists are those of Catholic descent who desire a reunion with the Republic of Ireland. Unionists are Protestants who desire to maintain Northern Ireland under British rule. Nationalist communities typically fly the Irish tri-color flag. Local unity is expressed in the green, white, and orange of its banners and signs. Unionist communities fly the red, white, and blue of the Union Flag, the symbol of English identity.

A point of tension still exists in the twenty-first century between Unionists and Nationalists in the use of name designations for cities, organizations, and even sports clubs. Choice of names often reveals the cultural, ethnic, and religious identity of the speaker. Unionist supporters call Northern Ireland Ulster while Nationalists most always use North of Ireland, or the Six Counties. The media generally use their community's preferred term or they mix the use of disputed names in a report. For example, the city of Londonderry may be referred to when introducing a story and then it will be called Derry for the rest of the report. Unionists prefer City of Londonderry, while Nationalists prefer Derry. When the Derry City Council voted to rename the city Derry, unionists objected and it officially remained Londonderry. To satisfy both sides the Council printed two sets of stationery and replies to its correspondence using whichever term the original sender used.

rigid and lacking common sense. Protestants thought the Catholics were arrogant and belligerent in school and other community activities. Fear and distrust of each other led to segregation (using laws or social customs to separate certain social groups, such as peoples distinguished by skin color or religious affiliation) at most levels of society. This separation led to real differences in terms of economic prosperity, education, and political opportunity. Schools were segregated. Even senior citizens' homes were separated by religion. The church usually organized social activities, so contact between the two religions was limited. Mixed-marriage couples often stopped attending church altogether. Because of prejudice against them, they were not accepted in either circle. Catholics were more likely to be unemployed, paid lower wages, and living in inferior housing. Without obvious physical differences like skin color, discrimination against a stranger was based on other signals. Centuries of discrimination against Catholics had left the majority of them poor members of the working class. Protestants, who identified more with British culture, were much more likely to be landowners or managers who hired and fired the workers. People judged others on the basis of their home address, school attendance, name, appearance, and speech. The organizations one belonged to and even the sports one played were also indicators used in discriminating against another person. The common hostility and fear between the two groups eventually led to a sense of deprivation and discontent by the Catholic minority.

The Catholic minority held very little power in government. The state was run on the basis of a Protestant majority with the parliament building located six miles east of Belfast in Stormont, a region populated by Protestants. The Anglo-Irish Treaty in 1921 established the location, and the Ulster Unionist Party had maintained complete control since that time. Individuals from these powerful, upper-class Protestant families were wealthy from businesses as well as land ownership. Protestants from a few individual families controlled the vast majority of Stormont seats under the Unionist party. To the Protestant community, Stormont became a symbol of power; to the Catholic community, it was a symbol of oppression. In the 1950s, the international media began to play a major role in publicizing the views and demands of the Catholic minority in Northern Ireland. The eyes of the world slowly began to focus on the troubled little island.

The troubles

As the world watched, the political situation in Northern Ireland became increasingly bitter and violent. Throughout the 1960s, violence between Catholics and Protestants increased at an alarming rate. By 1966, the constant clashes erupted into civil war between the IRA and a Protestant group called the Ulster Defense Association, formed in 1971. Sinn Fein and the IRA increased their efforts to make Northern Ireland part of the Republic of Ireland. The Republic of Ireland did little to deter IRA cross-border raids into Northern Ireland. Working in their favor was the deep cultural division that separated Irish citizens in the north. Catholic Nationalists publicly charged that they faced religious and political

Bomb debris scattered in a street in Belfast. © LEIF SKOOGFORS/CORBIS.

discrimination from Protestant Unionists. The long-running conflict between the two sides became known as The Troubles, and it reached its most violent phase between 1968 and 1994.

When Sinn Fein and the IRA combined forces in the early 1970s, they created a more militant, or radical, force to fight for Irish nationalism. Using terrorist tactics, such as shootings and bombings, they began a bloody campaign to drive the English out of Northern Ireland. They bombed police stations, army bases, courthouses, buses, and hotels in Northern Ireland and England. Their targets were army, police, and anyone else they saw as cooperating with the English. Hundreds in law enforcement were killed or injured, but many more innocent civilians suffered the same fate. In 1971, the English government began imprisoning as political prisoners those known or suspected of being members of the IRA. English troops were sent to Northern Ireland to reinforce security forces and maintain border controls between Northern Ireland and the Republic of Ireland. Despite rising economic difficulties at home,

England took control of the government in Northern Ireland in the spring of 1972 and suspended the Ulster Parliament at Stormont.

The English presence only increased the violence and political unrest in Northern Ireland. On July 21, 1972, the IRA set off twenty-six bombs in Belfast, killing nine people and injuring one hundred and thirty. Over the next few years, thousands of armed robberies, shootings, and explosions followed. The English responded by searching tens of thousands of homes belonging to IRA suspects. In 1974 the IRA exploded a bomb in the English Houses of Parliament, injuring eleven. Parliament responded with tougher anti-terrorist laws and outlawed the IRA, giving the courts authority to prosecute IRA members and sympathizers. Nonetheless, the violence continued through the year until a ceasefire was agreed upon through secret negotiations between the IRA and English security forces. It lasted until 1975, when the English government ended its internment policy and began criminal proceedings against IRA members guilty of crimes. The troubles continued, and on August 27, 1979, IRA terrorists assassinated British war hero and admiral of the British Fleet, Lord Louis Mountbatten (1900–1979).

Negotiating Peace

Sinn Fein became a serious political force in the early 1980s when it campaigned in support of IRA prisoners being held in British prisons in Northern Ireland. Maze Prison was a famous prison located ten miles west of Belfast in County Antrim. In March 1981, IRA members began a hunger strike in Maze that ended only after ten men had fasted to their deaths. The fasts dramatized the cause of Irish unity and brought worldwide attention on relations between England and Ireland. In November of 1981, an Anglo-Irish Intergovernmental Council was established to formalize regular official contacts between English and Irish government leaders to improve communication.

The IRA continued its acts of bombing, intimidating, and terrorizing for another decade. In October 1984, English prime minister Margaret Thatcher (1925–) narrowly escaped injury when the IRA exploded a bomb during a government conference in Brighton, England. Thatcher refused to be intimidated and opened the conference on schedule the next morning. Hoping to end the violence in Northern Ireland, the English Parliament approved an Anglo-Irish Agreement, the Ulster Plan, in November 1985. It allowed the Republic of Ireland government to participate as a consultant in Northern Ireland's political,

Demonstrators march in Belfast on May 4, 1981, carrying portraits of IRA activists currently on hunger strike. © MICHEL PHILIPPOT/SYGMA/CORBIS.

legal, and security matters. In return, the Irish government promised to actively deter IRA cross-border raids into Northern Ireland. The Agreement reaffirmed the Ireland Act of 1949, which gave a legal guarantee that Northern Ireland would not cease to be part of the United Kingdom without consent of the majority of its citizens.

Not everyone agreed with the Ulster Plan. The Ulster Unionist Party was openly opposed to it. Peace seemed unlikely as the world watched television footage of explosions and deaths on a regular basis in Northern Ireland. However, in August 1994, the IRA announced a temporary ceasefire and laid down their weapons. An uneasy peace existed until February 1996 when the IRA, unsatisfied that progress was being achieved toward a resolution, announced the end of the ceasefire and renewed violence. In 1997, peace talks began when Sinn Fein sat down to formal negotiations with the British government. The Northern Ireland Peace Talks proceeded slowly because of more

The bomb that damaged this hotel in England was intended to kill prime minister Margaret Thatcher and her cabinet in 1984. © BETTMANN/CORBIS.

killings on both sides, but they finally produced a settlement that appeared to be a good compromise. That compromise was known as the Good Friday Agreement.

On Friday, April 10, 1998, the Good Friday Agreement, or Belfast Agreement, was reached in Belfast. Voters in Northern Ireland and in the

Republic of Ireland approved the Agreement by a large margin with 71 percent supporting it in Northern Ireland and 94 percent in the Republic of Ireland. It provided for an elected Northern Ireland Assembly made up of representatives of all the main parties who would share power on an equal basis. It confirmed the Anglo-Irish Agreement of 1985, which acknowledged that the status of Northern Ireland could only be changed with the agreement of a majority of voters in Northern Ireland. Some serious obstacles remained over the issue of disarming terrorist groups of their store of weapons. Opponents of the Agreement continued with bombing raids. A new Northern Ireland government was finally established at Stormont on December 2, 1999. On July 28, 2005, the IRA declared an end to its campaign and removed its store of weapons from service. This act was performed in accordance with the Good Friday Agreement, and under the watch of the International Decommissioning Body and others. The end of violence and political unrest has opened the two Irelands to economic stability with tourists returning to the beautiful island. Since 1969 over 3,500 had been killed including 1,100 members of the various British security forces. Over 1,800 civilians had lost their lives. Some 47,000 were injured and almost 20,000 imprisoned.

For More Information

BOOKS

Christie, Kenneth. *Political Protest in Northern Ireland: Continuity and Change.* Berkshire, UK: Link Press, 1992.

Darby, John, ed. *Northern Ireland: The Background to the Conflict.* Syracuse, NY: Syracuse University Press, 1983.

Feeney, Brian. *Sinn Fein: A Hundred Turbulent Years.* Madison: University of Wisconsin Press, 2003.

McColgan, John. *British Policy and the Irish Administration, 1920–22.* London: George Allen & Unwin Publishers Ltd., 1983.

O'Brien, Brendan. *The Long War: The IRA and Sinn Fein, 1985 to Today.* Syracuse, NY: Syracuse University Press, 1993.

WEB SITES

Darby, John. "Northern Ireland: The Background to the Peace Process." *CAIN (Conflict Archive on the Internet)—University of Ulster.* http://cain.ulst.ac.uk/events/peace/darby03.htm (accessed on November 29, 2006).

PBS. "Chronology." *Frontline: The IRA & Sinn Fein.* http://www.pbs.org/wgbh/pages/frontline/shows/ira/etc/cron.html (accessed on November 29, 2006).

"Sinn Fein." *Nidex—Northern Ireland Politics.* http://www.sinnfein.org/index2.html (accessed on November 29, 2006).

21

Prejudice Against Hispanic Americans

Hispanic is a term that generally refers to individuals and groups who possess cultural or genetic links to people of Spanish-speaking origin. Usually this lineage in the Americas is traced to 1450, when Spanish explorers and conquistadors (soldiers) settled much of Central America, Mexico, and the southwestern region of what became the United States. Hispanics are also referred to as Latinos, a term understood to primarily include Mexicans, Puerto Ricans, and Cubans. However, Dominicans, South Americans, and Central Americans are also a part of this group.

This chapter will examine the historical experiences of Hispanics in the United States, their fight against prejudice (a negative attitude, emotion, or behavior towards individuals based on a prejudgment about those individuals with no prior knowledge or experience) for equality and civil rights, complicated immigration (the movement of people from one country to another with the intention to reside permanently in the new country) issues that continued into the twenty-first century, and the successes and struggles of a group that has contributed much to the American story.

The Mexican-American War

Tensions between the United States and Mexico grew steadily in the early nineteenth century as Americans began migrating west. The migration was largely triggered by U.S. president Thomas Jefferson's (1743–1826; served 1801–9) purchase in 1803 from France of a vast region west of the Mississippi River and east of the Rocky Mountains. Known as the Louisiana Purchase, the addition instantly doubled the size of the United States. The idea of "Manifest Destiny"—that the North American continent was a God-given gift to the American people and it was their destiny to expand westward—began to take root during this period. Manifest Destiny was a feeling of national exuberance after

WORDS TO KNOW

barrio: Spanish word referring to a neighborhood largely inhabited by people of Hispanic ancestry.

bracero: Spanish word meaning worker.

discrimination: A major consequence of prejudice by treating differently or favoring one social group over another based on arbitrary standards or criteria..

Hispanic: A term that generally refers to individuals and groups who possess cultural or genetic links to people of Spanish-speaking origin. Hispanics are also referred to as Latinos, a term understood to primarily include Mexicans, Puerto Ricans, and Cubans. However, Dominicans, South Americans, and Central Americans are also a part of this group.

immigrant: A person who leaves his country of origin to reside permanently in another.

prejudice: A negative attitude, emotion, or behavior towards individuals based on a prejudgment about those individuals with no prior knowledge or experience.

racism: Prejudice against people of a particular physical trait, such as skin color, based on a belief that the physical trait primarily determines human behavior and individual capabilities; social and cultural meaning is given to skin color or whatever other trait is considered important.

repatriation: Sending an individual, usually a prisoner of war, immigrant, or refugee, back to his country of origin.

segregation: Using laws or social customs to separate certain social groups, such as whites and blacks or women and men.

---

successfully defeating the British in the War of 1812 (1812–14) and having all the lands of the Louisiana Purchase available for exploration and settlement. The rapid expansion involved both violence and non-violence alike. In 1835 and 1845, the U.S. government offered Mexico $30 million to purchase California. Both times the offer was declined. Americans became frustrated at their inability to expand the borders of the nation. In addition, many Mexicans living in California resented the Mexican government's attempts to regulate trade with Americans in the territory. They wanted freedom to conduct business with the Americans as they wished.

Frustration, resentment, and disagreement between Americans and Mexicans was nothing new in Texas. After Mexico gained its independence from Spain in 1821, the Mexican government offered people the chance to populate the northern part of the country to provide a buffer from anticipated U.S. expansion efforts. The new settlers had to take an oath of allegiance to Mexico and convert to the national religion of

Catholicism. Thousands of Americans jumped at the offer. However, the American settlers soon became frustrated with what they saw as the inefficiency and lack of interest in the new frontier settlements by the Mexican government. In 1835, the Texas settlers revolted and gained their political independence as a republic the following year. However, many Mexicans refused to recognize the Treaty of Velasco that had stopped the fighting and gained Texas's freedom from Mexico. They claimed that the defeated Mexican general Santa Anna (1794–1876) had no legal authority to negotiate or sign a treaty with the Texan forces. The treaty provisions included the removal of the Mexican army from Texas and the return of prisoners and property such as horses and slaves taken by Mexican forces.

Violent border disputes erupted. Many Americans sympathized with the Texans while at the same time developing harsh prejudices and stereotypes (oversimplified prejudgments of others using physical or behavioral characteristics, usually exaggerated, that supposedly apply to every member of that group) toward the Mexican people. In 1845, the United States admitted Texas as the twenty-eighth state. The United States now claimed that the southernmost U.S.–Mexican border was the Rio Grande River. The next year, the new border became the issue of an international dispute and war between Mexico and the United States followed.

Despite suffering several defeats in major battles and the capture of much of its land, the Mexican government refused to give in. U.S. Army general Winfield Scott (1786–1866) executed what was at that point in time the largest amphibious (by land and water) assault in military history at Veracruz, Mexico, on March 9, 1847. The Americans captured Mexico City in September 1847.

Parts of Mexico join the United States

After several months of negotiations formal hostilities between the two nations officially concluded when the Treaty of Guadalupe-Hidalgo was signed on February 2, 1848. The treaty's terms gave the United States the vast territory of Upper California and New Mexico, including present-day Arizona. This area included what are now the states of California, Nevada, Utah, New Mexico, and parts of Colorado and Wyoming. In addition, Mexico formally recognized the state of Texas while fixing its southern border at the Rio Grande. The United States paid Mexico $15 million, recognized the prior existence of large land grants made to

The Rio Grande flows at the border of Mexico and Texas. Here, two Mexican women hold their children as they cross the river at the border of Ciudad Juarez, Mexico, and El Paso, Texas, in 1983. © DANNY LEHMAN/CORBIS.

settlers by the Mexican government in the Southwest, and offered U.S. citizenship to Mexicans already living in the area. The U.S. government also took responsibility for resolving all claims (formal requests for payment for losses) made by American citizens against the government of Mexico.

The U.S. government later revised the treaty, however, and removed the portion about recognizing the earlier Mexican land grants. Nearly five hundred thousand Mexicans found themselves renting their own land from the United States. As American settlers claimed these lands the U.S. court system made it easy for many Americans to evict Mexicans from what had been their land. As a result, many Mexican-Americans became tenant farmers (farmers renting their land from another person) or field laborers working for white landowners. They lived apart in Spanish-speaking enclaves known as "barrios" (the Spanish word for neighborhood). Retail shops and places of entertainment were also segregated, as were schools. The schools for Mexican American children lacked the funding and supplies that schools for white children enjoyed. There were also few teachers able to speak Spanish.

Immigration wave and U.S. policy

During the early 1900s, the economy of Mexico struggled and became progressively worse. Anger and resentment within the Mexican population toward its government ultimately resulted in the revolution of 1910. The conflict sent Mexico spiraling into political, economic, and social upheaval for a decade. The chaos and lack of job opportunities led thousands of Mexicans to look to the north as a means of escape.

Between 1910 and 1930, over 680,000 Mexicans immigrated to the United States. Most settled in the Southwest and found employment as laborers in factories and mines, on railroad lines, farms, and ranches. During U.S. participation in World War I (1914–18) in Europe, thousands of Mexican Americans served in the military under the American flag. Those who stayed behind took advantage of the booming wartime economy. They found employment as highly skilled laborers in construction and industry. While Mexican immigrants made great strides in the United States, housing and employment discrimination (treating one social group differently than another based on arbitrary standards or criteria) against them abounded and continued following the war. Many immigrants formed organizations and labor unions (an organized group of workers joined together for a common purpose, such as negotiating with management for better working conditions or higher wages) to combat prejudice and discrimination. Among those was a coalition group called the League of United Latin American Citizens (LULAC), the oldest Hispanic organization in the United States, formed in 1929.

In response to the massive arrival of immigrants, the U.S. government passed legislation to restrict immigration and control legal entry into the country. In 1917, Congress passed a law requiring all adult immigrants to demonstrate the ability to read and write in at least one language. The Bureau of Immigration established the U.S. Border Patrol in 1924 to guard against illegal immigrants filtering across the Mexican border. As a result of the tougher legislation, increased border security, and the onset of the Great Depression (1929–41), Mexican immigration declined. The Great Depression was a severe economic crisis that started in the United States in late 1929 and soon spread throughout the world. Throughout the 1930s, the Depression led to decreased business activity, high unemployment, and social unrest in many places. Only thirty-three thousand Mexican immigrants arrived in the United States during the 1930s while many stayed in Mexico where the economy was growing despite the Depression elsewhere in the world.

Still, prejudices against Mexican immigrants ran high. Many Americans believed that Mexican immigrants slowed the economy by holding low-paying jobs while native-born citizens suffered from high unemployment. Because of this growing prejudicial attitude and the potential problems it might cause, the governments of the United States and Mexico cooperated on a program of repatriation (returning immigrants to their original homeland).

Despite the program's objective of returning Mexican Americans to Mexico in a cooperative manner, many were involuntarily (against their will) deported by the United States. Those who were removed from the United States included many who had been citizens for as long as ten years. Their children were American citizens because they were born in the United States. They had no interest in living in Mexico. Many Mexican Americans—most notably in California—were placed in detention camps (guarded temporary camps with minimal provision for life's necessities). They reported harsh treatment such as beatings at the hands of government officials. By 1939, the United States had deported about 500,000 Mexican Americans. Those who remained faced segregated public facilities and schools that frowned upon use of the Spanish language. With the start of war production in 1939 in preparation for World War II, jobs became available again and the deportation efforts came to a close.

No longer needing Mexican workers, the U.S. government attempted a repatriation policy again in the 1950s. This time, the program focused on "wetbacks" (an ethnic slur used to describe illegal Mexican immigrants), immigrants who had remained in the United States after the war to earn higher wages. Mexico eventually pulled out of its agreement to the program because of the often harsh work conditions and racial discrimination the Mexican workers faced. Still, even more illegal immigrants flooded Texas and caused resentment among native-born Texans who were being displaced in the workforce, even if many of the jobs were those they considered too menial for them.

In July 1954, the U.S. government used the Immigration and Nationalization Service (INS), the U.S. Border Patrol, and the armed forces to begin a search and seizure operation into homes and businesses to find and remove illegal immigrants from Texas, a strategy named

The issue of illegal immigrants crossing the border has been a longtime problem. Here, an Arizona man shows his support for boosting funds and troops at the U.S.–Mexico border near Naco, Arizona. © SAUL LOEB/EPA/CORBIS.

Operation Wetback. The government claimed that over a million illegal immigrants were sent back to Mexico, though no firm figure was ever confirmed. The program wound down late in 1954. The U.S. government continued to patrol the borders into the twenty-first century and sent many illegal aliens back to Mexico and other countries. Yet millions of immigrants successfully got through by crossing the border in remote areas or through illegal smuggling operations. The issue again became the subject of intense national debate in Congress and throughout the nation in 2006.

World War II contributions

Despite the difficulties and barriers placed in front of them as a group, Mexican Americans continued to make progress within American society and contribute to the nation's economy and arts, while gaining a stronger voice in the quest for full equality.

As was the case in World War I, Mexican Americans answered the call to service as the United States became involved in World War II. More than three hundred thousand Mexican Americans served in the armed forces during the conflict. Close to five hundred thousand Hispanics served, including fifty-three thousand Puerto Ricans. Hispanics serving in U.S. forces around the world earned thirty-nine Medals of Honor during World War II, more than any other ethnic group. U.S. general Douglas MacArthur (1880–1964) described the 158th Regimental Combat team, a group comprised of mostly Mexican Americans and Native Americans from Arizona, as one of the greatest teams ever sent into battle.

Similar to World War I, the manufacturing industry opened new job opportunities for immigrants who were not with the military overseas. In addition, agricultural labor was in great demand during the war years as many American fieldworkers joined the military services and went overseas. Cooperating again on immigrant policy, the United States and Mexico established the bracero program. The program, developed in 1942, allowed braceros (day laborers) to legally enter the United States for seasonal work on farms and railroads. The program continued until 1964, bringing in almost five million workers from Mexico, even though working conditions were known to be often harsh such as working in the fields for long hours for low pay.

Civil rights

Hispanics who had served with honor and distinction in World War II had no desire to resume lives filled with prejudice and employment barriers for themselves or their families. Following the war, many political, business, and civil rights organizations formed to help fight discrimination, segregation (using laws or social customs to separate certain social groups, such as whites and people of color) and racism (prejudice against people of a particular physical trait, such as skin color). Two of the more prominent groups were the Mexican American Political Association and the American GI Forum. These early groups grew into larger and more influential groups such as the National Council of La Raza (see box) that organized in the 1950s and 1960s.

The plight of immigrant workers in the agricultural industry captured the nation's attention during the 1950s and 1960s thanks to the

National Council of La Raza

Organizations like the National Association for the Advancement of Colored People (NAACP) and the National Urban League helped with passage of civil rights legislation by bringing national attention to the racial prejudice that had long been plaguing African Americans. However, no such organization existed for Hispanics in the United States through much of the twentieth century. Much of the progress of the African American civil rights movement, while certainly improving conditions for racial minorities in general, was not felt as broadly within the Hispanic American community since the focus had been on African Americans.

Into this void stepped a group of young Mexican Americans living in Washington, D.C., in the early 1960s. Calling themselves the National Organization of Mexican American Services (NOMAS), they worked to provide technical assistance to the Hispanic civil rights organizations scattered about the country and to bring them together as a united group. Armed with a grant from the Ford Foundation to conduct the first major study of Mexican Americans, NOMAS researchers found that working-class organizations and national advocacy groups needed to grow in order to serve Mexican Americans better. Meetings to organize Mexican Americans led to the formation of the Southwest Council of La Raza in Phoenix, Arizona, in February 1968. It soon grew into a national organization known as the National Council of La Raza (NCLR) in 1972.

NCLR established a national office in Washington, D.C.

In the late 1970s, NCLR director Raul Yzaguirre (1939–) was instrumental in developing NCLR's programs and goals. Yzaguirre secured a continual core funding pledge from the Ford Foundation, a private organization dedicated to ending social injustice in the world. He also expanded the group's reach to all Americans of Hispanic descent rather than only Mexican Americans, began to acquire federal funds for private development, and assisted Hispanics with such issues as financial counseling. Yzaguirre focused on research and development of social policies aimed at benefiting Hispanics. He started the Policy Analysis Center, which studied issues such as immigration, welfare, education, and health care. The NCLR also began a public awareness effort geared toward presenting a positive image of Hispanics in the mainstream American media.

The policy initiatives of the NCLR changed following passage of federal welfare reform legislation in 1996. The legislation gave individual states the power to determine who should receive a broad range of public services. As a result, NCLR shifted many of its programs to the state level while continuing to maintain an influential presence in Washington, D.C., where it opened the Raul Yzaguirre Building as its headquarters. The NCLR's federal policy initiatives focused primarily on immigration reform legislation.

efforts of Cesar Chavez (1927–1993), who was born in Yuma, Arizona, near the Mexican border. Chavez spent most of his life working on farms for low wages alongside fellow Hispanic immigrants in California, including Dolores Huerta (1930–), who was instrumental in helping Chavez organize. Working conditions were less than adequate. Chavez began organizing workers into a union in order to demand higher pay

Cesar Chavez (center) and Dolores Huerta (far right) join other United Farmworkers Union board members at an event.
AP IMAGES.

and better working conditions. This union eventually became known as the National Farm Workers Association (NFWA). It was the first farm workers' labor union.

In 1965, Chavez and Huerta urged cooperation with another union, the Agricultural Workers Organizing Committee, in refusing to work for grape growers in Delano, California. In 1966, the two unions merged to form the United Farm Workers. The group chose a Mexican Aztec eagle as its symbol. The nonviolent strike, modeled upon the techniques and strategies of Indian leader Mahatma Gandhi (1869–1948), lasted five years. It resulted in a nationwide boycott (an organized effort to not buy certain products or use certain services in order to express disapproval with an organization) of California grapes that severely affected the industry. Chavez and the United Farm Workers garnered the support of influential political figures like Rev. Martin Luther King Jr. (1929–1968) and U.S. senator Robert F. Kennedy (1925–1968) of New York.

After five years the boycott ended in 1970 as the workers reached an agreement with the growers on improved working conditions.

Another grape boycott led by the United Farm Workers in the 1970s led to Congressional passage of the Agricultural Labor Relations Act of 1975. At the time a national public opinion poll showed that seventeen million Americans supported the grape boycotts. The law allowed for a collective bargaining by agricultural workers. Collective bargaining involves negotiations between representatives of employers and workers to reach agreement on working conditions, wages, and job benefits. Chavez remained active in workers' rights until his death in 1993. Chavez received numerous awards for his leadership including Mexico's highest award, the Aguila Azteca (The Aztec Eagle), in 1991.

Groups such as the United Farm Workers and National Council La Raza continued to advocate for equal rights and beneficial governmental policies on behalf of Hispanic Americans into the early twenty-first century.

Caribbean immigration and migration

Puerto Rican migration While the U.S. government was attempting to curb Mexican immigration in the 1950s through policies such as Operation Wetback, there was significant immigration from Puerto Rico as well as Cuba. While Puerto Ricans were primarily looking for employment, Cubans were fleeing the Communist dictatorship (a form of government in which a person wields absolute power and control over the people) of Fidel Castro Ruz (1926–). (Communism is a system of government where the nation's leaders are selected by a single political party that controls all aspects of society including all economic production. Private ownership of property is eliminated.)

In 1898, the United States claimed the island of Puerto Rico in the aftermath of the Spanish-American War (1898) (in which the United States gained control over the Spanish colonies of Cuba, Puerto Rico, and the Philippines). Puerto Rico's citizens could enter and exit the United States without restriction. Despite historical animosity (hostile resentment) toward the U.S. government for its indifferent (showing little interest) policies toward the island in the mid-twentieth century, many Puerto Ricans viewed the United States as a land of opportunity.

Between 1940 and 1960, economic recessions (period of lesser economic activity) on the island of Puerto Rico motivated over half a million residents to move to the United States in search of employment. Most

Puerto Ricans gravitated to New York City in large part because of a campaign by New York mayor Robert F. Wagner Jr. (1910–1991) to recruit Puerto Ricans to work in the city's factories. By 1960, almost 70 percent of Puerto Ricans living on the American mainland resided on the east side of Harlem in barrios of overpriced, substandard housing. Prejudice-driven discrimination existed. In many restaurant windows signs read "No dogs or Puerto Ricans allowed." Job opportunities proved not as plentiful as Puerto Ricans had hoped. Discrimination and suspicion of Puerto Ricans increased after a pair of Puerto Rican nationalists seeking to establish their country as a separate nation attempted to assassinate U.S. president Harry S. Truman (1884–1972; served 1945–53) in 1950. They acted in protest of American policies toward Puerto Rico.

Many other Puerto Ricans settled in large cities such as Chicago to work in industrial factories. Because of the unstable Puerto Rican economy, some 20 percent of the island's 3.5 million people were living in the United States by end of the twentieth century.

For those Puerto Ricans immigrating to the United States, unemployment remained very high. Being U.S. citizens, Puerto Ricans were eligible for welfare benefits. Suffering a high unemployment rate, Puerto Ricans became trapped in a vicious cycle of poverty and joblessness. In addition, the free movement back and forth from the island to the U.S. mainland contributed to a disruption of families and the lack of a foundation upon which to build a steady employment history.

As the American economy shifted to a more automated production of goods and services, the demand for lower-skilled jobs lessened. The new centers of employment increasingly left urban areas where Puerto Rican communities existed. Many Puerto Ricans found themselves isolated from the new economic sector and lacking the skills to compete in the new economy reliant on computer technology. Unemployment among Puerto Ricans hovered around 50 percent higher than the national average by the end of the twentieth century. The poverty rate was almost four times higher.

Persistent prejudice Puerto Ricans reported that they continued to be victims of prejudice and discrimination, especially by law enforcement officials, in terms of police brutality and sentence discrimination. One of the first Puerto Rican riots in a major city occurred in Chicago in 1966 in response to the city's police shooting of a Puerto Rican man. The riots lasted two days. Puerto Rican leaders and city officials came together to establish positive programs and communication between members of the community and law enforcement to help prevent further incidents. The

Puerto Rican community organizations that resulted from the riots allowed community concerns such as education, housing, health, and employment to be addressed. Puerto Ricans remained active in Chicago politics afterwards.

Puerto Rican Day parades have been held in the United States since 1958. The largest and most popular is the parade held in New York City every June. Aside from its celebration of Puerto Rican culture, the event has also provided opportunities for clashes with authorities over specific issues. For example, tensions between the Puerto Rican community and the police ran high in 2000 when the parade had an anti-U.S. theme that protested American military testing of weapons off the waters of Puerto Rico. The following year, police presence at the parade was high. Many Puerto Ricans accused the police of assaulting women and the city of reducing the number of marchers allowed in the parade. Groups such as the National Congress for Puerto Rican Rights legally pursued the complaints and publicly advocated equal treatment. The efforts were successful in raising public attention to cases of police brutality against Puerto Rico Americans in New York City and provided a lasting avenue for Puerto Ricans to pursue cases in which they believed they were treated unfairly in the criminal justice system.

A movement in both the U.S. and Puerto Rico to make Puerto Rico the fifty-first state of the union has existed since the 1950s. However, Congressional legislation has never gone very far since referendums (votes) held in Puerto Rico have always been won by those favoring the island's current political status. Since the early 1990s opinions on statehood within Puerto Rico are split nearly down the middle. Into the twenty-first century, inhabitants of the island of Puerto Rico continued to enjoy many of the benefits of American citizenship though they remained ineligible to vote in federal elections.

Fleeing a dictator The Cuban experience in the United States has dramatically differed from nearly any other immigrant group in American history. In 1956, Cuban nationalist Fidel Castro led a guerilla (an irregular military unit invasion of the island nation successfully overthrowing the government of Fulgencio Batista (1901–1973), an oppressive dictator. Castro and his followers believed that the Batista government was influenced too heavily by the United States in matters of business and politics. Castro's revolt eventually led Batista to abandon his government and his country. In 1959, Castro began transforming Cuba from an island paradise into a stark Communist state.

Castro pursued the nationalization (placing private business under control of the government) of Cuban businesses and agriculture leading some supporters, particularly the wealthy members of the upper and middle classes, to abandon their belief in Castro's vision. Castro was now seen as a direct threat to their economic well-being. Castro also began seizing control of U.S. business holdings in Cuba and formed a business and military alliance with the Soviet Union, the bitter global enemy of the United States. Soon Castro had established a dictatorship.

Between 1959 and 1962, about two hundred thousand Cubans fled the island for the United States. During the 1960s, the total number of Cuban immigrants in the United States reached five hundred thousand, as Castro's dictatorship became increasingly totalitarian (a highly centralized form of government that has total control over the population). Cuba was a place where free political speech and demonstrations were met with imprisonment or execution. As Castro's grip tightened, many Cubans escaped the island on homemade rafts and boats at considerable risk to reach the United States.

Cuban immigrants quickly settled mainly in south Florida. Because the first wave of Cubans to land on American shores were educated and wealthy, they adapted very easily to American life. The U.S. government furthered the ease of adaptation by granting political asylum (place of safety from some form of persecution). It offered federal assistance in finding homes, made potential job contacts, and helped businesses get established. Also, Cuban immigrants were the only immigrant group allowed to claim U.S. citizenship after only one year on American soil. Many future Cuban immigrants were relatives of this first group. They found a ready-made network of connections to help them adjust to life in a new country.

Taking immediate advantage of the opportunities afforded to them, Cuban immigrants quickly established themselves, most notably in Miami and the surrounding area in Dade County. The economic base was built around banking and small business. Many prominent business owners planned ahead for the day Cuba was once again a free-market nation. Twenty-five percent of all banks and five of the ten most successful businesses in Dade County were owned and operated by Cuban immigrants. The education achievement level among Cuban immigrants matched the U.S. national average. Unemployment and poverty rates were significantly lower than those of other Hispanic groups in the United States.

Not every aspect of Cuban immigration to the United States went smoothly, however. In 1980, Castro emptied his prisons of criminals and

A shrimp boat loaded with Cuban refugees returning from Mariel, Cuba, sails into the Key West Naval Base in Florida in April 1980. AP IMAGES.

the mentally ill and shipped them to the United States on boats leaving from the Cuban port of Mariel. The United States allowed the boats to dock at Miami, but government officials were shocked at the number of people and criminal element of the passengers. Many of the people, including the mentally ill, were eventually deported back to Cuba while some criminals faced imprisonment in the United States.

U.S. policy toward Cuban immigrants stiffened in the mid-1980s. The government announced that only long-term political prisoners and close relatives of Cuban Americans would be granted entry into the United States. This policy was later relaxed. In 1994, thousands of Cuban refugees attempted to land on U.S. soil. They were taken to military bases in the country of Panama and off the coast of Cuba at Guantanamo Bay. Most were settled in the United States, but because of their sheer number, many others were returned to Cuba.

Despite some of the difficulties involving Cuban immigration, Cuban Americans enjoyed more success and prosperity than any other group of American immigrants. While some in Florida, notably African Americans, objected to the increasing Latinization of Miami, the city and surrounding area took pride in joining American and Cuban culture and business so successfully.

Discrimination as a group

While the experiences in America of the different groups that make up the larger population of Hispanics in America vary greatly, some aspects of that experience are common in general and offer a broader perspective.

The rapidly shifting American economy of the late twentieth century made it difficult for people without the benefit of higher education to adjust to their new country and move forward. Hispanics were twice as likely to be living at or below the poverty level in America as non-Hispanic white Americans. Only about 6 to 8 percent of Hispanics attended college, and Hispanics earn only about 60 percent of the income that white Americans earn.

Elementary and secondary education remained areas of concern for Hispanic Americans into the early twenty-first century. Because many Hispanic children were primarily taught Spanish in the home and perhaps English as a second language in the schools, the barrier between students and teachers remained a problem much as it was during the first wave of significant Mexican immigration to the United States in the early twentieth century.

Many educators and administrators supported a bilingual (two-language) movement that gained strength in the late 1960s. However, few school districts experimented with bilingual education. It took a 1974 decision by the Supreme Court in *Lau v. Nichols* to require public schools to address the language problem for all students, not just Spanish-speakers, regardless of their first language. The decision required educators to provide instructions in the student's native language. Illiteracy rates among Hispanics, which were measured at a beginning elementary education level, were seven times higher than that of white Americans.

Several Hispanics felt they were singled out by law enforcement officials because of the ethnic heritage and darker skin. Police harassment was a common complaint at events such as Puerto Rican heritage parades in large cities. Many Hispanics believed U.S. Border Patrol officials and Texas Rangers, a statewide law enforcement agency, dealt with them unreasonably. In addition, there was very little affordable legal aid available to Hispanics who had legal problems in the United States aside from the Mexican American Legal Defense and Education Fund. Moreover, many court officials, lawyers, and judges did not speak Spanish. This caused problems at court hearings as confusion sometimes led to harsh consequences, such as tougher sentences than otherwise might occur.

Political and cultural progress

While Hispanic Americans have faced prejudice and hardship in the United States, many were still able to take advantage of the opportunities America afforded. They gained seats in the highest councils of American government and business.

Alberto Gonzales (1955–) was sworn in as the eightieth attorney general of the United States on February 3, 2005. Prior to being appointed as the nation's highest-ranking law enforcement official, Gonzales served as counsel to Republican president George W. Bush

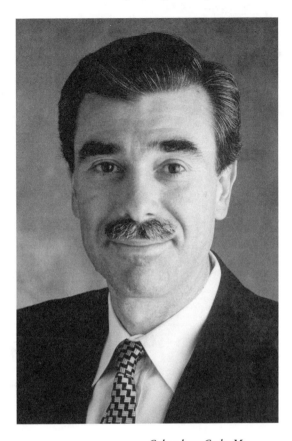

Cuban-born Carlos M. Gutierrez, U.S. secretary of commerce during President George W. Bush's second term. AP IMAGES.

(1946–; served 2001–) and was a justice of the Supreme Court of Texas. In addition, in November 2004 President Bush nominated Cuban-born Carlos M. Gutierrez (1953–) as secretary of commerce. He was confirmed two months later. Gutierrez had previously served as the youngest chief executive officer in the history of the Kellogg company at forty-six years of age.

U.S. senator Mel Martinez also was born in Cuba and fled Communist rule to live in America at age fifteen. He became the first Cuban-born U.S. senator when he took office in January 2005. Robert Menendez (1954–), who grew up as the son of immigrants in tenement housing (older multi-storied apartment buildings often in poor condition), became a U.S. senator representing New Jersey in 2006 after serving in the U.S. House of Representatives. Many Hispanic Americans served in the U.S. House of Representatives and in state legislatures across the nation by the late twentieth century. Governor Bill Richardson (1947–) of New Mexico was perhaps the most prominent Hispanic American state governor in the early twenty-first century having earlier gained national attention as foreign ambassador and U.S. secretary of energy during the administration of Democratic president Bill Clinton (1946–; served 1993–2001).

Hispanic Americans also gained wide respect and reverence in American popular culture. Musical acts such as Gloria Estefan, the late Selena, Shakira, and others sold millions of albums. Benjamin Bratt became a popular actor in the early twenty-first century, starring on television and in film. Jennifer Lopez successfully combined a musical career with an acting career. Comedic acts such as George Lopez star in television.

As have African Americans, many Hispanic American entertainers have become international celebrities, such as Cuban-born Gloria Estefan in music and actor Jimmy Smits of Puerto Rican heritage in film. However, critics often pointed out that some comedic entertainment did nothing but reinforce negative stereotypes of ethnic groups, perhaps most notably the movies by Cheech Marin and Tommy Chong. While that may have been the case at times, there is no doubt that Hispanics had an increasing presence in the music and entertainment industries while gaining more and more power in politics and business.

The ongoing question of immigration

In early 2006, hundreds of thousands of Hispanic immigrants marched in protest rallies across the United States. They were in opposition to legislation before the U.S. Congress that they believed would unfairly restrict immigrants and jeopardize their well-being.

At issue was the question of illegal immigration, long a source of contention between immigrant groups and the U.S. government. Frustrated citizens living near the American-Mexican border began volunteer patrols (calling themselves Minutemen in homage to New England patriots of the Revolutionary era) to search for illegal immigrants attempting to cross the border. These groups notified U.S. Border Patrol when they spotted individuals attempting to illegally enter the United States. They did not advocate or practice violence against the illegal immigrants, but their participation and willingness to use their spare time patrolling the border spoke to the passion the immigration issue aroused.

Many citizens, including legal immigrants and naturalized citizens who had gone through the citizenship process, opposed any sort of amnesty (granting official forgiveness to a large number of people for some illegal act) for illegal immigrants. They wished to impose financial and other penalties on the substantial number of employers who hired illegal immigrants at low wages. However, thousands of immigrants, both documented (holding an official paper allowing entrance) and undocumented, joined together to protest what was perceived as a nationalist passion within the United States against Hispanics. Defenders of the immigrants, arguing that Hispanic illegal immigrants performed work that Americans would not normally do because the wages were so low, charged that Hispanics should not be singled out by anti-immigrant groups simply because of their ethnicity. This been the case throughout history with most immigrant groups. Illegal immigrants numbering about eleven million in the United States in 2006 worked predominantly in service positions, such as cooks, construction laborers, hotel housekeepers, grounds workers, and agricultural laborers.

The first mass protest in the spring of 2006 took place in Los Angeles on March 25. Tens of thousands in other large cities, such as Chicago, New York, and Detroit, quickly followed suit. Perhaps the largest rally was held on the National Mall in Washington, D.C., on April 10 of that year. It included prominent speakers such as U.S. senator Edward Kennedy (1932–) of Massachusetts and prominent Hispanic American leaders. Many speeches were delivered in Spanish and marchers waved Mexican flags. Some protestors called for a *Reconquista,* or taking back of land the United States acquired in the treaty that ended the Mexican-American War.

Protestors objected to the passing of a resolution in the U.S. House of Representatives regarding immigration reform. The resolution ignored the wishes of the administration of U.S. president George W. Bush (1946–; served 2001–). Bush called for a guest worker program and a legalization process for illegal immigrants already living and working on U.S. soil. President Bush and others believed that deporting illegal immigrants was inhumane and would drastically impair the economy. Instead, the House language, championed by U.S. representative James Sensenbrenner (1943–), a Republican from Wisconsin, included requirements for a massive fence along the southern U.S. border and an increased border security presence. In September 2006 Congress passed a bill authorizing construction of part of the proposed fence, but did not provide sufficient funds at the time to accomplish the task.

About a half million Latino workers and immigrants march in downtown Los Angeles on March 25, 2006, to protest against an anti-immigrant federal bill that would instantly criminalize millions of undocumented aliens. © GENE BLEVINS/LA DAILY NEWS/CORBIS.

The U.S. Senate considered a compromise bill of its own that would have allowed illegal immigrants two years to begin the citizenship process, but the bill failed to pass.

The continuing lure

Hispanics continued to flock to the United States in search of opportunities that were not available in other nations. The high rate of immigration and the high birth rate among Hispanic immigrants made this group the fastest growing minority in the United States. According to the 2000 U.S. Census report, in the 1990s the Hispanic population grew sixty times faster than the total population of the nation. The census indicated that Hispanic Americans had become the nation's largest minority, slightly passing African Americans.

As the immigration debate of 2006 indicated, many non-Hispanic citizens of the United States resented the perception of illegal immigrants avoiding the law, the seeming lack of enthusiasm by Hispanics for assimilating into American culture by learning and speaking English, and the apparent willingness of U.S. lawmakers and politicians to not strictly enforce the immigration laws in hopes of attracting votes from the growing Hispanic population. Still others believed that illegal immigrants should be granted amnesty and a chance to participate in the process of becoming a legal citizen of the United States.

Use of the English language, historically an important issue, was no less so in the early twenty-first century. Twenty-five states passed legislation making English the official language of those states. A movement was building to pass a constitutional amendment making English the official national language, a symbolic gesture aimed against immigrants. Yet this language issue was merely a sidelight of the overall economic issues that were central to the illegal immigration debate.

The Hispanic American experience in the United States has long been one of struggle and triumph, and it continued to evolve into the twenty-first century. While issues such as use of the English language, educational opportunity, access to healthcare, proposed immigration laws, and strong racial and ethnic prejudices continued to pose difficult questions to be resolved by government and citizens alike, Hispanic Americans had broken barriers to personal success and contributed richly to American politics, business, and culture.

For More Information

BOOKS

Aguirre, Adalberto, and Jonathan Turner. *American Ethnicity: The Dynamics and Consequences of Discrimination.* Boston: McGraw-Hill, 1998.

Bruns, Roger. *Cesar Chavez: A Biography.* Westport, CT: Greenwood Press, 2005.

Dalton, Frederick J. *The Moral Vision of Cesar Chavez.* Maryknoll, NY: Orbis, 2003.

Eisenhower, John S. D. *So Far from God: The U.S. War with Mexico, 1846–1848.* Norman: University of Oklahoma Press, 2000.

Ferriss, Susan, and Ricardo Sandoval. *The Fight in the Fields: Cesar Chavez and the Farmworkers Movement.* New York: Harvest/HBJ, 1998.

Libal, Autumn. *Cuban Americans: Exiles from an Island Home.* Philadelphia: Mason Crest Publishers, 2006.

Meier, Matt, and Feliciano Ribera. *Mexican Americans, American Mexicans: From Conquistadors to Chicanos.* New York: Hill and Wang, 1994.

Shusta, Robert, Deena Levine, Philip R. Harris, and Herbert Wong. *Multicultural Law Enforcement.* Englewood, NJ: Prentice-Hall, 1995.

WEB SITES

Mexican American Legal Defense and Educational Fund. http://www.maldef.org (accessed on November 29, 2006).

National Council of La Raza. http://nclr.org (accessed on November 29, 2006).

United Farm Workers. http://www.ufw.org (accessed on November 29, 2006).

22

Apartheid of South Africa

Until the discovery of diamonds in 1867, Southern Africa had an agricultural economy (main income is by farming). Then the discovery of gold came in 1886. The newfound wealth drew broad interest from foreign investors and laid the foundations of future apartheid (a formal policy of racial separation and discrimination (treating some differently than others or favoring one social group over another based on prejudices). The struggle for land at the turn of the twentieth century resulted in the creation of the Union of South Africa as part of the British Empire. The South African colonial government (government ruled by a foreign nation) passed laws after 1909 restricting land ownership and residence for all people of non-European ancestry. Later in the twentieth century, following two world wars, the racial tension in the country reached a dangerous level. The government of the nation of South Africa responded by officially adopting the policy known as apartheid. Through apartheid, South Africa became a key example of racial prejudice in the twentieth century.

Apartheid, which means "separateness" in Afrikaans, one of eleven official languages spoken in South Africa, began in 1948 and remained in effect for over forty-two years. However, not everyone supported the government and its policy. Within South Africa, the struggle for liberation began with peaceful protests but soon escalated into a campaign of defiance against unjust laws driven by racial prejudices (a negative attitude towards others of a particular physical trait, such as skin color, based on a prejudgment about those individuals with no prior knowledge or experience) and growing oppression. The African National Congress, an organization established in 1912 to promote the rights of black Africans, and other groups opposed to apartheid formed the Congress of the People in 1955 and adopted The Freedom Charter that declared the goals of a future democratic government they sought in South Africa. Decades of violence followed before apartheid was dismantled in the face

WORDS TO KNOW

apartheid: A policy of racial separation and discrimination.

boycott: To refuse to have dealings with a person, store, or organization in order to express disapproval.

discrimination: To treat differently or favor one group over another on a basis other than individual merit.

racism: A belief that race primarily determines human behavioral traits and capabilities and that

racial differences produce an assumed superiority of a particular race.

reservation: A tract of public land set aside for a special purpose.

segregation: Using laws or social customs to separate certain social groups, such as peoples distinguished by skin color—whites and blacks.

of international demands. The Republic of South Africa ended the twentieth century without the burden of official apartheid. However, it was faced with an overwhelming task of reconciling and uniting all people equally in South Africa.

Colonial conquest

White Europeans first permanently settled in southern Africa in the mid-seventeenth century when the Dutch established a colony on the southwestern tip of the continent called the Cape. They became known as Afrikaners, a distinct ethnic group in South Africa composed of Dutch colonists and other early settlers from Europe. Afrikaners spoke Afrikaans, which was closely related to the Dutch language.

Beginning in the 1830s some of their descendants, primarily farmers, moved into remote areas to escape from expanding British rule and establish new settlements. Those who moved called themselves Boers (the Dutch word for "farmers"). They established two republics, Transvaal in the far north and the Orange Free State in the middle of the territory. Early in the nineteenth century, the Cape Province in the south became an English colony, along with the province of Natal on the western coastline. Europe's colonial powers expressed a renewed interest in southern Africa in the nineteenth century when diamonds were discovered at Kimberley and gold was found at Witwatersrand. By the turn of the twentieth century, most African tribes had lost their land through

Signs like this are an example of the extreme racism that blacks had to endure under apartheid. GETTY IMAGES.

conquest or settlement. The white colonizers had reduced the status of native people to that of servants and tenants on land that had once been their own.

In 1899, the English sought to establish dominance in the South African region. They went to war against the Boers. The Anglo-Boer War (1899–1902) resulted in an English victory over the Boers. However, the English failed in their attempts to attract large numbers of English immigrants to populate the land. The Boers, determined to preserve their own culture and language, retained a deep hostility toward their English rulers. Less than five years after the war ended, the Boer republics were largely self-governing once again. As a result, England granted the

The Colour Bar

A "colour bar" was used in South Africa to determine a person's rights within the law. Racial prejudice divided people into color groups based on the distinction between whites and non-whites. Non-whites were further divided into black, Indian, and colored designations. Legally, the color groups were supposed to be categorized into specific groupings.

The white population was of European descent. Most came from the Netherlands (Dutch), but large numbers of immigrants also came from France and Germany. They were called Afrikaners and their population was concentrated in the Western and Eastern Cape province and in Natal on the Eastern coast.

Native Africans, or blacks (also called Bantu), made up the largest population of people. Blacks were further divided into groups based on language and cultural backgrounds. Examples included the Swazi, Venda, Tswana, and the Zulu.

The Indian designation in the color bar mostly included those of Indian ancestry, but also included all people of Asian descent. Most Indians were originally brought from India to South Africa to work on sugarcane plantations. The largest Indian population lived in the province of Natal.

Colored South Africans were people of mixed race. They were descendants of the first Dutch settlers and the native population of South Africa, called the Khoisan. The Khoisan had been militarily defeated and absorbed early in South African history by black migration from the north and white migration from the south. The races further mixed when Malayans and East Indians were brought to South Africa in the eighteenth century. Colored people had their own cultural heritage and generally lived in the Cape region.

colony independence within the British Empire and established the Union of South Africa in 1910. Dutch was recognized along with English as an official language of the Union. Elections placed former Boer generals in high government positions. Two main political parties emerged, and both were opposed to racial equality for native Africans. Most Boers supported the Nationalist (or National) Party. Most English-speakers and industrial employers supported the Unionist (or United) Party in the new government.

Although the state government was now centralized, the provinces remained deeply segregated because of racial prejudice. People were divided into groups based on the distinction between whites and non-whites in the so-called "colour bar" (see box). Non-whites were not allowed to vote outside of the Cape Province. Therefore, the rights of the black majority, representing over 70 percent of the population in South Africa, were not considered nationally. The white minority introduced a group of laws in order to enforce the policy of racial separation.

The Native Land Act set aside reservations for native Africans. © DAVID TURNLEY/CORBIS.

The Mine and Works Act of 1911 secured the best jobs for white workers by limiting blacks to menial work, such as field laborers. This policy guaranteed a steady supply of cheap labor for mining and the construction of railways and roads used for industrial transportation. An endless need for laborers existed for the construction of buildings, commerce, and in domestic services, such as housemaids, for the rapidly expanding economy. Asian workers provided another source of cheap labor for industry in South Africa. Earlier in 1860, East Indian slaves had been introduced to southern Africa to work on the sugarcane plantations. In much the same way, Chinese laborers had been imported in 1904 to work in the gold mines in South Africa.

In 1913, the South African government established the Native Land Act. The act set aside reservations (a tract of public land set aside for a special purpose, such as placement of an undesired social group away from mainstream society) for native Africans. Their land ownership was restricted to these reserves that covered approximately 13 percent of the country. The government's land policy forcibly uprooted communities and set in place a migrant (worker who moves from job to job as they become available) labor system. Because the land could not support everyone, some men sought work in the mines located outside their reservations. Wives and children were not allowed to accompany the men. So families would often be separated for most of the year. In 1913, the government also passed the Immigrants Regulation Act, which prohibited Indians from moving out of the province in which they were born. Severely limited social, political, and legal rights finally prompted non-whites to organize and work toward racial equality.

The African National Congress

At the turn of the century, several movements formed to promote equal rights for all citizens in South Africa. Most were fairly conservative groups that urged people to work within the political system to effect change. In 1902, the African Political Organization (APO) was founded. Though it was open to all races, it had a predominantly non-white membership that failed to gain wide support because of a general lack of concern for non-whites among the whites.

After years of petitions and protest meetings against segregation, several hundred prominent Africans including John Dube (1871–1946) joined together to form the South African Native National Congress, later renamed the African National Congress (ANC). Dube was the organization's president for its first years until 1917. The ANC brought together all the native provinces at its inaugural (first) conference in 1912. At first, the ANC was politically conservative and attempted to work within the existing government system. Change seemed hopeful because the policy of segregation was never fully accepted throughout the country.

However, progress against segregation at the political level was severely disrupted with the outbreak of World War I (1914–18). South Africa joined the war effort on the side of the British. By the time the war ended, so had the passive acceptance of racism (prejudice against people of a particular physical trait, such as skin color, based on a belief that the physical trait primarily determines human behavior and individual capabilities) by black Africans. Fighting as allies with democracies in the world such as the United States highlighted the inequalities of segregationist policies. They formed associations to promote religious, political, industrial, and social advancement for native Africans.

In 1919, Unionist Party leader Jan Smuts (1870–1950) became prime minister (a position similar to that of president) of South Africa. An Afrikaner who was hailed as an international statesman, Smuts represented South Africa at the Paris Peace Conference in 1919. At that time, he also played a leading role in establishing the League of Nations. The League was an international organization whose purpose was to prevent future world wars and improve global welfare. However, the League was given far less power than Smuts had argued for and was largely replaced by the stronger United Nations following World War II (1939–45).

After decades of political fighting, Smuts's goal was to present South Africa as a united nation, ready to take its rightful place as a respectable member of the international community. Smuts's Unionist Party began to move away from the enforcement of segregationist laws, despite a deep conviction on his part about the virtues of European superiority. Smuts would later write to a friend in a letter that was printed in Martin Meredith's 1988 book *In the Name of Apartheid: South Africa in the Postwar Period,* "I am a South African European proud of our heritage and proud of the clean European society we have built up in South Africa, and which I am determined not to see lost in the black pool of Africa."

In 1920 Smuts passed the Native Affairs Act, which focused on the question of separate political representation for blacks and whites in South Africa. The act brought the issue of racism back to the center of attention in the country. It was a controversial act that deeply divided people on both sides of the issue. Those in favor saw it as a great step forward in race relations. Those opposed saw it as a barrier to their goal of apartheid. In order for apartheid to work, political separation of the races, not just physical segregation of people, was necessary.

The next decade saw a sharp rise in black political awareness and an increase in the number of protests aimed at political and economic reforms in South Africa. Africans created the South African Council of Non-European Trade Unions. Among other things, they demanded equal pay for equal work. Labor strikes occurred until 1926, when the Masters and Servants Amendment Act removed Africans' right to strike in most situations.

Between 1921 and 1936, thousands of black African men moved from reservations to towns and cities seeking employment. Urban areas were officially reserved for white populations. Native Africans were permitted only as long as they served a specific need, such as work for white Africans. They were allowed to temporarily live in camps on the outskirts of town, but their real homes were still officially listed on the reservations. Due to the growing number of blacks in the cities as well as the increase in political protests, the white minority sought more stringent controls. Officials set up a legal system that regulated entry into urban areas by requiring all black African men to carry a pass book, or passport, at all times. Police raids were regularly organized to ensure the pass laws were maintained. The raids often turned violent. Those caught without valid passes were arrested and sent to jail. Eventually, they would be sent back into the rural areas away from white-only areas.

Not directly represented in government, Africans' interests were handled by the Native Affairs Department (NAD). The NAD depended entirely on African taxes that paid for the expenses of education, social services, and economic development for native people. In 1936, African voters in the Cape Province lost their right to vote, a right they had held for more than eighty years. The reason given was that their right to vote could eventually lead to demands for the African vote in the northern territories. In exchange for losing their vote in general elections, Cape Province Africans were allowed to vote for selected white delegates who were suppose to represent them before the South African government. Liberty for native Africans was not progressing well and was about to get worse as the world faced another world war.

The world at war

The South African population was divided over entering World War II in late 1939 when war first broke out. Racial and political issues brewing at home caused many to favor neutrality (not choosing a side). Afrikaners in the Nationalist Party considered it another of England's wars that did not concern them. They also questioned opposing Germany, which seemed sympathetic to Afrikaner nationalism. On the other hand, Smuts's allegiance to England, along with his international leadership ambitions, supported South African participation in the war. The country had the most advanced economy in Africa with its vast mineral wealth. In addition, its control of the Cape shipping routes made it strategically important in the war effort. Smuts and his Unionist Party won out and South Africa went to war.

Native Africans' efforts for greater participation in political life were somewhat interrupted by the war. Thousands who were hoping to escape the poverty of the reserves flooded into urban areas. They were drawn to

South African president and activist Nelson Mandela's words and actions helped put a face on apartheid. © REUTERS/CORBIS.

the cities by the booming wartime industries, but their presence only increased the existing tensions. Authorities extended pass laws controlling African movement in an attempt to gain control of Africans entering into urban areas. Despite their efforts, large camps grew outside such cities as Johannesburg and Durban. Activist movements grew inside these settlements. The movements' members became increasingly critical of the government because of their poor living conditions. By the mid-1940s, nearly half of all Africans employed in commerce and private industry had joined labor trade unions.

In 1943, the ANC drew up a Charter of Rights to increase political pressure on the government. They proposed a fair distribution of land, voting rights for non-whites, and full political participation. Young members of the ANC, including future South African president Nelson Mandela (1918—), formed an African Youth League. They advocated non-cooperation with the war effort in order to bring about social change in South Africa. At the same time, the South African Indians (SAI) elected a new group of leaders who promised to organize the Indian community to resist the government's policy of segregation.

Postwar labor unrest

African trade unions became more aggressive as a series of strikes broke out. Emergency war regulations passed in 1943 had ended the legal right of Africans to strike in any and all circumstances. Despite the law, tens of thousands of mineworkers went on strike over wages and poor working conditions on April 12, 1946. It was the largest labor protest in South Africa's history to date. The government's response to the strike was severe. Armed police were called in to break down the miners' resistance. Black and Indian tobacco workers marched in support of the striking miners. White citizens were alarmed as the media dwelt on the dangers of allowing such demonstrations. The leaders of the mineworkers' strike were arrested and five days after it had all begun, the strike was over. The strike had failed in its goals but the very attempt showed to whites and non-whites alike how non-white workers were improving their ability to organize and act collectively. In 1947, the ANC and the SAI made a joint declaration of unity in demanding political and social rights.

Debates over race relations

Prime Minister Smuts was facing extreme pressure within South Africa from white citizens who were protesting against the rights of the Indian population to buy land. Indians, on the other hand, were demanding more political and social rights. Smuts's solution was to offer Indians limited representation in government while restricting their rights on how much and where they could purchase land. This solution did not satisfy either side and the conflict soon became an international issue when it was placed on the agenda of the United Nations (UN) General Assembly in October 1946. Smuts argued that it was an internal matter to be dealt with by South Africa alone, but the Assembly passed a resolution condemning South Africa's Indian policy. Europe's colonial powers were leaning toward the idea of racial equality. The UN resolution served to focus the world's attention on South Africa's racial practices.

Smuts returned home politically weakened. The Unionist Party government took steps to move away from strictly enforcing segregation-ist laws. They set up the Fagan Commission in 1948, which recommended segregation in the cities be gradually ended. The commission proposed a system that moved toward the races being equal, but still separate (see Jim Crow chapter 17) under South African government rule. In response, Unionists argued that territorial separation of the races was impractical in the mid-twentieth century and Africans should be accepted as a permanent part of the urban population.

The Nationalist Party responded with a commission of its own. The resulting Sauer Commission created in 1948 proposed a system of separate development between the races. It gave the name apartheid to the system. The Nationalist Party solution called for total racial segregation, giving native Africans their own separate states with political independence from white South Africa. The Nationalists argued that the reservations already in place were the proper homelands of native Africans and that social and cultural differences should keep the races separate whenever possible.

Divide and rule

The general election of 1948 was set for May. It was to determine the direction South Africa would take as a nation following World War II. Europe's colonial powers had begun to dismantle discriminatory laws. But the war had only increased the existing tensions between the white minority and the black majority in South Africa. The Nationalist Party, campaigning on its policy of apartheid, won an election victory over Smuts's Unionist Party. They set about to establish their own version of racial discrimination, which would maintain its hold on the country for decades to come.

The Nationalists quickly put laws in place to impose apartheid. The Population Registration Act of 1950 required all citizens to register with the government as white, Indian, Colored, or Bantu (the government term for Africans). The Bantu group was further broken down into groups based on language. Each was assigned a homeland, or bantustan. For example, those who spoke Zulu would be assigned a different homeland than those who spoke Sotho, creating two smaller divisions. The fact that whites often spoke different languages was not considered and assured them majority status. The government established complex criteria to determine racial groupings and created a board to rule in questionable cases. This separation by race sometimes resulted in members of the same family being classified in different racial groups and assigned different homelands. The Nationalist Party quickly passed legislation in 1948 enforcing racial purity by outlawing interracial marriages.

Apartheid's purpose was to guarantee political and economic privilege for the English-speaking minority. Not everyone in politics agreed with the policies of the new government, but resistance was quickly

The Reservation of Separate Amenities Act of 1953 created separate beaches, buses, hospitals, schools, and libraries for the races. GETTY IMAGES.

crushed. For example, the Communist Party in South Africa attempted political resistance to apartheid and was banned in 1950.

The Group Areas Act was passed on April 27, 1950, and became the backbone of apartheid. The act formally separated racial groups into separate states throughout South Africa. Around 87 percent of the country was reserved for whites, Indians, and Coloureds. The remaining land was assigned to the Bantu, who comprised 60 percent of the population. Scattered acres of land, mostly in the north and east, made up the ten designated Bantu homelands. Most of these homelands contained barren land that did not hold any of the wealth or key resources of the country, such as the gold and diamond mines. In 1951, the Bantu Authorities Act created separate government structures for native Africans in each of the homelands. The act laid the foundation for Africans to be declared citizens of Bantustans, not of South Africa, even if they physically lived in other parts of South Africa.

The Reservation of Separate Amenities Act of 1953 created separate beaches, buses, hospitals, schools, and libraries for the races. It prohibited people of different races from using the same public amenities, such as restrooms and drinking fountains. Non-whites were prohibited from entering white areas without specific permission and a pass. A pass was only issued to a person with approved work. Spouses and children were not included in the passes, which meant families remained separated if living outside the homeland. Those without a pass were arrested, tried, and deported to their homeland, where poverty was widespread. Over the decades, millions of Bantus were arrested under laws controlling their movement.

Resistance builds

Non-whites tried unsuccessfully for decades to end segregationist policies in South Africa. When the Nationalist Party implemented its policy of apartheid through government laws, it became apparent to non-whites that increased resistance was necessary. In the 1950s, several opposition groups, including the Coloured People's Congress, the SAI, and the white Congress of Democrats came together under the leadership of the ANC. They joined in a campaign of defiance over unjust laws. For the first time they advocated open resistance to unfair practices in the form of strikes, work stoppages, and protest marches.

When the government passed the Bantu Education Act (see box) in 1953, a boycott (an organized effort to not buy certain products or use certain services in order to express disapproval with an organization) of schools resulted. Not all whites were in favor of the apartheid system. In 1955, the Black Sash, an organization of white women wearing black sashes in protest of social injustice against black Africans, formed a movement to promote nonviolent resistance to apartheid. In the mid-1950s, the government extended the pass laws. Now every Bantu over sixteen years of age was required to carry a passport in order to visit, live, or work in a white area. On August 9, 1956, over twenty thousand women marched on government offices and demanded to see the prime minister. He refused to meet with them and, despite nationwide protests, the pass laws were extended. The protest sparked an annual event known as South Africa Women's Day. Referred to a National Women's Day, in 1994 the date of August 9 was proclaimed one of seven South African holidays that is celebrated every year.

The Congress of the People

Those opposed to the policies and practices of apartheid gathered outside Johannesburg on June 25, 1955, for a Congress of the People. Over three thousand delegates assembled from various parties and organizations. Their purpose was to create an alliance and draft a freedom charter for the

Bantu Education Act

Until apartheid, African schools were divided into four categories. These included private schools run independently by religious communities, mission schools founded by church organizations but funded and controlled by the state, tribal schools operated by African communities, and government schools.

The Bantu Education Act of 1953 brought all native African schooling under the administrative control of the government. It effectively ended all other types. This allowed the Education Ministry to determine budgets, examination requirements, and curriculum, or the course of study for Bantu children. The ministry also controlled building location and maintenance, fees, teacher assignments, and pupil-teacher ratios.

The apartheid government's educational policy was a key example of racial discrimination. The potential of a student was not based on individual merits, but rather on membership in a racial group which had been assigned certain characteristics. The Bantu Education Act was designed to insure African children received the type of education that the ministry had decided was best suited for unskilled labor. Bantu education therefore kept black children at a very low standard. Students were assigned a curriculum that included such subjects as dish washing and the weeding of flower beds.

By the 1970s, the pupil-teacher ratio for Bantu education was around sixty to one. In schools for whites it was around twenty to one. School attendance for whites was mandatory but it was optional for Africans at the primary level. African students who went on to secondary school were required to pay for their own education, textbooks, and supplies. Salaries for teachers in Bantu education were about half that of white teachers with the same qualifications. Many Bantu teachers were forced to work a double shift because of the lack of faculty and facilities. Because of the general poverty of native African homes and their distance from schools, the student dropout rate in Bantu education was very high. After 1959, higher education for Bantu was available only in separate colleges and universities.

democratic South Africa of the future. The following day, the Congress of the People met and adopted The Freedom Charter (see box).

The Nationalist Party reacted to The Freedom Charter by arresting 156 individuals and charging them with treason (attempting to overthrow the government). Ninety-one blacks were actually taken to court in 1958 in what became known as the Treason Trials. The ANC responded with boycotts and strikes. By the time the trial ended in 1961, international attention was once again centered on the racial situation in South Africa. All of the defendants were found not guilty. In 1962, the UN established the Special Committee against Apartheid to monitor racial policies in the country and to promote an international campaign to support the end of apartheid.

The Freedom Charter of 1955

In June 1955, the Congress of the People, consisting of over three thousand delegates opposed to apartheid, assembled to draft a freedom charter for a future democratic South Africa. They created The Freedom Charter. The preamble to The Freedom Charter states, "We, the people of South Africa, declare for all our country and the world to know: That South Africa belongs to all who live in it, black and white, and that no government can justly claim authority unless it is based on the will of the people...And we pledge ourselves to strive together, sparing nothing of our strength and courage, until the democratic changes here set out have been won."

The Charter demanded:

The People shall govern.

All national groups shall have equal rights.

The People shall share in the country's wealth.

The land shall be shared among those who work it.

All shall be equal before the law.

All shall enjoy equal human rights.

There shall be work and security.

The doors of learning and culture shall be opened.

There shall be houses, security and comfort.

There shall be peace and friendship.

A new nation struggles

South Africa maintained ties with the British monarchy (the king or queen who holds supreme governmental power) until it acquired independence as the Republic of South Africa on May 31, 1961. The continuing turmoil within the country alarmed foreign economic investors, who were concerned that the new government was about to fall. If black resistance continued unrestricted, the Nationalist Party leaders feared these investors would take their money out of South Africa.

Demonstrations against the hated pass laws grew violent on March 21, 1960. A large group of blacks congregated outside a police station in Sharpeville. The protesters were not carrying their pass books. They intended to make a statement by offering themselves up for arrest. Police grew intimidated by the crowd and opened fire, killing 69 and injuring 186. The event became known as the Sharpeville Massacre and led to the banning of the ANC and other black organizations by the government. In response, the ANC switched its tactics from nonviolent to violent resistance, which would prove much more effective against apartheid policies through the next thirty years.

Dead bodies scattered on the ground in the aftermath of the Sharpeville Massacre in 1960. © HULTON-DEUTSCH COLLECTION/ CORBIS.

In 1961, Nelson Mandela and others from the ANC formed Umkhonto we Sizwe, which is translated as The Spear of the Nation. The underground movement began a campaign of sabotage (to secretly disrupt activities) against the government. In 1963, Mandela and seven other leaders of the underground resistance were arrested and sentenced to life in prison.

An isolated nation

During the 1970s, public opposition increased as new trade unions, women's groups, and youth and student organizations united in their efforts against apartheid. In 1976, students in Soweto went on strike when the government ruled Afrikaans would be the new official language in African schools. Police responded with gunfire to rock-throwing students who gathered in protest. Before the violence ended, twenty-three students were officially listed as dead, but accounts of witnesses say hundreds more were killed in what became known as the Soweto Riots. It was a defining moment in the future of apartheid by increasing world attention on South Africa's racial policies.

Police dragging a protestor away at an anti-apartheid demonstration. © WILLIAM CAMPBELL/SYGMA/CORBIS.

The UN had been monitoring the situation in South Africa since 1946, but not until the 1976 Soweto Riots did it have enough international support to establish apartheid as a crime. The International Criminal Court was formed to prohibit any other state from adopting the practices of racial domination and oppression practiced in South Africa. International action against South Africa included oil and arms embargos (stoppages), sports and cultural boycotts, and a campaign to release political prisoners opposed to the system. South Africa was culturally and economically isolated from the rest of the world.

Violence prevails

In order to enforce apartheid, the South African government had dramatically increased its military spending. Authorities were allowed to detain opponents of apartheid indefinitely. Many died in custody or were deported. Agents of the government assassinated leaders of the liberation movement in a further effort to end the opposition. Armed resistance by The Spear of the Nation increased in response. It directed attacks on police stations, military bases, power stations, and government offices used to administer apartheid. The government responded by declaring a state of emergency in 1985, effectively turning South Africa into a police state (police are given greater powers to suppress activities that conflict with governmental policy).

Between 1985 and 1988, the country endured its most violent times. Many white South Africans fled the country for fear of being attacked on the streets or in their homes. The need for change was now evident to everyone. Archbishop Desmond Tutu (1932–), an Anglican cleric (a priest of the Church of England) from Cape Town, led the newly formed United Democratic Front (UDF), which called for the elimination of apartheid.

Apartheid ends

In 1989, F. W. de Klerk (1936–; served 1989–94) was elected president of South Africa. In his opening address to parliament, de Klerk announced he would overturn discriminatory laws and lift the ban on the ANC and others. After forty-two years, apartheid was officially ended. De Klerk released political prisoners of apartheid, including Nelson Mandela, who had served twenty-eight years of his life sentence. Over the next few years, the laws of apartheid were repealed, one at a time. The last whites-only vote was held in 1992. The vote gave the government the authority to negotiate a multi-racial government transition and a new constitution. Elections were called and took place peacefully in 1994 with the ANC winning all but two provinces. Nelson Mandela became the new president of South Africa. Those who still sympathized with apartheid policies were largely resigned by now to the changes in South African society.

Mandela and de Klerk were awarded the Nobel Peace Prize in 1993 for their peaceful termination of the apartheid regime and their work to promote a new democratic (a political system built on social equality in which citizens hold the nation's supreme power) South Africa. In addition to its issues of racial equality, the apartheid years left the country with serious economic problems and a high crime rate; the new government had serious work to do. The Promotion of National Unity and Reconciliation Act of 1995 set up the Truth and Reconciliation Commission to help South Africa transition to a full and free democracy by exposing all the

Nelson Mandela, left, and F. W. de Klerk were awarded the Nobel Peace Prize in 1993 for their peaceful termination of the apartheid regime and their work to promote a new democratic South Africa. © REUTERS/CORBIS.

atrocities that occurred during the apartheid era. Chaired by Archbishop Tutu, the commission began hearings to hear about particular injustices in April 1996. The committees of Human Rights Violations, Reparations (compensation), and Amnesty (pardon) heard thousands testify on life under apartheid. With the power to grant amnesty (official forgiveness), it was hoped this path would heal wounds more quickly, but its effectiveness in actually bringing about reconciliation between blacks and whites proved limited. South Africa entered the twenty-first century as an ethnically diverse nation steadily progressing toward democratization after years of discrimination.

For More Information

BOOKS

Anti-Apartheid Movement. *Racism and Apartheid in Southern Africa: South Africa and Namibia.* Paris: UNESCO Press, 1974.

Desai, Ashwin. *We Are the Poors: Community Struggles in Post-Apartheid South Africa.* New York: Monthly Review Press, 2002.

Dubow, Saul. *Racial Segregation and the Origins of Apartheid in South Africa, 1919–36.* London: Macmillan Press Ltd., 1989.

Finnegan, William. *Crossing the Line: A Year in the Land of Apartheid.* New York: Persea Books, 2006.

Louw, P. Eric. *The Rise, Fall, and Legacy of Apartheid.* Westport, CT: Praeger Publishers, 2004.

Meredith, Martin. *In the Name of Apartheid: South Africa in the Postwar Period.* London: Hamish Hamilton Ltd., 1988.

Suttner, Raymond, and Jeremy Cronin. *30 Years of the Freedom Charter.* Johannesburg: Ravan Press, 1986.

WEB SITES

African National Congress: South Africa's National Liberation Movement. http://www.anc.org.za/ (accessed on November 29, 2006).

Apartheid Museum. http://www.apartheidmuseum.org (accessed on November 29, 2006).

Black Sash: Making Human Rights Real. http://www.blacksash.org.za/ (accessed on November 29, 2006).

Where to Learn More

The following list focuses on works written for readers of middle school and high school age. Books aimed at adult readers have been included when they are especially important in providing information or analysis that would otherwise be unavailable.

Books

Aguirre, Adalberto, and Jonathan Turner. *American Ethnicity: The Dynamics and Consequences of Discrimination.* Boston: McGraw-Hill, 1998.

Allport, Gordon W. *The Nature of Prejudice.* Reading, MA: Addison-Wesley Publishing Co., 1979.

Altman, Linda J. *Hitler's Rise to Power and the Holocaust.* Berkeley Heights, NJ: Enslow, 2003.

Baird, Robert M., and Stuart E. Rosenbaum, eds. *Bigotry, Prejudice, and Hatred: Definitions, Causes and Solutions.* Buffalo, NY: Prometheus Books, 1992.

Bell-Fialkoff, Andrew. *Ethnic Cleansing.* New York: Palgrave Macmillan, 1999.

Brown, Mildred, and Chloe Ann Rounsley. *True Selves: Understanding Transsexualism: For Families, Friends, Coworkers and Helping Professionals.* San Francisco, CA: Jossey-Bass, 2003.

Brown, Rupert. *Prejudice: Its Social Psychology.* Cambridge, MA: Blackwell, 1995.

Burgan, Michael. *The Japanese American Internment: Civil Liberties Denied.* Minneapolis, MN: Compass Point Books, 2006.

Chafe, William H. *Remembering Jim Crow: African Americans Tell About Life in the Segregated South.* New York: W.W. Norton, 2001.

Chessum, Lorna. *From Immigrants to Ethnic Minority: Making a Black Community in Britain.* Burlington, VT: Ashgate, 2000.

Davidson, Tish. *Prejudice.* New York: Franklin Watts, 2003.

Dawa, Norbu. *Culture and the Politics of Third World Nationalism.* New York: Routledge, 1992.

Dovidio, John F., Peter Glick, and Laurie A. Rudman, eds. *On the Nature of Prejudice: Fifty Years After Allport.* Malden, MA: Blackwell Publishing, 2005.

Duckitt, John. *The Social Psychology of Prejudice.* New York: Praeger, 1992.

Ferriss, Susan, and Ricardo Sandoval. *The Fight in the Fields: Cesar Chavez and the Farmworkers Movement.* New York: Harvest/HBJ, 1998.

Flexner, Eleanor, and Ellen Fitzpatrick. *Century of Struggle: The Woman's Rights Movement in the United States.* Cambridge, MA: Belknap Press, 1996.

Fonseca, Isabel. *Bury Me Standing: The Gypsies and Their Journey.* New York: Knopf, 1995.

Frank, Anne. *The Diary of a Young Girl.* New York: Doubleday, 1995.

Friedan, Betty. *The Feminine Mystique.* New York: Norton, 2001.

Friend, Marilyn. *Special Education: Contemporary Perspectives for School Professionals.* New York: Pearson Education, Inc., 2005.

Gilbert, Martin. *The Holocaust: A History of the Jews of Europe during the Second World War.* New York: Holt, Rinehart, and Winston, 1986.

Greer, Germaine. *The Female Eunuch.* New York: Farrar, Straus and Giroux, 2001.

Hirsch, H.N. *The Future of Gay Rights in America.* New York: Routledge, 2005.

Hobsbawm, E. J. *Nations and Nationalism Since 1780.* 2nd Ed. New York: Cambridge University Press, 1992.

Jones, James M. *Prejudice and Racism.* New York: McGraw-Hill, 1997.

Jones-Brown, Delores. *Race, Crime, and Punishment.* Philadelphia: Chelsea House, 2000.

Kedourie, Elie. *Nationalism.* 4th Ed. Cambridge, MA: Blackwell, 1993.

Kent, Deborah. *Cornerstones of Freedom: The Disability Rights Movement.* New York: Children's Press, 1996.

Lattarulo, Lori A. *Disability, Society, and the Individual.* Gaithersburg, MD: Aspen Publishers, 2001.

LeGates, Marlene. *In Their Time: A History of Feminism in Western Society.* New York: Routledge, 2001.

Lesch, Ann M., and Dan Tschirgi. *Origins and Development of the Arab-Israeli Conflict.* Westport, CT: Greenwood Press, 1998.

Levi, Primo. *Survival in Auschwitz: The Nazi Assault on Humanity.* New York: Collier Books, 1993.

Levinson, David. *Ethnic Groups Worldwide: A Ready Reference Handbook.* Phoenix, AZ: The Oryx Press, 1998.

Lieberman, Benjamin. *Terrible Fate: Ethnic Cleansing in the Making of Modern Europe.* New York: Ivan R. Dee, 2006.

Louw, P. Eric. *The Rise, Fall, and Legacy of Apartheid.* Westport, CT: Praeger Publishers, 2004.

MacMaster, Neil. *Racism in Europe, 1870–2000.* New York: Palgrave, 2001.

Manzo, Kathryn A. *Creating Boundaries: The Politics of Race and Nation.* Boulder, CO: L. Rienner, 1996.

Matthiessen, Peter. *In the Spirit of Crazy Horse.* New York: Penguin Books, 1992.

Meier, Matt, and Feliciano Ribera. *Mexican Americans, American Mexicans: From Conquistadors to Chicanos.* New York: Hill and Wang, 1994.

Mencken, H. L. *Prejudices.* Washington, DC: Ross and Perry, Inc., 2002.

Molnar, Stephen. *Human Variation: Races, Types, and Ethnic Groups.* 2nd Ed. Englewood Cliffs, NJ: Prentice-Hall, 1992.

Monague, Ashley. *Man's Most Dangerous Myth: The Fallacy of Race.* 6th Edition. Walnut Creek, CA: AltaMira Press, 1997.

Muse, Daphne, ed. *Prejudice: Stories About Hate, Ignorance, Revelation, and Transformation.* New York: Hyperion Books for Children, 1995.

Naimark, Norman M. *Ethnic Cleansing in Twentieth-Century Europe.* Cambridge, MA: Harvard University Press, 2002.

Packard, Jerrold. *American Nightmare: The History of Jim Crow.* New York: St. Martin's Press, 2002.

Perlmutter, Philip. *Divided We Fall: A History of Ethnic, Religious, and Racial Prejudice in America.* Ames: Iowa State University Press, 1992.

Plous, Scott, ed. *Understanding Prejudice and Discrimination.* Boston: McGraw-Hill, 2003.

Richards, David A. J. *The Case for Gay Rights.* Lawrence: University of Kansas Press, 2005.

Rudolph, Joseph R., Jr., ed. *Encyclopedia of Modern Ethnic Conflicts.* Westport, CN: Greenwood Press, 2003.

Scherrer, Christian P. *Genocide and Crisis in Central Africa: Conflict Roots, Mass Violence, and Regional War.* Westport, CT: Praeger, 2002.

Shapiro, Joseph P. *No Pity: People with Disabilities Forging a New Civil Rights Movement.* New York: Three Rivers Press, 1994.

Solomos, John. *Race and Racism in Britain.* 3rd Ed. New York: Macmillan Palgrave, 2003.

Steinberg, Stephen. *The Ethnic Myth: Race, Ethnicity, and Class in America.* Boston: Beacon Press, 2001.

Sullivan, Andrew. *Same-Sex Marriage: Pro and Con.* New York: Vintage, 2004.

Waller, James. *Prejudice across America.* Jackson: University Press of Mississippi, 2000.

Washburn, Wilcomb E., ed. *Handbook of North American Indians: History of Indian-White Relations Vol. 4.* Washington, DC: Smithsonian Institution, 1988.

Weine, Stevan M. *When History is a Nightmare: Lives and Memories of Ethnic Cleansing in Bosnia-Herzegovina.* Piscataway, NJ: Rutgers University Press, 1999.

Wolfson, Evan. *Why Marriage Matters: America, Equality and Gay People's Right to Marry.* New York: Simon & Schuster, 2004.

Wormser, Richard. *The Rise and Fall of Jim Crow.* New York: St. Martin's Press, 2003.

Web Sites

American Civil Liberties Union (ACLU). http://www.aclu.org/ (accessed on January 18, 2007).

American Indian Movement. http://www.aimovement.org/ (accessed on January 18, 2007).

Amnesty International. http://web.amnesty.org/report2005/rwa-summary-eng (accessed on January 18, 2007).

Anti-Defamation League. http://www.adl.org (accessed on January 18, 2007).

Apartheid Museum. http://www.apartheidmuseum.org (accessed on January 18, 2007).

Disability Rights Education & Defense Fund. http://www.dredf.org (accessed on January 18, 2007).

"Enable." *United Nations.* http://www.un.org/esa/socdev/enable (accessed on January 18, 2007).

Gay & Lesbian Alliance Against Defamation. http://www.glaad.org (accessed on January 18, 2007).

Human Rights Campaign. http://www.hrc.org (accessed on January 18, 2007).

Human Rights Watch. http://www.hrw.org/ (accessed on January 18, 2007).

Genocide Watch. http://www.genocidewatch.org (accessed on January 18, 2007).

"Islam: Empire of Faith." *Public Broadcasting System.* http://www.pbs.org/empires/islam/faithtoday.html (accessed on January 18, 2007).

Japanese American National Museum. http://www.janm.org (accessed on January 18, 2007).

Mexican American Legal Defense and Educational Fund. http://www.maldef.org (accessed on January 18, 2007).

National Civil Rights Museum. http://www.civilrightsmuseum.org/ (accessed on January 18, 2007).

National Congress of American Indians. http://www.ncai.org/ (accessed on January 18, 2007).

National Organization for Women (NOW). http://www.now.org (accessed on January 18, 2007).

The Prejudice Institute. http://www.prejudiceinstitute.org (accessed on January 18, 2007).

"Slavery and the Making of America." *Public Broadcasting System.* http://www.pbs.org/wnet/slavery/ (accessed on January 18, 2007).

Understanding Prejudice. http://www.understandingprejudice.org/ (accessed on January 18, 2007).

United Farm Workers. http://www.ufw.org (accessed on January 18, 2007).

United States Holocaust Memorial Museum. http://www.ushmm.org (accessed on January 18, 2007).

United States Immigration Support. http://www.usimmigrationsupport.org/ (accessed on January 18, 2007).

War Crimes Tribunal Watch. http://balkansnet.org/tribunal.html (accessed on January 18, 2007).

"World Factbook." *Central Intelligence Agency.* https://www.cia.gov/cia/publications/factbook/index.html (accessed on January 18, 2007).

Index

Italic indicates volume number; illustrations are marked by (ill.)

S